DOWNFALL

ANDREW, EPSTEIN & THE END OF PRIVILEGE

NIGEL CAWTHORNE

GIBSON SQUARE

Also by Nigel Cawthorne

Virginia Giuffre
The Extraordinary Life Story of the 'Plaything' who Pursued and Ended the Crimes of Jeffrey Epstein and Ghislaine Maxwell

Ghislaine Maxwell
Epstein and the Fall of the World's Most Famous Socialite

Windsor Spares
The Prince Harry and Prince Andrew Soap Opera

Prince Philip
'I Know I Am Rude, but I Like It'

Call Me Diana
The Princess of Wales on the Princess of Wales

This first edition published by Gibson Square.

email: rights@gibsonsquare.com
website: www.gibsonsquare.com

A catalogue record for this book is available from the Library of Congress and the British Library.

 This is an entirely updated, revised and reset edition previously published in 2020 as *Prince Andrew, Epstein and the Palace*.

Prince Andrew by Donald Edgar, *Prince Andrew: Warrior Prince* by Graham and Heather Fisher, *Andrew: The Playboy Prince* by Andrew Morton and Mick Seamark, *Prince Andrew* by Nicholas Courtney, are gratefully acknowledged. Picture credits: Anwar Hussein, Getty, BBC. Copyright holders are urged to come forward.

CONTENTS

Legal Bombshells 5
19 February 2026 8

1. Betting The Firm 21
2 The Trouble with Andrew 31
3 Baby Grumpling 41
4 Mummy's Boy 57
5 Girls, Girls, Girls 73
6 When Andrew Met Fergie 86
7 'Never Heard of You' 98
8 Who Was Jeffrey Epstein? 114
9 Sex Slaves and Puritans 130
10 Nemesis 144
11 BBC Newsnight Car Crash 151
12 Fallout 165
13 The Mysterious Ms Maxwell 182
14 'Only One of Us Telling the Truth' 189
15 Federal Witness 193
16 Buckingham Palace Retreat 198
17 Andrew's Counter-Attack 209
18 A Throne in Peril? 216

Index 222

LEGAL BOMBSHELLS

On the morning of Thursday 19 February 2026, a seismic shockwave reached the gates of Buckingham Palace that shook the monarchy to its core. Entering the royal Sandringham Estate without prior warning at 8am, British police arrested Andrew, the king's younger brother who once was the second in line to the throne. The fact that a former senior member of the royal establishment was escorted to the local police station dominated news cycles around the world—particularly when he was photographed leaning back ashen-faced in the car that took him home after 10 hours of questioning. The surprise arrest at dawn on his sixty-sixth birthday was made on suspicion of misconduct in public office after the latest FBI release of 3.5 million files belonging to Jeffrey Epstein, the sinister billionaire who died in police custody in 2019. This was not the first earthquake to unsettle the British royal family in relation to Andrew. On Monday 9 August 2021, Virginia Roberts Giuffre filed a lawsuit for sexual misconduct in a New York State court against him, when he was still a prince and eighth in succession to the throne as Queen Elizabeth's second son. These were both unprecedented events. In the long history of the British monarchy from 1066, there was no one like Andrew. Never before had a British royal been challenged on such charges without the courtesies to which British royals had grown accustomed over a millennium. In fact, siblings of the monarch had only ever been arrested by fellow royals (the last was Elizabeth by her sister Queen Mary in 1554). They had never before faced civilian criminal charges. By extension, the exceptional breach of royal privilege indicated a tectonic shift that would cause havoc as the most respected royal family in the world was ever deeper embroiled in the Epstein affair. I had raised tough questions for

Epstein's high-profile friends such as Andrew even though they—Andrew included—strenuously denied any knowledge of Epstein's sordid and reprehensible acts involving minors.

Giuffre's allegations had circulated in the press since January 2015 and consistently been denied as untrue in statements by the palace, Andrew and Andrew's close friend Ghislaine Maxwell. Even so, Giuffre's fifteen-page-long claims that she submitted in 2021 to the court of federal judge Lewis A. Kaplan were hair-raising. Giuffre accused Andrew of sexually abusing her at convicted paedophile Jeffrey Epstein's mansion in Manhattan and at other locations in 2001 when she was seventeen. Giuffre stated she 'was compelled by express or implied threats by Epstein, [Ghislaine] Maxwell, and/or Prince Andrew to engage in sexual acts with Prince Andrew, and feared death or physical injury to herself or another and other repercussions for disobeying Epstein, Maxwell, and Prince Andrew due to their powerful connections, wealth and authority'. She further alleged that the prince knew she was a sex-trafficking victim and that she suffered—and continued to suffer—'significant emotional and psychological distress and harm'.

Normally, Giuffre's civil claims against the prince would have floundered after the lapse of some twenty years under New York State's statutes of limitations. But in 2019 the New York State Legislature had passed the Child Victims Act that gave survivors of sexual abuse a one-year window to file a civil case no matter how long ago they had been abused. Following the corona lockdowns, its deadline had been extended and Giuffre's explosive legal allegations were dramatically lodged only days before the window finally closed on bringing litigation under the act.

Previously, Andrew had 'absolutely and categorically' denied having sex with Giuffre from when this was first reported and Buckingham Palace called her statements 'false and without foundation'. But both the palace's and Andrew's response to Giuffre's legal filing caused great confusion.

The day after the filing, Andrew left his Windsor home to join the Queen and her advisors at Balmoral—his mother's 50,000-acre estate in Scotland where she was on holiday. When Giuffre's legal team sought to serve papers on the prince at his residence, Royal Lodge in Windsor, the full-time security staff on duty refused to accept them. Her team had also sent them to his lawyers and posted them to him by Royal Mail, on the assumption that the service would have no trouble delivering to one of its namesakes.

The palace's refusal to accept the papers created a major standoff between the

Queen's second son and the US legal system. It appeared to some observers as if he was above US law. David Boies, the star US lawyer representing Giuffre, did not take kindly to the royals' cat-and-mouse game and warned, 'ignore the courts at your peril', adding, 'It would be very ill-advised for Prince Andrew to ignore judicial process'.

While multiple attempts were made, Andrew remained at the Queen's Balmoral estate with his ex-wife Sarah Ferguson some five hundred miles away. It was reportedly said, 'Andrew was going stir-crazy inside Royal Lodge for the past few weeks. He wasn't going horse riding and couldn't step outside because of attempts to serve him with the legal papers. He knows he is far safer up at Balmoral.'

The direct aftermath in 2021 of Giuffre's allegations had raised many pregnant questions, including many that were potentially constitutional in nature. What did (then) heir to the throne Charles know? How did Queen Elizabeth II end up as her son's shield against the US legal system? Was Britain's monarch prepared to undertake further measures against a family member, or was a senior royal somehow considered to be above laws promulgated in the name of the Crown? Why had Scotland Yard never proceeded to a full police investigation into Giuffre's complaint to Scotland Yard in 2015 as to what happened to her in London as a minor?[1] Were there two measures of justice when public figures such as Harvey Weinstein, Kevin Spacey (coincidentally both friends of Andrew's), and media personality Russell Brand, became the subject of 'a full' police investigation in the UK following complaints to the police?[2] How and where was the palace's link to the Epstein Affair going to end up for both Andrew and the royal family? What had been moot questions in 2021 had nudged closer to inevitable ones in 2026 as Andrew's arrest had left the privileges, behaviour and demeanour of the entire royal establishment open to accusations of hypocrisy with piercing constitutional scrutiny of the entire institution lying ahead.

1 '[I]n November 2016, a decision was made that this matter would not proceed to a full criminal investigation,' Metropolitan Police—28 November 2019; 11 October, 2021; 15 February, 2022; 13 December, 2026.

2 The investigation against Weinstein was stayed given his incarceration in the US, Spacey was tried and found not guilty in the UK in 2023, and Brand was charged and pleaded not guilty in February 2026.

19 FEBRUARY 2026

Having in February 2022 settled Virginia Roberts Giuffre's civil case under the New York Child Victims Act against him for a reported £12 million, Andrew had ducked out of his day in court. It had been his one chance to clear his name and he had not taken it. Instead he followed the palace rule book—for once—keeping his head down and keeping his name out of the news. Even so, there was now a groundswell of popular opposition against Andrew from the inhabitants of the areas associated with his royal titles—such as 'Duke of York', created for him on his wedding day by his mother. York City Council voted unanimously to have his freedom of the city revoked. He was the first person to suffer such ignominy. They also called for him to relinquish the title Duke of York. Earlier, in 2019, the people of Inverness had started a petition to strip Andrew of the title Earl of Inverness, another wedding present of the Queen. He was also Baron of Killyleagh and the people of Killyleagh felt the same, petitioning he be stripped of his barony.

In 2021, Buckingham Palace itself had taken steps against Andrew to be seen to respond to the conviction in a New York federal court of his close friend Ghislaine Maxwell on charges of sex trafficking minors in association with her former partner Jeffrey Epstein. Andrew could no longer 'use' his titles and HRH style in public. But, in private royal circles it was a different matter. He remained the Queen's favourite son and rock. He was the Queen's chaperone to the memorial service for Prince Philip in Westminster Abbey, which took place with great pomp and circumstance in March 2022. He also took part in the private celebrations of the Garter Day ceremony in June—the dinner and the induction of new members behind closed doors to the highest noble order in Britain founded in 1382. Nonetheless, Charles and Prince William had insisted that Andrew be excluded from the public procession and to this the Queen had agreed—perhaps reluctantly it was rumoured.

Yet Andrew was by now playing for time. The Queen, his greatest and absolute protector, celebrated her platinum jubilee on the British throne in June; but then she died on September 8 at the age of ninety six. While his royal siblings wore the usual military uniforms the Windsors put on display at ceremonial events, Andrew was seen wearing civilian clothing to walk behind the Queen's coffin at a procession in Edinburgh. As a filial gesture to his deceased mother, the new King Charles III gave Andrew a special dispensation to wear his Royal Navy uniform—the Queen had made him an honorary Vice Admiral on his fifty fifth birthday in 2015—at the 'vigil of the princes' where they stood around their mother's coffin in Westminster Hall.

However, Andrew could not expect fraternal leeway to reach the same height as his mother's now that Charles was the new king. Andrew was no longer allowed to use his suite of rooms in Buckingham Palace. Following Maxwell's conviction and Andrew's failure to have Virginia Giuffre's civil case against him dismissed, his security had already been downgraded—which put an end to his round-the-clock protection by armed police. The police would ultimately be replaced by private security guards, costing an estimated £3 million per year that was paid for by the crown. By October 2024, however, Charles III stopped funding Andrew's private security guards. He would have to pay for them himself, though no one knew where he would get the money. Charles also tried to force Andrew to leave Royal Lodge where he was paying a 'peppercorn rent'—that is to say, nothing—to the Crown Estate. Charles's idea was that Andrew move into Frogmore Cottage, also on the Windsor grounds, with its more modest five bedrooms compared to thirty at Royal Lodge. Andrew, however, decided he wouldn't budge.

By now, in 2024, it seemed that the headlines were running out of steam. The palace appeared, at last, to have succeeded in keeping the lid on further calls for action against the king's brother.

Had courtiers really taken the gravity of the longstanding Andrew problem to heart, many still wondered, however? Buckingham Palace's response to the previous years' news about Andrew looked like more window dressing. Instead of addressing the real issues—the allegations of rape and sexual abuse, behaviour in public office and other financial issues that, though strenuously denied as untrue, might on some future day lead to further news—the palace had concerned itself more with battling column inches around the beleaguered Andrew. At any rate, its measures had to do with dusty matters of etiquette and palace paraphernalia that mattered only in royal stage-setting: the levels of usage of titles, what esoteric regalia Andrew was or was not allowed to wear, and pressure on where (but not whether) he ought to live on Crown land, and so on. The nickname of the royal family is The Firm, but it seemed from the outside that not much had actually changed in Andrew's privileges as eighth in the Firm's line of succession.

In the end, was Charles III's approach that different from his mother's, or indeed from how the king himself had dealt with similar news in the past? There was Peter Ball, former Bishop of Gloucester—the bishop had admitted an act of gross indecency with a nineteen-year-old man (who was to commit suicide in 2012) and received a formal police caution for it in 1993. Two years later, Charles had written to Ball saying: 'I wish I could do more. I feel so desperately strongly about the monstrous wrongs that have been done to you and the way you have been treated.' Later Charles, then Prince of Wales, arranged for the Duchy of Cornwall to buy a house to be rented by Ball and his identical twin, Michael, also a bishop. In 2015, Ball was sentenced to thirty-two-months' imprisonment for misconduct and indecent assault after admitting the abuse of eighteen young men. Further charges of indecent assault of boys aged thirteen to fifteen remained on file. Then there was British TV personality Jimmy Savile. Charles and Savile had been friends since the 1970s, with frequent correspondence between the two until Savile's death in 2011. But Savile had first been investigated for sexual offences in 1958 and there were allegations of child abuse in 1963, as well as admissions of numerous instances of sexual misconduct in Savile's 1976 autobiography *Love Is an Uphill Thing*.

If Buckingham Palace stood accused of decades of indolence—continuing to sit on its hands under a new monarch who still appeared to lack a full grasp of the situation's gravity—and a misplaced reliance on pageantry, it was in for a sharp awakening with the re-election of Donald Trump. The palace's house of cards was once again to teeter as a result of past mistakes and its anachronistic deference to royals.

One of Trump's MAGA election platforms was that he would have the FBI finally release the entire Epstein file. In office, President Trump would prove perhaps less unequivocal, cancelling release decisions several times—dismissing the Epstein affair as a 'Democrat Hoax' or as a distraction to the great things he was doing—before reinstating them again, in part at least. But whatever would be released would likely cast an ugly light on Andrew's past behaviour and some of Andrew's more unusual statements about Virginia Giuffre's allegations made during the prince's notorious own-goal 2019 interview with the BBC. Congress itself was putting pressure on Donald Trump to release the FBI's Epstein files. It was a rare moment of bipartisan action that would eventually result in the Epstein Files Transparency Act of November 19, 2025.

As it turned out a hurricane of bad news headed towards Buckingham Palace in 2025, not least because Virginia Giuffre's memoirs *Nobody's Girl* was listed for publication in October 2025. Criticism of Andrew widened as a result of increased spying by China. In December 2024, questions were raised about Andrew's dealings with Chinese businessman Yang Tengbo, also known as Chris Yang, who had been invited to events at royal residences in 2018. Yang had subsequently been denied entry to the UK on the grounds that he was a spy for the Chinese Communist Party. Nonetheless, Andrew's secretary wrote to Yang in the year he was banned, 'You should never underestimate the strength of that relationship... Outside of [Andrew's] closest internal confidants, you sit at the very top of a tree that many, many people would like to be on.' It was then revealed that Andrew had met with Cai Qi who turned out to be a high-ranking member of the Secretariat of the Chinese Communist Party. At the same time, Andrew's former wife Fergie was being supported with Chinese money through Hong Kong businessman Dr Johnny Hon who had strong ties to mainland China.

The bad news for the palace started in January 2025 when an email exchange between Andrew and Epstein emerged as part of disclosures in a financial investigation by the FCA into one of Epstein's friends, Jes Staley, a banker at JP Morgan and subsequently Barclays. The exchange appeared to shatter Andrew's credibility.

In his notorious BBC interview, Andrew had said about a December 2010 stay of several days at Epstein's New York mansion, 'I never had any contact with him from that day forward.' Asked why he had gone to stay with a convicted sex offender, Andrew said he felt it was 'the right thing to do' to meet him in person to say 'terribly sorry... I can't see you [any more]'. He seemed to claim the high ground as an 'honourable' person and continued to explain a photograph in Central Park of the two of them in animated conversation: 'We had an opportunity to go for a walk in the park... I said to him, I said, "Look, because of what has happened, I don't think it is appropriate that we should remain in contact".'

Yet the FCA disclosures revealed that on February 28, 2011, Andrew emailed Epstein and discussed the articles in the press about the visit and Giuffre, writing: 'Keep in close touch and we'll play some more soon!!!!' The day before this exchange, the infamous photograph of Andrew with his arm around Virginia's bare waist in Maxwell's London home had been published by the *Mail on Sunday.*

Case 18-2868 unsealed papers, US District Court, Southern District of New York. The photograph of Prince (then) Andrew, Virginia Roberts Giuffre, Ghislaine Maxwell, apparently taken by Jeffrey Epstein and first made public by the Mail on Sunday on 28 February 2011 (months before Prince William and Kate Middleton got married).

Then, on 25 April 2025 came the news as a bolt from the blue that Virginia Giuffre had committed suicide, aged just forty one. At first her father accepted this, but then said he thought that 'someone got to her'. This was the second dramatic suicide after Jeffrey Epstein's in 2019 by a key actor in the affair. It meant that Ghislaine Maxwell was the only principal figure in the affair who remained alive.

Royalists were secretly relieved as Giuffre would no longer be around to level accusations at Andrew and they knew Ghislaine would shy away from self-incrimination. Others wondered, however, how much Andrew, who had stated to the BBC he could not recall meeting Giuffre but settled rather than fought her New York lawsuit, and London police force Scotland Yard, who had not taken her allegations seriously enough for further investigation, had preyed on her state of mind. Scotland Yard had on three occasions publicly declined to reopen its investigation into her 2015 complaint of having been sex-trafficked to Ghislaine Maxwell's London flat in 2001 when she was a minor. Despite Maxwell's conviction in 2021 and serving a sentence of twenty years, Scotland Yard had continued to keep the investigation into Giuffre's allegations closed.

Just when the palace thought it could not get any worse, the US Congress also began to call for action against Andrew, despite his strenuous denials of Giuffre's allegations. First Congresswoman Nancy Mace called for: 'A cold dark cell. Prince Andrew in handcuffs. This is an image sending the right message. No one is above the law, victims deserve justice and Americans deserve confidence our system works as it was intended.'

Interest in the case was fanned further by the publication of extracts from an album Ghislaine Maxwell had compiled on the occasion of Epstein's fiftieth birthday in 2003. The album was made up of letters of congratulation from Epstein's friends. One of them was a drawing of an outline of a naked woman with an imagined conversation between Trump and Epstein, concluding with: 'Happy Birthday—and may every day be another wonderful secret.' The woman's pubic hair appeared to be Trump's signature. Trump denied the drawing was his and sued the *Wall Street Journal* and its owner, Rupert Murdoch, for $10 billion.

US Deputy Attorney General Todd Blanche, formerly Trump's personal lawyer, went to question Maxwell in the Federal Correctional Institution in Tallahassee. During the two-day interview, Maxwell said that Trump had not done anything of concern in her presence. She was then transferred to a minimum-security camp in Bryan, Texas. No reason was given for this highly irregular move. The White House insisted she received no preferential treatment and there was no quid pro quo. The US House Oversight Committee investigating the Epstein Affair was seeking to uncover the names of co-conspirators and subpoenaed Maxwell to testify under oath about her dealings with Epstein and his circle. In response, she demanded immunity from further prosecution and said very little when she gave video-evidence from Federal Prison Camp Bryan, Texas.

In October, as Giuffre's *Nobody's Girl* was published posthumously, another leaked email appeared to show that, on 27 February 2011, Andrew had written to Ed Perkins, Queen Elizabeth's deputy press secretary, that he had asked one of his close protection officers to find out information about Virginia Giuffre. 'It would also seem she has a criminal record in the [United] States,' Andrew wrote to Perkins. 'I have given her DoB [date of birth] and social security number for investigation with [XXX], the on duty ppo [personal protection officer].' The email was sent just hours before the infamous photograph of him with his arm around Virginia's waist was published in the *Mail on Sunday*. The implication of the email was furthermore that he wanted the police to use this material to smear Giuffre in 2011. Virginia had no criminal record and it is not clear if the officer complied with the request. This time the Met did look into the matter as it involved one of their own policemen.

The pivotal question was, how did Andrew have the date of birth and the social security number of a woman that he could, in his 2019 BBC interview, not recall ever meeting? At the same time, and even more embarrassingly for Buckingham Palace, since the email exchange between Andrew and the senior courtier only emerged publicly in 2025, the palace seemed to share a lack of recollection from 2011—one that mirrored Andrew's. The leaked DoB email appeared to confirm an article published in *Vanity Fair* fourteen years earlier. *Vanity Fair* described in narrative detail the negotiations with the palace and how Sian James had made her approach over the phone the day before the exchange (Friday) and provided Virginia's name and the exact extent of her claims against Andrew. More details followed. Four months later the DoB email turned up in the FBI's Epstein datasets released in 2026 as Andrew had forwarded the entire chain to Epstein. It also contained the palace's response to Andrew: 'The *M[ail]o[n]S[unday]* have now come back to us and say they will make no reference to any sexual impropriety.' Two hours before the palace had responded 'lawyers primed' after Andrew wrote to Perkins, 'I've just had a short conversation with [G]hislaine and she says [Virginia Giuffre] is a lying so and so'. The FBI's Epstein files confirmed that both Andrew and the palace had been unwavering throughout in 'categorically' denying Giuffre's claims.

Another part of the email that Andrew sent to Epstein on 28 February, the day after the Virginia photograph was published in 2011, now gained public attention. Andrew did not only write to Epstein, 'Keep in close touch and we'll play some more soon', he had also written, 'we're in this together.' Was this the irrefutable evidence that Andrew had lied on the BBC about his relationship with Epstein and that he hadn't gone to New York to break off their friendship in a 'morally acceptable' way? In addition, a 2011 email from Andrew's wife Sarah Ferguson to Epstein also emerged calling him her 'supreme friend' and apologising for her public criticism of him that year.

In desperation, Buckingham Palace reached for another range of symbolic measures to be seen to censure Andrew. It announced that Andrew had agreed to stop using the title Duke of York and other titular forms of address. Two weeks later this was followed by the news that he would give up his membership of the Order of the Garter and that Charles III had decided to formally remove all Andrew's remaining royal styles and honours. On 3 November 2025, he issued letters patent removing Andrew's style as Royal Highness and title of prince. Andrew's name was also removed from the Roll of the Peerage. While this did not revoke his ducal and earl peerages (only an Act of Parliament can as peerages are considered property) it meant they could not be used in official contexts. In conjunction, Fergie was forced to give up the patronage of several charities and ceased using the courtesy title Duchess of York on her public media. It seemed to many that this was tantamount to another flurry of paper pushing that should have happened a long time before.

From 3 November, Andrew was plain Mr Mountbatten Windsor. Later, the hyphen would be returned, making his surname Mountbatten-Windsor. Andrew had at first been asked how he wanted it to be spelled. But the hyphen was how the family name had been designated in the proclamation his father Prince Philip had insisted on when Andrew was born on 19 February 1960 (Philip wanted to see his surname placed before the Queen's family name on the birth of their second son). Andrew, it turned out, had no choice in the matter.

Andrew and Fergie—who had continued to live together despite their divorce—were now forced by the Crown Estate, directed by Charles III, to move out of Royal Lodge, Andrew's seventy-five-year lease notwithstanding. The repair clause in the lease made this possible: in case of failure to keep the building in good repair, the lease could be forfeited by the Crown. Andrew had not done or paid for any maintenance since 2002 and Royal Lodge was in an execrable state.

Why this clause wasn't invoked earlier was not clear, and some pointed to the fact that since Andrew's removal only happened in the middle of yet another barrage of disreputable revelations it suggested that the palace's actions were merely a veneer for hypocrisy.

Fergie would find her own accommodation, and Andrew would be exiled to Sandringham in Norfolk, Britain's equivalent of Siberia. Andrew would be confined, it was thought, to the five-bedroomed Wood Farm—once the out-of-the-way home for his father Prince Philip's more intimate affairs. In the end, he was assigned the slightly more modest Marsh Farm on the estate but moved into Wood Farm temporarily from Royal Lodge while Marsh Farm was being renovated. Siberia it might be, but it was reported that the former royal would still have a cook and a footman, though it was unclear who was paying for this—and that Andrew was to be addressed as 'Sir' by them.

Once Andrew had been stripped of his royal titles, Democrats on the US House Committee on Oversight and Accountability wrote to him to testify before them. 'Well-documented allegations against you, along with your long-standing friendship with Mr Epstein, indicate that you may possess knowledge of his activities relevant to our investigation,' the letter said. 'In the interest of justice for the victims of Jeffrey Epstein, we request that you co-operate with the committee's investigation by sitting for a transcribed interview with the committee.' The committee's letter also said it had identified 'financial records containing notations such as "massage for Andrew" that raise serious questions'.

Congress's powers were not as far reaching as those of the US government—which had previously requested Britain's assistance under the Mutual Legal Assistance Treaty in the FBI's Epstein investigation (a request that was made public by Donald Trump himself during his first presidency; it was ostensibly never withdrawn and the request appeared to be unresolved—a highly unusual situation). As a foreign national resident abroad, Congress could not subpoena Andrew to force him to testify.

When Andrew did not respond, Suhas Subramanyam, a Democrat on the committee, said Mountbatten-Windsor 'has been hiding from us, and I think he will continue to try to hide from people doing meaningful investigations of this matter'. 'It seems like every time we find more evidence, Prince Andrew [sic] seems to be in the documents. And so I think if he is hoping that the story will just go away by ignoring us and being silent, he will be sorely disappointed as we continue to pursue this over the next year and beyond.'

In Britain, Liberal Democrat leader Sir Ed Davey picked up the cudgel and waved the flag. '[Andrew] should also give evidence to our Parliament. The public deserve answers and full transparency about this scandal,' Davey wrote in a post on X. There were wider calls for Parliament to investigate Andrew's fiscal probity in public office. There was evidence that, while being UK trade envoy, he had amassed considerable wealth doing deals on the side. As a matter of settled custom, Parliament does not discuss members of the royal family. But there were rumours that MPs would be given 'carte blanche' to discuss Andrew's affairs.

This opened an entirely new and potentially dangerous can of worms for Buckingham Palace. If Members of Parliament were going to start looking into the financial affairs of Andrew, courtiers feared they might also take an interest in those of Charles III and Prince William. This was not an imaginary worry, particularly after the financial investigations by the *Sunday Times* and Channel Four's *Despatches* that showed Charles's and William's deep and troubling financial connections with the NHS, schools, the armed forces, public bodies and charities.

The Democrats on the House Oversight Committee then released three explosive emails. One from Epstein to Maxwell mentioned 'the dog that hasn't barked'—an apparent reference to the Sherlock Holmes short story *The Adventure of Silver Blaze* where the fact that a dog didn't bark was a crucial clue. Epstein's email went on to say that Virginia Giuffre 'spent hours at my house with him [Donald Trump]'. To journalist Michael Wolff, Epstein wrote 'of course he knew about the girls as he asked Ghislaine to stop'.

In retaliation, Republicans on the committee then released another 23,000 documents with many names, including those of former US president Bill Clinton. This batch contained an email sent in March 2011 by Andrew, some two months after he had claimed on the BBC to have broken off all contact with Epstein. Andrew wrote to both Epstein and Maxwell: 'I can't take any more of this,' in response to the allegations put to him further to the picture of him with Virginia, the girl he couldn't recall.

Maxwell had famously claimed in her submissions in her criminal case of 2021 that the picture with Giuffre was a fake. But the Republican batch of 23,000 Epstein emails contained one by Epstein to a reporter, saying, 'yes, she [Giuffre] had her picture taken with Andrew'. It seemed to confirm that the picture was genuine—Virginia always said Epstein himself had taken the picture. In fact, in the same email, Epstein offered the journalist a whole menagerie of pictures—'would you like photos of donald and girls in bikinis in my kitchen' he asked. He added, 'ask my houseman about donald almost walking through the door leaving his nose print on the glass as young women were swimming in the pool and he was so focused he walked straight into the door'. These words from beyond the grave appeared to place the US president himself once again at the heart of the crime scene as a witness.

When a bill demanding the release of the FBI's Epstein files was certain to pass in the House of Representatives, President Trump reversed his reluctance to get behind it and asked Republicans in the House to vote in favour of the release bill. The vote was unanimous but for one maverick, 427-1. The Senate followed suit and Trump promised he would sign the act into law when it reached his desk rather than use his veto to kill it. He said, at the same time, that he could have released the records all along; he did not actually need Congressional consent.

The act proved to be a watershed for many, including Andrew. Public opinion of him stood already at an all-time low. Although he was a war hero of Britain's 1982 Falklands War, it was reported that commemorative plaques on the Falkland Islands erected after the war were being stripped of his name.

The FBI had evidently not yet started work on redacting victims' names from the 3.5 million documents they were going to release, but this work began in earnest after the Epstein Transparency Act became law. It led to a release in three batches over two months. Each one cast a harsh light on the web of influence created by Epstein involving a myriad of leading figures around the world, as well as on further sordid details of the secret sex ring he and Maxwell had invented. In some cases, it seemed possible that those two worlds met as when Elon Musk begged Epstein to be invited to his island with his then wife Tallulah. 'What day/night will be the wildest party on your island?', he wrote in 2012, though it was unclear whether he and his wife actually ever visited.

The third release on 30 January 2026 contained the death knell for Andrew. There was an email with a draft statement by Maxwell sent to Epstein for approval on 10 January 2015. This was shortly after Virginia Giuffre (as Jane Doe 3), had filed a complaint against Maxwell—Virginia's first allegation that she had been forced to have sex with Andrew.

According to the release, Giuffre's attorneys submitted: 'Epstein also sexually trafficked the then-minor Jane Doe, making her available for sex to politically connected and financially powerful people. 'Epstein's purposes in "lending" Jane Doe (along with other young girls) to such powerful people were to ingratiate himself with them for business, personal, political, and financial gain, as well as to obtain potential blackmail information.' 'For instance, one such powerful individual Epstein forced Jane Doe to have sexual relations with was a member of the British royal family, Prince Andrew (aka Duke of York).' The legal submission added that Giuffre was 'forced to have sex with Prince Andrew when she was a minor in three locations: London, New York and at an orgy with numerous other underage girls on Epstein's private island in the U.S. Virgin Islands.'

Maxwell's draft statement was meant to counter this allegation in line with Andrew's strenuous denials. 'It was in London when [Virginia] met a number of friends of mine including Prince Andrew. A photograph was taken as I imagine she wanted to show it to friends and family'. This was remarkable as Maxwell had publicly stated the exact opposite—'I don't believe it is real for a second, in fact, I'm sure it's not'—in a 2023 interview with TalkTV from her prison. The draft continued to state that 'G Maxwell' did not see 'anything improper that took place at my home.' The third release also contained an email to a journalist by Epstein of 9 July 2011 in which he said the same as Maxwell, 'Yes [Virginia] was on my plane, and yes she had her picture taken with Andrew'.

Another email of the same day cast a further savage light on Andrew's claim not to recall Virginia or meeting her at Maxwell's London home. After consulting her lawyer, Maxwell emailed Epstein saying: 'I have to distance myself from you in statement too. And they need me to say I was not aware of massage w/andrew in my house. These things they have to stay along w/meeting [Virginia] and rebutting those allegations. I needs [*sic*] it asap.' Epstein replied: 'I am on the phone with another attny getting you an answer.' Maxwell wrote, 'they need me to say I was not aware of massage w/andrew in my house' and they appear not to have wanted her to state simply that Andrew did not get a 'massage' in her London house.

In his 2019 BBC interview, Andrew himself had said, 'Nobody can prove whether or not that photograph has been doctored but I don't recollect that photograph ever being taken.' He also claimed that he was not in London, and was having a pizza with his daughter on account of her birthday on the day of the photograph in Woking, a town near Windsor. In his 2019 BBC interview, Andrew remembered this event as follows, 'the 10th of March [2001], I was at home, I was with the children and I'd taken Beatrice to a PizzaExpress in Woking for a party at, I suppose, sort of four or five in the afternoon… Because going to PizzaExpress in Woking is an unusual thing for me to do, a very unusual thing for me to do. I've never been… I've only been to Woking a couple of times and I remember it weirdly distinctly.' As to the photograph with Virginia of that day, he had added, 'I don't believe it's a picture of me in London because... when I go out in London, I wear a suit and a tie. That's what I would describe as… my travelling clothes... if I'm going overseas.'

The third batch of the 3.5 million Epstein documents contained more unusual photographs of Andrew. The images showed him in his 'travel clothes' in one of Epstein's homes crouching on top of a woman, holding her stomach, and grinning with enlarged pupils. It was unclear what the situation portrayed, but it proved a culmination of the problems Andrew was facing.

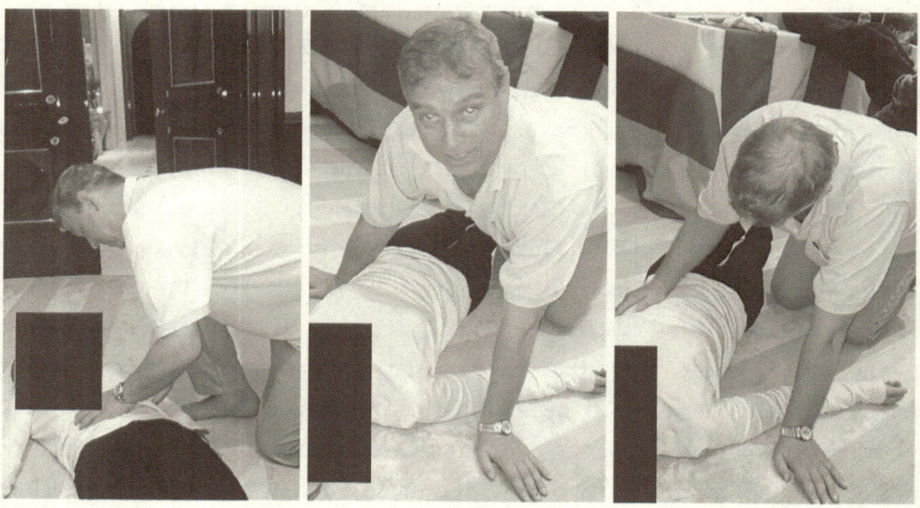

Department of Justice, Epstein files release of 28 January 2026.

The third batch also opened a window on Andrew's financial affairs.[3] It turned out that Andrew had shared confidential information with Epstein while he was the UK's trade envoy. This was an expenses-only office he had held until the release of the photograph with Giuffre in 2011. To Buckingham Palace's dismay, the floodgates now truly seemed to open. Nine local police forces said

3 As well as those of many others, including former UK Ambassador to the US Lord Peter Mandelson, also arrested on suspicion of misconduct in a public office on account of the Epstein files, questioned and released without being charged.

that they were investigating Andrew—though Scotland Yard declined to include Giuffre's 2015 complaint. The denouement was swift. On his sixty-sixth birthday, 19 February 2026, Andrew was arrested at 8am on suspicion of misconduct in public office. He was released hours later after questioning and without being charged. In a photograph taken by Reuters when he returned to the Sandringham Estate from his arrest, he reclined in the back of his car with a stunned face white as a sheet.

Painfully for Buckingham Palace, not even King Charles had been given prior warning of the arrest of his own brother in his name as Britain's monarch, it seemed. This did not mean the palace did not get involved. As a rule, arrests are not made a matter of public record by the British police. It was however a palace release to the BBC in the afternoon that pointed the media to the arrest and searches of Andrew's former home, Royal Lodge. Even so, it seemed that as a result of its handling of Andrew, the palace might have to pay the piper in the future. Many argued that the palace's antiquated handling of Andrew over a twenty-five-year period—if not longer—signalled the dawn of an era where royal privilege has no place, and that a major change was needed for a clean break with the past. It seemed to many that the assumption that the royal family's word was a bond of honour was deeply flawed and that a fortress around family members of the head of state should no longer be tolerated. But would Charles III draw the conclusion that royal privilege is not just a matter of arcane court etiquette but rather a heavy constitutional burden—one so degraded over decades, including his own reign, that he might consider abdicating in favour of William to leave the future of The Firm in safer, unspoilt hands?

1

BETTING THE FIRM

The first warning sign of a severe reckoning aiming for Buckingham Palace came on 6 July 2019 when billionaire businessman Jeffrey Epstein was arrested on federal charges related to sex trafficking. Twelve years earlier he had pleaded guilty to Florida State charges of soliciting girls as young as thirteen for prostitution and served nearly thirteen months in low-security Palm Beach County Jail. The sixty six year old now faced as much as forty-three years in a federal jail. Though guards were supposed to check on him every thirty minutes, he was found hanged in his cell on 10 August. Verdict: suicide.

Most of Epstein's influential friends, including Donald Trump, Bill Clinton, and Elon Musk, distanced themselves from him after his first fall from grace. However, for another friend—Prince Andrew—it was too late.

The US Appeals Court in New York City released two thousand pages of papers from a defamation suit by Virginia Roberts Giuffre that included her claim that Epstein had used her as a sex slave while underage and had forced her to have sex with Andrew on three occasions. Even before these allegations, a photograph had surfaced of the prince with his arm around the seventeen year old's naked midriff.

Also in the picture was Andrew's close friend Ghislaine Maxwell, Epstein's girlfriend and daughter of disgraced media mogul Robert Maxwell, who died under mysterious circumstances after he went missing from his yacht Lady Ghislaine off the Canary Islands in 1991. In a lawsuit, Giuffre claimed Maxwell had procured her when she was fifteen for Epstein and worked at Donald Trump's Mar-a-Lago estate in Florida for $9 an hour, and that Maxwell was Epstein's accomplice in trafficking her to Andrew and others. Maxwell denied the allegations outright when she was deposed under oath and called Giuffre a liar, leading Giuffre to sue for defamation. An attempt to get the prince to testify under oath in the defamation case failed. When Giuffre's lawsuit was settled in May 2017, its court papers were sealed, only to be released in part by the New York Court of Appeals the day before Epstein died.

The first weeks of August 2019 dramatically changed Andrew's life and forever changed the light in which these allegations placed the royal family. All of a sudden, the Queen's favourite son stood at the heart of the Epstein Affair and became someone US law enforcement was interested in talking to. The sex crimes the billionaire orchestrated, involving up to a hundred victims by now, remained under FBI investigation—despite his death. Andrew became the first British royal ever whose extradition to the United States was mooted in the press.

But the scandal went well beyond the fate of one man. Ex-New-York federal prosecutor and Columbia Law School professor Jennifer Rodgers said, 'In theory, if he comes to the US, he could be arrested pursuant to a material-witness warrant'. Could Andrew ever return to America under these circumstances? Though strenuously denied, Giuffre's accusations against Andrew now threatened Britain's monarchy as a whole—an institution reliant on broad public support for its very existence—in an unprecedented way. Like the catholic church, Buckingham Palace found itself yet again engulfed by headlines connected to an underage-sex scandal.

The renewed media scrutiny and the attendant furore that shook the royal family to its core all stemmed from the prince's relationship with Jeffrey Epstein. Each time the Epstein allegations bounced back into the ether as a result of new facts, the media storm gathered in potency, and the monarchy looked increasingly at risk of its half-cocked handling of the crisis.

In 2011, it had first been reported that the prince had partied with Epstein at the paedophile's New York mansion—three months after the financier had been released from Florida State custody and house arrest at his New York home. Alongside the news, the press had published hand-written telephone messages from high school girls for Epstein that had been retrieved in 2005 as material evidence from the billionaire's Palm Beach home. It included one that said, 'She is wondering if 2.30 ok cuz she needs to stay in school'. Another girl, 'Colleen', phoned to tell Epstein, 'Going into class—will be out in 45 min'. 'Sarah', a further message read, 'doesn't know at what time she must come this night for the massage'.

Epstein threw the intimate dinner party in December 2009 for fifteen at his $80 million Manhattan townhouse. Located on 71st Street, just off Central Park, it was considered the largest private residence in Manhattan. The prince was guest of honour and stayed at the mansion for a few days. Also present at the bash were Woody Allen, the subject of sexual misconduct against his seven-year-old daughter since the 1990s, and Charlie Rose, the CBS anchor who would later lose his job after numerous allegations of being a sexual predator. The prince was then photographed strolling with Epstein in Central Park during his stay. Both were deep in conversation.

Epstein's New York mansion, Manhattan's largest private residence

In 2019, Prince Andrew again strenuously denied Giuffre's allegations and those of Johanna Sjoberg, whose unsealed evidence first became public the day before Epstein died. Sjoberg claimed that the prince had groped her at Epstein's

New York house in 2001. 'I just remember someone suggesting a photo, and they told us to go get on the couch. And so Andrew and Virginia sat on the couch', Sjoberg had testified. As she herself reluctantly sat on Andrew's lap, someone touched Virginia's breast and then Andrew groped hers, Sjoberg stated under oath.

She, too, said that Andrew's close friend Ghislaine Maxwell 'lured her from her school to have sex with Epstein under the guise of hiring her for a job answering phones'. At Epstein's mansion, she found out that her duties included being a masseuse. He then induced her 'to perform demeaning sexual services,' she said.

Despite these allegations, the Queen made a show of support for Prince Andrew by sitting alongside him in a Rolls Royce as she headed for Sunday morning worship in Balmoral the day after Epstein died.

The following week the *Mail on Sunday* released a video showing Andrew waving goodbye from the mansion's fifteen-foot tall oak doors to a young brunette as she left Epstein's Manhattan home. Buckingham Palace promptly issued a statement saying: 'The Duke of York has been appalled by the recent reports of Jeffrey Epstein's alleged crimes. His Royal Highness deplores the exploitation of any human being and the suggestion he would condone, participate in or encourage any such behaviour is abhorrent.'

The mystery brunette was later named as Katherine Keating, the then twenty-eight-year-old daughter of Paul Keating, former prime minister of Australia. Keating had come forward herself as she was 'deeply upset' about the speculation. Although Keating conceded she knew Epstein, she had only met the prince for forty five minutes 'for a cup of tea' that day and did not meet Epstein on this occasion.

Keating had met the prince at a lavish party in Dubai celebrating the 2010 opening of the Meydan Racecourse and they were seen together several times that March weekend. Keating was a public relations guru—something much needed by Andrew and his New York host. The twenty eight year old was also a friend of Ghislaine Maxwell's. She spoke at a high-profile party in New York organised by Maxwell in 2013 and later Keating persuaded her to give a rare-as-hen's-teeth radio interview in 2014 on her programme for Huffington Post.

Giuffre repeated her claim first made in 2015 that, from the age of seventeen, she had had sex with Andrew three times—in London, at Epstein's New York home, and at an orgy on his private island in the Caribbean. Given the popular outcry in Britain, the palace unequivocally stated the allegations were 'false and without any foundation', adding, 'Any suggestion of impropriety with underage minors is categorically untrue.'

At the end of a torrid week of more battering by the media, the palace took the unprecedented step of issuing a second statement. This one—even more unique—was from the prince himself, who must have felt cornered by the negative headlines. In it Andrew expressed 'tremendous sympathy for Epstein's alleged victims'. The prince added: 'I met Mr Epstein in 1999. During the time I knew him, I saw him infrequently and probably no more than only once or twice a year. I have stayed in a number of his residences. At no stage during the limited time I spent with him did I see, witness or suspect any behaviour of the sort that subsequently led to his arrest and conviction.'

However, the prince's words merely intensified the cloud of questions that engulfed him. It seemed that Andrew had known Epstein for a lot longer than he would admit. In March 2011, the prince's private secretary Alastair Watson wrote to *The Times* in response to the 'widespread comment' about his employer's relationship with the paedophile, saying that the prince had known Epstein 'since being introduced to him in the early 1990s'.

It was not easy to see how Andrew did not suspect Epstein. When the police raided Epstein's Palm Beach mansion in 2005, the walls were plastered with photographs of naked and scantily clad young girls. As these even decorated the hallway, they would be hard to miss and Andrew had stayed there. The police identified at least forty victims, one as young as fourteen, though the total would double over the years.

He had also stayed on Epstein's private island in the US Virgin Islands, Little Saint James or 'Little Saint Jeff'. After the lawsuits it had become popularly known as 'Orgy Island', 'Paedophile Island' or the 'Island of Sin'. Epstein's home there was decorated like his place in Palm Beach.

'There were topless photos of women everywhere,' said Steve Scully, a former phone and internet contractor for Epstein from 1999 to 2005. 'They were on his desk, in his office, in his bedroom.'

Guests at Epstein's home in Manhattan said it was impossible not to notice the number of young girls going in and out. Visitors were often offered a massage on arrival.

Somehow Andrew had missed all of this. The palace's second statement acknowledged that Andrew met Epstein again in 2010 after he had been released from jail.

'I have said previously that it was a mistake and an error to see him after his release in 2010 and I can only reiterate my regret that I was mistaken to think that what I thought I knew of him was evidently not the real person, given what we now know,' the prince said. 'This is a difficult time for everyone involved and I am at a loss to be able to understand or explain Mr Epstein's lifestyle.'

Former palace press secretary Dickie Arbiter said: 'It is unusual for Buckingham Palace to put out not just one statement, but two statements. But the palace felt that they had to do it.' Four statements were made in all.

Virginia Giuffre asked the prince to own up. She told the press, 'He knows exactly what he's done and I hope he comes clean about it.'

Things got more doom-laden for Buckingham Palace on 5 September when *The Times* reported that more documents from the Giuffre-Maxwell lawsuit could be unsealed.

Then, on 21 October, Channel Four's Dispatches aired The Prince and the Paedophile in which it was revealed that Epstein had no fewer than thirteen phone numbers for Prince Andrew, including, interestingly, the direct line to his computer's modem—then the way to connect to the internet—and a direct line to Buckingham Palace. In fact, they turned out to be numbers from Ghislaine Maxwell's address book, which state police had taken in evidence during their raid of Epstein's Palm Beach home in 2005. The prince's friend was the paedophile's walking rolodex.

In June 2000, the billionaire was close enough to Prince Andrew to get an invitation to the Dance of the Decades, marking Andrew's fortieth birthday, the Queen Mother's hundredth, Princess Margaret's seventieth and Princess Anne's fiftieth. It was hosted by the Queen herself at Windsor Castle. Epstein attended with Ghislaine Maxwell.

Andrew's relationship with Epstein appeared to be very friendly. Over their long acquaintance, Andrew stayed with Epstein at his various residences, sometimes spending days on end with him. Epstein was also in contact with Sarah Ferguson, Duchess of York—aka Fergie—speaking regularly on the phone. Dispatches had obtained the flight log for Epstein's private jet, which showed that on 16 April 1998 Epstein met 'Princess Sarah Ferguson and kids' at Nassau in the Bahamas. In February 1999, 'Prince Andrew' himself appeared in the log for the first time, flying into the Virgin Islands. A few days later, he flew out again with

'JE'—Jeffrey Epstein; 'GM'—Ghislaine Maxwell; and a number of other people. And Andrew flew on Epstein's private jet from Luton to Edinburgh with Ghislaine Maxwell on 1 September 2006, six weeks after Epstein had been arrested on charges of soliciting prostitution.

The programme pointed out that, even before he met Epstein, Prince Andrew's reputation had already been called into question. Once praised for his service in the Falklands War, he became known as 'Randy Andy', the 'Playboy Prince' with a series of high-profile girlfriends. He was mocked on the satirical TV programme Spitting Image as the 'prince who can't say no'.

The documentary then re-examined the court papers which claimed that Epstein and Andrew had group sex on Little Saint James. In evidence given to a Florida court in January 2015, Giuffre said: 'The third time I had sex with Andy was in an orgy on Epstein's private island in the US Virgin Islands. I was around eighteen at the time. Epstein, Andy, approximately eight other young girls and I had sex together. The other girls all seemed and appeared to be under the age of eighteen and didn't really speak English. Epstein laughed about the fact they couldn't really communicate, saying that they are the "easiest" girls to get along with.'

In her deposition, she continued, 'A group of Russian girls who didn't speak a word of English turned up with a modelling agent who was a friend of Jeffrey's. That night there was a dinner and Andrew was there. He said "Hi" to me. Jeffrey directed us with hand gestures because the Russian girls didn't speak English. We were told to start kissing and touching and to use sex toys on each other. The girls obviously had been trained. Jeffrey and the prince were laughing… and then they undressed and then I performed a sex act on them—Jeffrey first and then Andrew. It was disgusting. There was no pleasure in it.'

Prince Andrew did not testify as he had left the US the previous night and the judge ordered Giuffre's remarks to be struck from court records. Nevertheless, her allegations under oath hit the news pages.

On the back foot, Buckingham Palace had issued its first-ever public Epstein-denial in January 2015 and, at a press conference in Davos, Andrew himself said: 'I think I must, [and] want, for the record, to refer to the events that have taken place in the last few weeks, and I just wish to reiterate and to reaffirm the statements which have already been made on my behalf by Buckingham Palace.'

Having run this statement for Dispatches through the DecepTech Voice Stress

Analysis Machine, a computerised version of the Psychological Stress Evaluation used by more than fifty law enforcement agencies in the US, expert Michael Sylvestre concluded: 'He's lying. Andrew knows the statement made by Buckingham Palace was not true.'

A few days after the programme, Giuffre signed a sworn statement saying: 'I did have sexual contact with him as I have described—under oath. Given what he knows and has seen, I was hoping that he would simply voluntarily tell the truth about everything. I hope my attorneys can interview Prince Andrew under oath about the contacts and that he will tell the truth.'

Dispatches also claimed that medical records from New York Presbyterian Hospital show Giuffre was admitted on 9 July 2001 after three weeks of vaginal bleeding. In response to the 2019 documentary, Buckingham Palace yet again issued a statement defending Prince Andrew which said: 'It is emphatically denied that the Duke of York had any form of sexual contact or relationship with Virginia Roberts [Giuffre].'

Despite the rebuttals, the documentary prompted calls in the press for the police to investigate her accusations. Giuffre was seventeen when she said she first had sex with Prince Andrew. While that is not underage under English law, it is underage in Florida and the US Virgin Islands, where the age of consent is eighteen.

Nonetheless, the pregnant question for the British police was whether she had been trafficked to the UK for the purposes of sex—a criminal offence under British law. It was a politically-sensitive offence as it had recently been codified in the Modern Slavery Act, a piece of 'globally leading' trophy legislation sponsored by Prime Minister Theresa May herself.

At the beginning of November it was then revealed that the US TV network ABC had been sitting on an interview with Virginia Giuffre that had not been aired due to pressure from Buckingham Palace.

'I tried for three years to get [the interview] on to no avail and now it's coming out and it's like these "new revelations" and I freaking had all of it,' the host of 20/20 Amy Robach complained. 'First of all, I was told "who's Jeffrey Epstein? No one knows who that is, this is a stupid story." Then the palace found out that we had her whole allegations about Prince Andrew and threatened us a million different ways. We were so afraid we wouldn't be able to interview Kate and Wills, that also quashed the story.'

Buckingham Palace realised that they looked ragged. It was decided that the way to stop all speculation about the duke's connections to Epstein was for him to go in front of the TV cameras with BBC Newsnight presenter Emily Maitlis and give his testimony on Giuffre's accusations to her. This lost the prince the services of Jason Stein, the spin doctor he hired in September 2019 to restore his reputation. Stein had advised against going on air, favouring instead a drip-drip strategy that included a great deal of charity work and interviews with print outlets to mark the duke's upcoming sixtieth birthday. Courtiers took no notice of this caustic vote of confidence by a media professional and pressed on with preparations for the BBC interview.

Andrew's ex-wife Sarah Ferguson also urged Andrew to go on television. She thought that it would be his chance to address the negative headlines head on and present his version of events rather than leave the allegations unanswered.

Fatefully, Buckingham Palace signed off on the plan and that it was to be held in the Queen's part of the palace lending the prince the gravitas and weight of the British head of state. The Newsnight team would be taken to her private South Drawing Room, through the Queen's Entrance, surrounding the BBC crew and the prince with the paraphernalia and high symbols of Britain's monarch. It would be an unmitigated disaster.

Perhaps the palace thought it could ride out the connection between a prince and a paedophile by merely impressing the people with pomp and circumstance. Like the Vatican, it had a tin-ear record of dealing with sexual scandals. Prince Charles had been a friend of TV personality Jimmy Savile, who was posthumously exposed as a serial predatory paedophile. Savile had been allowed to make unannounced visits to Kensington Palace and had been invited to Charles's fortieth birthday party. Charles had even sent Savile a box of Havana cigars—a gift from Fidel Castro—with a note saying: 'Nobody will ever know what you've done for this country, Jimmy.'

Charles also expressed sympathy for another sexual offender. He allowed Peter Ball, the Bishop of Lewes and Gloucester, to live in a property in Somerset provided by the Duchy of Cornwall despite the prelate's admission that he had sexually abused boys, one as young as twelve. Documents revealed that the police had cooperated with leaders of the Church of England, particularly the Archbishop of Canterbury George Carey, to 'prevent a scandal', partly because Ball was 'friendly with Prince Charles'.

'I wish I could do more,' Charles wrote to the paedophile in 1995, angry that Ball had not been re-appointed as bishop. 'I feel so desperately strongly about the monstrous wrongs that have been done to you and the way you've been treated.' Ball was jailed in 2015—the year that Giuffre accused Andrew.

The royal family had sailed through these scandals relatively unscathed. But the Epstein imbroglio was not going to go away. There were at least fifteen lawsuits by victims against Epstein's estate and the FBI were on the track of possible accomplices. There was also Jean-Luc Brunel, the Epstein insider who found models for the billionaire. He seemed to have turned sides and in a pivotal breakthrough provided, in the words of Giuffre's lawyer, 'first-hand accounts of Epstein engaging in sex with minors inside and outside of the US—describing nothing less than an international sex scheme'.

Buckingham Palace and the prince were adamant, however, the allegations were untrue and the palace was preparing to bet The Firm.

2

THE TROUBLE WITH ANDREW

There is a very good reason for a book on the scandal caused by the man behind the princely title and its ramifications for Britain as a nation. Behind the scenes, the duke has not only become one of Britain's most influential royals since Prince Philip's retirement from public life in 2017, but he is also the son whom the nonagenarian monarch considers her 'rock' and 'tower of strength'. These affectionate epithets, the latest in many over the years, transpired in January 2020 when reporters were briefed during the media frenzy surrounding the move of Prince Harry and his wife Meghan Markle to Canada.

Not long before the storm-in-a-teacup crisis surrounding Prince Harry, Andrew himself had been swept up in the much more sordid scandal of his own making. The scandal was further inflamed by the November 2019 TV interview with the duke on BBC Newsnight in Buckingham Palace. The interview had been mooted for six months by palace officials with BBC Newsnight producer Sam McAlister.

In fact, there seemed to be a connection between the two royal crises. The palace had known for months, as well, about the Sussexes' desire to step back from their roles as senior royals were secretly negotiating the implications of such a move with the couple. Was it a coincidence that, shortly after the Newsnight interview spectacularly misfired, the emigration of Harry and Meghan, his wife of African-American descent, to Canada was leaked? It was such big news globally that, if it didn't drown out the prince's TV catastrophe completely, it at least directed a lot of the turbulence around the palace towards a different, much lighter royal subject.

Already on the day of the Newsnight interview there was a report of Prince Harry 'dropping out of the royal family'. Was it an early plant by the palace? Once the top of the royal family had cleared Andrew's interview, courtiers had to have a contingency plan ready in case the prince's reputation would not be burnished the way the royal family hoped it would. While royals themselves were evidently persuaded by Andrew's impending success, opinions were certainly divided among palace staff as to what the net result would be of appearing on the BBC's most famous inquisitorial programme.

Following the green signal for the interview, the Charles-William faction among the royal staff likely saw the Harry-Meghan diversion as a move that would both protect the Queen and the monarchy while saving the prince from himself in case he became the media's sitting duck.

At worst, a plant might nudge the ongoing negotiations with the Sussexes to a conclusion. At best it could result in trimming the expanding monarchy, a long-standing objective among the faction. The news reception would decide the fate of three independently-minded HRHs. One would fall, or not, depending on his TV performance, and the Sussexes would have to make a decision as to what exactly they wanted—remain or leave. The royal family, bound by family affection, would of course not personally be involved in this part of the palace's job.

The first sign of storm clouds had gathered on the horizon when billionaire Jeffrey Epstein was arrested at a New Jersey airport on federal charges of sex trafficking minors. The federal arrest followed Epstein's guilty plea eleven years earlier in 2008 to a State of Florida charge of soliciting a sixteen-year-old girl and an eighteen-month largely suspended prison sentence.

The prince, notwithstanding Epstein's underage sex charges, was photographed in 2010 with the registered sex offender after his release. This was followed by news in 2011 that his ex-wife had accepted money from the paedophile and the prince resigned thereafter from his official function within the UK government.

On the same day of Epstein's arrest in July 2019, the FBI searched Epstein's Manhattan townhouse. What they found was truly explosive. The agency uncovered photographs of underage girls as well as a fake passport belonging to Epstein, among many other pieces of potential evidence that the billionaire had secreted away at his New York home. In a desperate bid to restore their client's freedom, Epstein's lawyers offered to post bail of 100 million dollars. The request was denied by the presiding federal judge.

Not long after, the first domino stone tumbled. Alex Acosta, one of Donald Trump's cabinet members, had to resign for having engineered Epstein's generous guilty plea in Florida in 2008. The plea had been advocated by Alan Dershowitz and Kenneth Starr on Epstein's behalf in exchange for his immunity from prosecution in the other cases. Some forty minors had originally come forward to the police, including the fourteen year old who had made the first complaint. The youngest girl was thirteen. Nonetheless Epstein's guilty plea related to one sixteen year old only and he was allowed to leave prison on work release during his sentence. Julie Brown of the *Miami Herald* would later identify up to eighty victims, including twelve-year-old triplets flown in from France, in a 2018 article about Acosta's handling of the Epstein charges.

By this time, the opposing sides of Giuffre's case and that of the other Epstein victims split into a who's who of America's establishment. Giuffre's lead lawyer was David Boies, one of America's most high-profile lawyers. He had fought on Al Gore's side at the Supreme Court in Bush v Gore on dangling chads and the presidency, and he had won gay-marriage equality in US v Windsor. Alan Dershowitz had defended OJ Simpson and himself was a frequent traveller on Epstein's private plane. In 2020 he and Giuffre still had a mutual defamation suit open against one another according to one of her lawyers. Orbiting the case were US Attorney General William Barr, whose father had given Epstein his first job, and US President Trump, who knew Epstein, Prince Andrew and Ghislaine Maxwell, well.

Fortunately for Epstein's powerful sex friends, the sixty six year old died under mysterious circumstances while in custody. The Trump administration's official investigation into the matter reckoned it was an unlucky confluence of Epstein's suicide by auto-strangulation and prison-regulation 'screw-ups'. Days later the criminal trial was dismissed as a result of Epstein's demise and his victims were denied their day in court.

The prince, however, had been implicated in Epstein's sex ring in 2015 when Giuffre opened her libel suit against Maxwell. Four days before Epstein's arrest in July 2019, a federal court had ordered that documents be unsealed in the Giuffre vs Maxwell case. The unsealed papers revealed the second accuser of the prince, Johanna Sjoberg, who stated he had groped her breast while both she, he and Giuffre were posing for a picture. Sjoberg had not wanted to give evidence originally, but Giuffre had convinced her through her charm, persistence, and courage to take on powerful people.

In a separate twist, Richard Dawkins's literary agent John Brockman revealed late August that he had witnessed a man called 'Andy', whom he later realised was Prince Andrew, receive a foot massage by two Russian women at Epstein's Manhattan mansion.

In 2013, Brockman wrote in an email to one of his authors, 'I walked in to find [Epstein] in a sweatsuit and a British guy in a suit with suspenders, getting foot massages from two young well-dressed Russian women.'

The man in the suit was talking about the Swedish authorities and their rape charges against Julian Assange which had been issued the month before in November 2010.

'We think they're liberal in Sweden, but it's more like Northern England as opposed to Southern Europe', the Brit complained. 'In Monaco, Albert works 12 hours a day but at 9pm, when he goes out, he does whatever he wants, and nobody cares. But, if I do it, I'm in big trouble.'

At this point Brockman realised that the man talking was Prince Andrew. Sometime later, he saw his new British friend again but this time on the front page of the *New York Post* walking with Epstein in Central Park, under the headline 'The Prince and the Perv.'

It was soon revealed by a royal source that the prince 'does enjoy massages' and the press found Monique Giannelloni who had been introduced to Andrew in 2000 by Maxwell and Epstein as a masseuse. The booking had been made by the prince's secretary, who also paid Giannelloni after the massage in his bedroom at Buckingham Palace. To her surprise, the prince appeared in the nude, Giannelloni told the *Daily Mail.*

Over the years, the prince vigorously denied impropriety and flatly denied these accusations via the palace press service. Indeed he has denied ever meeting the women who accuse him, the scene Brockman described, being in the same photograph, or even having himself seen anything that might have hinted at Epstein's sex crimes during his visits to the billionaire's houses.

At Epstein's bail hearing, the presiding judge asked the US prosecutor, 'Do you anticipate that there may be other defendants in this proceeding?' and received the response, 'It certainly is possible down the road.' And, notwithstanding the close of Epstein's prosecution on account of his death, the FBI went on the record that it continued to investigate the billionaire's sex trafficking of minors and was interested to speak to the prince.

There was no indication at all that the US prosecutor was thinking of Prince Andrew or anyone else in particular. Then the prince volunteered his own-goal BBC Newsnight interview. Not long after, the interview led press pundits to debate the issue of extradition.

There is only one nation in the world that will extradite its own citizens to the US, no questions asked, and that country is the United Kingdom. This extraordinary state of affairs was the result of the Extradition Act 2003, a piece of legislation some legal experts at the time described as a disgrace. Railroaded through parliament under Tony Blair's government, it simplified and automated the extradition of UK citizens to America. Any incoming US extradition request is merely vetted by the Home Secretary on being a genuine request and sent on to the Westminster Magistrates Court, where the extradition judge will issue an arrest warrant without considering such evidence as there may be in support of the request.

The new law solved the difficulty of removing extremists from British soil, but at a cost no other government in the world was willing to countenance on behalf of its citizens.

US courts considered 'aliens' to be a flight risk and denied bail as a rule. It meant immediate custody upon arrival on US soil with extremely limited access to lawyers—usually only a few hours a week—and the outside world. In practice, therefore, an extradition request was virtually tantamount to a guilty verdict because the accused wouldn't be able to prepare a decent defence.

Used in 2004 finally to extradite Abu Hamza smoothly without judicial review, the Act would now subject the Queen's second son to the same skimpy process if matters ever came to a head. And if that were to happen, the event would tarnish the reputation of the British royal family from one of the most preeminent in the world, to a far sleazier one where the word 'prince' and 'arrest' were never far away. The stakes were high indeed.

Under the 2003 Act, it doesn't matter whether no British law was broken. The only defence that the prince could try to plead against a potential extradition request was immunity from prosecution as a government official or as a member of the household of the Queen, Britain's head of state—or, indeed, both. Although this exception was not expressly written into the Act, it was accepted that it was the one get-me-out-of-a-US-jail card before one gets shunted into the American legal system.

Legal experts considered it very unlikely that such a request for immunity would succeed in a British court, if only because the prince waived his protection as a witness by speaking publicly about the allegations against him. Under UK law, moreover, it was not sufficient merely to be one of the heirs to the throne to be considered part of the head of state's household. In 2018, an additional exception was eked out by the Court of Appeal around personality disorders. It followed years of British outrage over pending extradition of a hacker described as suicidal, Asperger's-suffering, with eczema, and a student at Glasgow University. That was also not very likely to apply to the prince.

What were Andrew's chances of immunity under US law? As it happened, his older brother Charles had cleared the way. The Prince of Wales was sued in 1977 after a ten-minute address he gave at the opening of the University of Cleveland's law faculty new building. After a long and tenacious lecture by its dean on the British origins of due process, Charles's own speech was short, 'witty, urbane and self-effacing', according to a student in the audience who said he would have happily taken the twenty-nine-year-old prince out for a beer.

However, the editor of the law faculty's student newspaper, Jack Kilroy, was also there and remained standing after the ovation for the prince, stepped forward and asked, 'Prince Charles when is the British government going to stop torturing political prisoners in Ireland?' One of six invited students, IRA buttons pinned to his lapels in solidarity with the three hundred or so protesters outside, Kilroy was bundled off within seconds by federal agents while Charles pointedly quizzed the assembled dignitaries, 'Are there any more Irish here?'

The ITN photographer present thought 'it was the joke of the year' but the confused Cleveland constabulary asked Kilroy, 'You are the law student, what do you think we should charge you with?' Declining to sign a waiver, he instead sued Charles for having deprived him of his freedom of speech. Before it could go any further, however, the US State Department intervened and extended sovereign immunity to Charles as a high-ranking representative of the British head of state—which meant that the case was dismissed. The prince had set a frequently cited precedent that would now be the best chance of avoiding extradition for his younger, loquacious brother.

Most presidents would not get involved, but Donald Trump was not like most presidents. Nonetheless, would he be such great friends with Prince Andrew that, almost half a century later, he would extend the immunity the heir to the throne enjoyed to the very junior prince as well if things came to a head under his presidency? On this occasion, the underlying extradition facts would involve a case of sex with minors rather than a witty speech.

Kilroy and Prince Charles, 1977

Trump had a tendency to drop friends like hot potatoes when there was no longer any publicity upside and merely downside of their acquaintance.

Indeed, Trump was accused in 2016 by one woman, 'Katie Johnson', of having violently raped her when she was thirteen during an orgy organised by Epstein in 1994. The $100 million lawsuit cited two of Epstein's party planners as witnesses but was dropped days before the election. Furthermore, Giuffre had claimed to work at Mar-a-Lago when she was recruited as a fifteen year old by Maxwell, and her alleged encounters with Andrew took place in 2000 and 2001 when many photos were taken of a beaming Trump with Epstein and Maxwell at his exclusive Florida club.

In 2002, Trump still went on the record with the words, 'I've known Jeff for fifteen years. Terrific guy'. In 2017, he said of Epstein, 'I wasn't a fan'.

The omens for Andrew were not very favourable. Asked in December 2019 whether he knew the duke, Trump said, 'I don't know him, no'. This was even though they had had lunch half a year earlier at Buckingham Palace and had known each other since at least February 2000, when they were photographed at his Mar-a-Lago club—together with Epstein, Maxwell and his future wife Melania. The prince had also flown on his private jet.

Donald, Melania, Andrew, Epstein, Maxwell, Mar-a-Lago, 2000

The extradition issue begged the more important question for the United Kingdom whether Prince Andrew Epstein's Affair could end the monarchy in its existing, traditional form.

It was not difficult to imagine a situation that would create a crisis as serious as the one caused by Edward VIII's closeness to American divorcee Wallis Simpson. Prince Andrew was by far the least favourite member of the royal family in a YouGov poll of 13 January 2020. Only 17 per cent of respondents had a positive opinion of the prince and 45 per cent had a 'negative opinion' of him. The same poll found that 74 per cent were positive about the Queen, which made her the most popular royal.

Yet, in a poll a month later almost 80 per cent of respondents disagreed with the Queen's decision to ring the bells for her favourite son's sixtieth birthday on 19 February. When Melanie Dawes, as one of her last acts as the Prime Minister's local government secretary, sent an email out to local councils reminding them to fly the flag for the royal, there was uproar from the councils. 'The Government doesn't appear to be noticing what has happened recently, or factoring in the mood of the nation', was one livid response.

If there were further legal ramifications, however mild, the pressure could become irresistible for Prince Andrew to actively cooperate with the US federal authorities investigating the transgressions surrounding Epstein's associates. At the same time, as will become clear from the chapters below, there was no chance that the Queen would allow her favourite son to be sacrificed—even for the survival of The Firm. Prince Andrew's Epstein Affair thus had the potential ingredients for a full-blown constitutional crisis.

These exceptional developments would by themselves be a good reason for the first book on this long royal crisis. But there was another reason.

Once, the prince was perceived in a very different way. In an earlier part of his life he was the one royal who seemed to do no wrong. The man, who since then bested his father's self-confessed foot-in-mouth disease by becoming a scandal-prone duke, once was the poster boy for the monarchy. As the handsome, self-confident, straightforward foil to his older brother—the diffident, complicated, and plain-looking Prince of Wales—Andrew appeared to have it all as a young man. A long career as Britain's most popular prince and the monarch's most powerful brand ambassador seemed assured for the Queen's favourite son. Teenage girls and young mothers once lined the streets shouting, 'We want Andy', fainting as if he was a popstar, and being lifted over the crowd for medical attention as if at a concert. How did this fairytale prince raised at the pinnacle of the world's leading royal family, with the best and most exclusive education money could buy, get seduced into friendship by an American hustler from the Bronx who some described as 'a bit creepy'?

Following in his father's and older brother's footsteps at the Spartan Gordonstoun, he had enrolled in the Royal Navy. He trained as a helicopter pilot, a personal interest stimulated by watching his father behind the cyclic as a young boy. His navy career progressed in a steady if not exemplary fashion thereafter. His postings in the nation's internationally-admired war machine were real enough.

Nothing made this clearer than the 1982 Falklands War, during which the Queen overruled Margaret Thatcher's government and ensured that Andrew would serve in action as a helicopter pilot. It was only four years into his training; his service earned him a favourable accolade from his squadron commander. His Falklands involvement had also drawn the attention of the Argentinian government, which allegedly formed plans to have him assassinated, according to

1983 news reports. It made him seem an even more heroic figure.

Andrew then also proposed to the no-nonsense, friendly and photogenic Sarah Ferguson, a choice that was popularly received with jubilant headlines. While his working life spoke of diligence and duty, his family life was the epitome of domesticity with two small, bouncy daughters, a carbon copy of his grandfather George VI's—who was also the second son with two small daughters, one of which would unexpectedly become the Queen after the abdication crisis following Edward VIII's decision to marry Wallis Simpson.

How did this attractive young prince, who seemed to have handled his life of royal privilege ostensibly so well, become the Andrew we are now familiar with? The prince's life was also a test case of Buckingham Palace in action.

One of the surprises was that the monarchy projects an image of long-standing and immutable traditions, but in fact was quite flexible and opportunistic in what it did. The palace often just made it up as it went along, while dressing decisions up as if this was how it was done since time immemorial.

The palace operatics surrounding Prince Andrew's nephew Harry were a case in point. While trying to wrest back royal titles gifted to the Sussexes on their marriage, the palace justified one of its 'returns demands' by the apparently self-evident reason that their 'title is one of the ancient royal dukedoms'. Many around the world might find it slightly curious to be asked to hand a wedding gift back to the donor—however old the present they received. Furthermore, knights and members of the house of lords are rarely stripped of their titles upon something far more disreputable than emigration: such as conviction of a crime. In any case, though there was a 'King of Sussex' until 827 AD, the dukedom itself dates back to 1801—old like the arch-ducal title of the Battenbergs, or Mountbattens, but not quite ancient.

A notorious stickler for the vagaries of protocol, the palace also announced its new form of address for Meghan, now that she was no longer an 'HRH'. She was to be styled 'Meghan, Duchess of Sussex'. Unfortunately, it overlooked that her new style was identical to the one she would receive—and get to keep?—if she and Harry were to divorce. Not much later an announcement followed that the palace's guidance would be 'updated'.

Likewise, Prince Andrew's life resembled that of a pinball in a royal game controlled by flappers.

3

BABY GRUMPLING

Born on 19 February 1960, Andrew was a handful from the beginning. His nanny, Mabel Anderson, called him 'Baby Grumpling' for his temper tantrums, mischief and obstinacy. He led her a merry dance and she struggled to teach him rudimentary manners. It took all her willpower to not make him scoff his food as fast as he could to go back to his games.

Andrew's name for his nanny was 'Mamba'. Originally, the infant prince was loved by other palace staff who called him 'Andy Pandy' after a popular puppet programme on TV. But that affection for him didn't last long. He got obstinate if he didn't get his way and after his sister Anne left for Benenden and until his younger brother Edward joined him in the nursery, he was the king of his solitary domain. Shouts, laughter, and angry cries would make his presence known, and he would want to know what was going on. His new nickname among palace staff was 'that young imp' when he removed the back of 'Mamba's' radio and took out the valves.

Prince Philip named Andrew after his father, Prince Andrew of Greece and Denmark, and called him 'The Boss' as he was wilful and self-possessed. Philip's father was twice exiled from his native Greece, estranged from his wife and son, as well as his daughters, who all married Nazis. At the end of his life Andrew of Greece could mainly be found on board his mistress's yacht or in casinos in the South of France and died in a hotel room in Monaco. It was not an auspicious name.

The young Andrew was special, even amongst royalty. His birth in 1960 was the first to a British reigning monarch since Queen Victoria. All of Victoria's nine children were born during her long rule, but her last and youngest child was Princess Beatrice—who was born in 1857, twenty years into Victoria and Albert's marriage.

Beatrice loomed large in royal family lore. Although Victoria cut herself off from her children after Albert's death, Beatrice remained her trusted companion from the day she was born. Privy to all Victoria's secrets, Beatrice was her literary executor and edited the queen's scrupulously candid daily diary entries, copying them in long-hand and cutting and sanitising the material by a good two thirds—destroying the originals, to her nephew George V's powerless distress—over a thirty-year-long period.

Andrew was always acutely aware of this unique quirk in his royal pedigree and he named his first child Beatrice after this distant but symbolically important relative. Born thirteen years into the Queen and Philip's marriage, fussed over quite a bit in the palace by the maids and ladies-in-waiting, the prince was also his parents' favourite baby—as Beatrice had been Victoria and Albert's. His birth came ten years after Anne was born, and Andrew was the affirmation that the Queen and Philip had overcome the difficulties in their union. Originally he and Fergie had picked the name Annabel, but dropped it when the Queen said she thought it was too 'yuppie'.

Philip's enjoyment of Andrew had not been a foregone conclusion, as he had complained about having more children, 'The last thing the world needs is more royal mouths to feed.' But when the baby turned out to be a boy, Prince Philip's enthusiasm knew no bounds. Too impatient to take the elevator, he ran up the stairs two at a time to tell Anne that she had a brother and then rang the Queen Mother to tell her the news.

To his further joy, Prince Philip soon recognised the spitting image of himself in the little boy's quirks and took immense pleasure in Andrew's increasingly confident cocky streak. Philip's relatives agreed that he and Andrew were identical twins separated in time. Philip's mother, living in Buckingham Palace at the time, recognised the hunched shoulders when either would be perplexed or excited. Philip was much more protective and lenient towards Andrew than his oldest son who, as a toddler, was an 'exceptionally sweet-natured boy' but would clam up if shouted at. Andrew was not put out by his father's commands and bonded closely with him.

Philip had fretted over his third child's surname even before 'the second round' arrived, and in a hard-fought exchange got the Queen to agree to insert his 'Mountbatten' before her 'Windsor' just before Andrew's birth. This was quite a departure from the birth of Charles and Anne. Winston Churchill as prime minister had firmly resisted any change in name, but his successor relented to the queen's diplomacy. Heavily-pregnant, the Queen had applied pressure on Harold Macmillan to yield on the issue that 'had been irritating her husband since 1952'.

In fact, the Queen's concession was one of principle rather than practise. Royals don't really use surnames, unless they are travelling incognito—in which case they make them up anyway. Windsor was still the name of the royal House and the surname would only apply to male-descendants of the Queen without royal styles or titles, i.e. those in need of a surname. Nonetheless, Andrew was Philip's first son born with the surname Mountbatten-Windsor.

Though this was seemingly a modest prize, it was a crucial moral victory for Philip. George V was the first-ever British monarch to adopt a surname—the weight of nine centuries of tradition dispatched, *ad hoc*, at the stroke of a pen—and he had picked 'Windsor' for his male descendants in a rebranding exercise that yielded to Britain's violent anti-German sentiment at the beginning of World War I.

Almost half a century later, Philip had forced an exception on the foremost royal family in the world, distinguishing his male descendants from any other male royal Windsors that walked the earth. There was to be no doubt. Andrew was his son. By his own estimation, Prince Philip was no longer 'some sort of amoeba', as he had complained bitterly before. Indeed, if the titles and HRH style were ever to be taken away from the Duke of York by a future monarch, Andrew would have to start using the surname his father picked for him. Currently only the Queen's unmarried female descendants have no choice in the matter.

Where Charles was tentative as a child, Andrew thrived. His early years marinated in the opulence and splendid isolation that surrounded the monarch. He had at least seven nurseries in four palaces and, unlike his two elder siblings, from the start his life consisted of sumptuous surroundings with footmen and priceless art, endless royal Rolls Royces, while the royal train and yacht would take him wherever on the yearly 'royal migration'—London,

Windsor, Sandringham, Balmoral—always accompanied by a detective for his protection. There were royal celebrations at the palaces, such as shooting parties and banquets, and his mother's birthday would be celebrated by uniformed parades and other pomp and circumstance.

By palace convention, his nanny had two footmen and maids waiting on her. It was a Victorian and Edwardian tradition that only Diana would end when raising William and Harry herself—the first of many disagreements she and Prince Charles (who had loved his devoted but severe nanny, Helen Lightbody) had about their children.

At Balmoral with his mother

Yet it was a strange life for the little prince, who lived over a hundred yards away from his parents' bedrooms. At set times, things just materialised for him. 'Things always turned up on time, and I remember well that if I didn't turn up to breakfast within five minutes of the appointed time, there would be none',

Andrew recalled. The terror of missing breakfast meant that he could only have breakfast at exactly 8:30 in the morning for the rest of his life. Diversions were laid on for the prince. 'I remember great tea parties at Buckingham Palace... all sorts of expeditions to museums, taxis to the shops, and going on the Tube.' Only in summer would the whole family, including Charles and Anne, be together in relatively close quarters at Balmoral Castle.

Although Andrew was not often around children his own age, he did have his mother's undivided attention. This was again very different from his elder siblings. Nanny Lightbody ruled with an iron fist over Charles's and Anne's nursery and even the Queen had to obey Lightbody's rules, which were meant to create habits like clockwork for royal babies and toddlers. The Queen rarely saw her oldest son in his infancy and did not attend his first three birthdays. It was only when Nanny Lightbody overplayed her hand by refusing the Queen's request for a special birthday dish that she was replaced by a new nanny, Mabel Anderson. Mabel relaxed the rules on the Queen's limited influence over the royal nursery and Charles and Anne in general.

With Andrew, the Queen was entirely different and he was entirely different with her—gone was the little boy with tantrums. He would often play quietly in her study with a puzzle or picture book while visitors on official business came round, and the Queen would go for walks and watch him play in the sandpit and climbing rack built for him. She also taught him the letters of the alphabet, how to tell time on one of the palace clocks, gave him lessons on Mr Dinkum, his first pony, and looked forward to bathing him and giving him her undivided attention on the days that Mabel had her night off.

The special bond she had with their second son strengthened as he grew older. Before a state banquet his mother, in her tiara and gown, and father, in white tie, would come down to the nursery to chat to Andrew and later Edward. The almost Victorian Nanny Lightbody would never have allowed such a casual interruption of Prince Charles's sacrosanct nursery schedule. The Queen was not welcome unless Lightbody condoned a visit.

Andrew himself recalled of his childhood, 'My parents made huge efforts to make sure they were with us a lot. That meant a huge sacrifice for them. I remember my mother would look after Edward and me in the evenings in the palace, alone, quite happily.' In his estimation, 'It was a proper family.'

It made Andrew very confident and extroverted in comparison to the self-conscious Charles. Once, while the whole royal family were watching Coronation Street and the busty Bet Lynch got into an argument, Andrew erupted, 'Oh God, look at all those common people.' Raised in between his nanny and mother, Charles would never let himself go like that, let alone think like that.

It did not go down well. Prince Philip instantly gave his son a rocket, saying, 'If it wasn't for people like that you would not be sitting here', flicking Andrew's ear. The young prince fell quiet and for once he was far from the boisterous tornado who was always 'chatting to housemaids or favoured visitors' of his mother's. Philip was to give his favourite son many a rocket over the years and decades that would follow.

The young Andrew played endless practical jokes on the staff, hiding the knives and forks when a footman was laying the table, and tying sentries' shoelaces together, knowing they wouldn't be able to move—literally—or chastise him. Using a silver tea tray he tobogganed down the stairs in the palace and broke the greenhouse windows with a football. In the nursery, after taking 'Mamba's' radio to bits, he went missing, only to be found contentedly asleep in the airing cupboard. Sparring with Prince Philip, he punched his father in the eye. Attending a film premiere that night, Philip pointed to his eye and said: 'That was The Boss.' Everyone thought he meant the Queen. Andrew later said airily, 'Every now and again a pane of glass got broken, but I don't think we ever broke a piece of Meissen or anything like that'.

His mischievousness gathered pace as he grew into a youth. He gave the Queen Mother a whoopee cushion, sprinkled itching powder in his mother's bed and once climbed onto the roof of Buckingham Palace to turn the TV aerial so that when the Queen sat down to watch her favourite show—horse racing from Sandown Park—she couldn't see a picture. The palace maintenance man was called to do something about it or she'd have missed the three thirty. Meanwhile Andrew was hidden away laughing before telling his mother what he had done. There were stink bombs, and bath soap sneakily poured into the Windsor Castle swimming pool (Andrew didn't admit to being the culprit). Even the Queen sighed, 'He is not always a little ray of sunshine about the home.'

Nor did Andrew share his mother's other delight—he being her first passion. Once he interrupted a spirited discussion of his friends about horses, the one subject that could rival the Queen's attention for him. Screwing up his face jokingly in contempt, he complained to them, 'Horses, bloody horses. I am sick of hearing about them. Can't you talk about anything else.' He might as well have been chiding his mother for not paying enough attention to him.

His first schooling was with his nephew, Viscount Linley, and a few others, to whom he was aggressive and bossy. He would upset them when in a black mood. Only one of them, a young girl called Kate Seymour, the daughter of a courtier, dared to stand up to him.

Rather than following the tradition of previous generations—including Prince Charles—who had been taught by private tutors, the Queen's 'second brood' were to attend school. This was in order to raise them as 'ordinary children' in the words of Prince Philip, a man who grew up in palaces.

Nonetheless, they remained hedged in by privilege on all sides. To raise them as if they were ordinary was always going to be a matter of accents rather than a real break with the past—certainly in the case of Andrew. He had all the privileges but none of the responsibilities that Charles had.

At the age of eight, he was sent to Heatherdown, a prep school in Ascot, which is not far from Windsor, and where he was soon known as one of the wilder boys and a bruiser. At Heatherdown he organised midnight feasts and mixed up everyone's shoes in the dorm. He was blamed when a shirt appeared flying from the top of the school flagpole.

In going to Heatherdown, Andrew followed in the footsteps of Prince Charles. So everything he did, Charles had done first and usually better. He nonetheless aped his elder brother's antics, which earned him the nickname 'Action Man Two' after Charles's sobriquet in the media at the time. Andrew could be rude and aggressive to both boys and teachers if the mood took him, but he was treated with kid gloves, as he was at the palace. Disciplining him could only be done through a procedure especially designed for him that had to involve the headmaster.

He and his younger brother Edward were taken to Lords to be taught how to play cricket by Britain's best coach and praised for having promise, taken to Wimbledon for tennis by one of its former champions, and given private lessons in ice skating in Richmond after other skaters had been cleared off the rink by security staff so that the boys had the entire area for themselves to spread out. Their gym was the one at the Chelsea Barracks, and both Andrew and Edward were also given ballroom dance instruction by Madame Vacani, a poor warm-up for the disco floor at London private-members club Tramp later in Andrew's life.

All that special attention created a bit of a career as a bully for Andrew. But his mother called it, 'Andrew isn't a bit shy', and Prince Philip put it that Andrew 'was a natural boss'. Philip's relatives, also turned a blind eye and said, 'sometimes naughty but never nasty'—as they had said about Philip himself at that age. The Queen's own prophesy had been fulfilled. She had written to her cousin, 'the baby is adorable. All in all, he's going to be terribly spoilt by all of us, I'm sure.'

Sharing a dormitory at Heatherdown with six others, Andrew complained that he was not allowed to watch the TV programmes he watched at home. But he was spanked following a school outing to the Natural History Museum in London where there was a brawl with a group of teenagers who, Andrew's schoolmates claimed, approached them and demanded money. The staff at Heatherdown was not heart-broken to see the prince leave after his exams.

There were lots of other special perks his doting parents showered on him from an early age. One of the greatest circus legends, veteran clown Charlie Cairoli, entertained at Andrew's birthday party. The prince was given a one-off miniature replica of the Aston Martin driven by James Bond in Goldfinger and a pony on another birthday. There were sailing lessons at Cowes and he was taught salmon fishing by the Queen Mother, while the Bishop of Norwich took him to see Norwich City play Chelsea FC. He was given a guided tour of New Scotland Yard with an Iranian prince and, during a visit to King Olav of Norway, sailed up the coast to visit Prime Minister Per Borten at his farmhouse near Trondheim Fjord. His mother sent a plane to pick him up from school to go to the wedding of his sister at Westminster Abbey and the reception for royal relatives arriving from all over the world, which was massively televised.

These special treats meant little to Andrew, however. When Charles graduated from Cambridge, got his RAF wings, and went out on a naval mission with destroyer HMS Norfolk all in the same year, Philip had to cheer Andrew up that his time would come. When he went to help his father retrieve game grouse-hunting, he wanted his own gun.

In fact, at this time Andrew himself, as the second in line to the throne, was one of the trophies hunted by the IRA. As a boy Charles had merely needed protection from over-enthusiastic members of the public and the press, but Andrew's formative years coincided with the height of brutal IRA terrorism. As far as the security forces were concerned, he was one of the crown jewels whose life needed the highest level of protection. They once surrounded Heatherdown as there was credible intelligence that there was an imminent execution plot. One of the security officers taught the prince how to handle a gun while it was going on.

Andrew was sent to Gordonstoun, the tough remote boarding school in the bleak north of Scotland where both his father and Charles had excelled. Founded a few years after the Great War, the school was for (largely German) aristocrats and plutocrats who were to be trained in the art of becoming selfless rulers, living and dying for the common good, through asceticism, cold showers, no pocket money, community work and the like. As a rule, a few ordinary people on scholarships were accepted to inoculate the noble children against greater hubris. The pupils trained on the school's own fire engine and it had its own sea-worthy yacht.

Thirty girls had been admitted for the first time in the year before Andrew arrived, prompting Charles to say about his brother's school work, 'He's enjoying himself immensely'. A court observer would spikily summarise what the admittance of girls at the school meant: 'In the old days at royal courts there would have been maids-of-honour or ladies-in-waiting to provide company for the young princes'. At any rate, Gordonstoun's new headmaster advertised that in addition to female pupils they now had central heating and even a heated pool. As with life at the palace, Andrew's Gordonstoun was a lot more mellow than the dour regime Charles and Philip had endured.

Andrew shone neither academically nor in sports, saying of his *alma mater*: 'The beds are hard and it's all straw mattresses, bread and water—just like a prison.'

Other pupils called him 'boastful' and 'big-headed'. One said: 'He had a bit of the "I am the Prince" about him when he arrived. He soon had it knocked out of him. The ribbings he got were unmerciful.'

When Edward later went up to Gordonstoun he was wisely placed in a different house, as he did not want to be 'tarred with the same brush'. He knew his older brother's swagger well. Unlike he-man Andrew, his peers said of Edward he 'didn't ram who he was down your throat'.

To endear himself to the other boys, Prince Andrew regaled them with blue jokes, earning himself the nickname 'The Sniggerer'. One classmate said: 'By the time he's finished a joke he's laughing so much you can't understand the punch line.'

During the holidays, the prince learnt to ski in Switzerland, visited his cousins in Germany, sailed on the royal yacht Britannia and, finally, learnt to fly at RAF Milltown. Charles had been given naval-helicopter training and Andrew was again envious despite the eleven-year age difference.

Since he was, until Charles would have a son, the second in line to the throne, part of Andrew's education, involved preparation as a 'spare', in case he might become the future monarch. Two of the previous three kings had been second sons, and the odds were not considered to be particularly long.

At sixteen, he went with his parents to the 1976 Montreal Olympics, where girls clearly began to take an interest in him. And it didn't escape the Canadian press how at ease Andrew was around girls and women, whereas Charles was always a little circumspect and stood out because of his ears. When asked, the Prince of Wales was forced to concede that Andrew was the 'one with the Robert Redford looks'. His chubby younger brother had started to look like a fairy-tale prince.

One Canadian newspaper called Andrew 'six feet of sex appeal'. He was bombarded with requests for dates, invitations to parties and telephone numbers. This boosted his already dizzying self-confidence. He flirted with the female competitors in the Olympic Village and took a shine to his minder, a bubbly blonde named Sandi Jones who accompanied him everywhere, saying to her: 'Call me Andrew, not "Your Royal Highness".'

His name was also connected with that of Silvia Sommerlath, who had been a hostess at the 1972 Munich Olympics. However, she married Carl Gustaf of Sweden in 1976 and became his queen. When Andrew, travelling as Andrew Cambridge, returned to Canada in 1977 for an exchange year at Lakefield College School for boys near Toronto, dozens of young girls turned out at the airport. They screamed, blew kisses and chanted: 'We want Andy.' The exchange was semi-official to create photo opportunities that strengthened the ties of the House of Windsor to Canada and he was met by the Lt-Governor of Ontario getting off the plane. But, as his official car pulled out of the airport, he wound down the window to chat to some of the girls. Asked about them in the subsequent press conference, he said: 'I like them as much as the next chap.'

Andrew, Lakefield, Canada

When he played rugby at Lakefield, more girls turned out on the touchline to cheer his every move, wearing sweatshirts emblazoned with the slogans 'I'm an Andy Windsor girl' and 'Andy King'. The school itself had a strict protocol: staff called him 'Prince', governors would call the seventeen year old, 'Sir', and the chairman would say 'Your Royal Highness'. But the boys could call him Andrew, which soon became 'Randy Andy'. 'He really attracts the ladies', one fellow pupil complained.

He surprised everyone when he invited Sandi Jones to come to the first school dance at Lakefield and danced cheek to cheek with her. It did not go down well with the other girls invited to the dance. Schoolgirl Patricia Foy complained: 'It was unfair that he had one girl all the time. A lot of us wanted to dance with him.'

The following day on the ski slopes, he managed to ditch his Canadian minder, a Mountie, so he could spend time alone with Sandi. They met up later at a jazz concert in Toronto and had dinner together at the Harbour Castle Hotel after the show.

In a school production of Oliver, he tried to revive the stricken Nancy. His performance wasn't as electric as Charles's school-rendition of Macbeth, but Andrew did have an effect on his fellow thesps. 'My heartbeat shot up to about a hundred miles an hour when he put his fingers on my wrist,' said Gillian Wilson, who was playing the part of Nancy. He had a similar effect on the teenage Linda Sergeant, who bumped into him while jogging on the college playing fields. 'He was a real charmer,' she said. 'I really fancied him.'

Despite the adulation, something changed in Canada. Andrew dressed differently. Gone was the princely armour of a suit and tie and in came the Marlboro-man look with jeans, a big-buckled belt and open-necked seventies shirts. He even smiled more and was a little less brazen in a country that saw him as a curiosity rather than someone who had to live up to a different standard from their own. Andrew could let his hair down.

He returned not long after to attend the 110th anniversary of Canada's independent status in the year of his mother's Silver Jubilee. The photogenic, sporty Andrew was the third most senior royal and he knew the country. So it was logical that he was the Queen's companion of choice for the trip. This time, he received full official honours as the Queen's second heir travelling across the vast country. At a party given for him at Government House in Ottawa, he spent the night dancing with star figure skater Lynn Nightingale, and was given a new name, Soya Hun, by the Algonquin tribes. In Vancouver on Canada day, he was cheered by bevies of young girls. At a rodeo hostess Gillie Newman called him: 'A real prince charming', others called him 'cute' and 'even better than Prince Charles.' Then he teamed up again with Sandi Jones for a survival tour of wildlife parks, where the threat of an IRA attack was less great.

Was young love in the air and were Andrew and Sandi an item? Sandi complained that there 'wasn't much romancing under the eye of Andrew's bodyguards'. With terrorism rife in the UK, neither the Canadian nor the British government were taking any chances. With some justification. A year later, Prince Philip's uncle, Lord Mountbatten, would be blown up by the IRA while boating at his Northern Ireland retreat.

Nonetheless, Sandi admitted candidly that 'we managed to give them the slip on occasions. Andrew can be extremely resourceful. He's just an ordinary guy who wants to have fun with his girlfriend.' When he flew home, Andrew told the press that his time in Canada was 'the most wonderful experience I've ever had I think.'

At the age of eighteen, he received his first handout by the state when Parliament granted him £20,000 a year (worth comfortably over £100,000 in today's money) but that did not improve his performance at Gordonstoun, which now had 120 girls to over 300 boys. Fellow pupil Lucilla 'Lulu' Houseman said: 'He didn't shine at anything. He loved having a good time. In fact the story that went round the school was that he failed some O levels because he spent all his time reading trashy magazines and comics. Having started school in the top stream he gradually slipped down the rankings in all subjects except in French, which he was very good at. He gave up Latin and went down a set in maths. This was partly because he was very talkative. If there was laughter in the refectory Prince Andrew was bound to be the centre of it.'

Both his father and elder brother had been made head boy, or Guardian, at Gordonstoun. He was pipped at the post by Lulu Houseman's sister Georgina, the first girl to be made Guardian. This failure bothered him, even though he had been idle.

However, he was a great success with the girls and knew after Canada how to lay on the charm when he had to. Although the sex ratio was one girl to every three boys, his conquests were effortless and the many girls he took out became known as 'Andy's Harem'. Lulu Houseman reported: 'He had several girlfriends at Gordonstoun as well as many friends who happened to be girls. His girlfriends were quite good for him because he took them fairly seriously and serious relationships are a steadying influence.' At any rate, it was the beginning of many a revolving-door girlfriend.

The first was Clio Nathaniels, the daughter of an architect who lived in the Bahamas. She left school unexpectedly and fled back to Nassau after he dropped her.

'Andrew was very embarrassed about the whole affair,' said her mother.

He then turned his attentions to Clio's school friend, eighteen-year-old Kirsty Richmond. They shared a love of tennis and skiing, and wrote to each other during the holidays. She was a hit with the Queen and was invited to spend Christmas at Sandringham two years running.

The other girls dismissed the affair, saying: 'It was just Kirsty's turn.' Besides Andrew was involved with another girl at Gordonstoun, an American beauty named Sue Garnard.

According to school friends: 'She is Andrew's long-term girlfriend. She doesn't mind Andrew taking Kirsty home because she knows she is just a friend.' He also took Sue home to meet the Queen during the vacations.

In London, he spent time with Julia Guinness usually in the posh nightclub Annabel's. 'He is a bit of a flirt but the most charming person you could hope to meet,' she said about him.

He also hung out at the more edgy Tramp and Tokyo Joe's in Piccadilly, or Wedgies in the King's Road. Newspapers began carrying pictures of him emerging from nightspots with various blondes.

They were all part of what the girls at Gordonstoun called 'Andy's Harem'. Those on the outside scoffed, 'Who's on the royal rota today?' But for those on the inside, the feeling was not very different. Though sworn to secrecy, some girls said, disheartened, 'he knew how to spread himself around. One minute he's making you feel really great that you're the only one that matters. The next minute, just as you really think you're getting somewhere, he's off with someone else.'

Although his disco dancing got mixed reviews, all agreed that his 'technique' was excellent. 'He knows how to make a girl feel special.'

Technique notwithstanding, it was becoming clear that the prince's love life was hampered by two obstacles. There was the fear of the media instilled by his parents. What if there were a kiss-and-tell story? Could he trust his conquest to be discreet? Many royals had to walk that tightrope. But Andrew had another wall to climb for all the female attention that he so easily gathered at that age.

It had everything to do with the ever rising temperature of terrorism by the IRA, which had called their murder of Lord Mountbatten an 'execution'. If it was that, it was a very messy one. After fog prevented a sniper's bullet intended for Mountbatten alone, an assassin's bomb also killed a fifteen-year-old boat hand, Mountbatten's fourteen-year-old grandchild and ninety-three-year-old mother—apart from seriously injuring three further family members on the boat.

Andrew himself found it totally normal to have a police detective within arm's length of him who was keeping an eye out on what he was doing to intercept an IRA attack on his life. He didn't even notice it. But his love interests did not have a lifetime of growing up and being watched and waited on by servants at every step of the way, however intimate. And in this it didn't help the teenage prince that he was more attracted to the untitled than to the titled. Invariably at some point his love interests felt inhibited by the presence of his police minder hovering like a substitute parent. Whatever sexual chemistry there was would lead no further. 'He's a real passion-killer, if you will pardon the phrase,' said one of his escorts of the prince's bodyguard.

The media was hooked, however. Around this time, press reports started appearing that he was 'the most outstanding boy in the royal trio' of the Queen's sons. He was credited with 'diplomacy' and even 'charisma' as a result of his Canadian exploits. During the Queen's Silver Jubilee celebration in Northern Ireland, Andrew found himself talking to Nobel Prize winners Mairead Corrigan and Betty Williams, founders of the Northern-Ireland Peace Movement and both in their thirties. Corrigan said, 'He is a really handsome young man with charming manners and I was swept off my feet. Betty Williams embarrassed me by asking if he was spoken for as "I was still single and available if asked". He was deeply interested in the situation and in finding out what the problems are.' Similarly, in a Belfast walkabout there were dozens of 'starstruck' girls to meet.

As Charles didn't seem close to getting married, constant comparisons continued to be drawn between the two bachelor brothers. It helped that little was still publicly known about Andrew in comparison with Charles and that his film-star looks far outshone those of his older brother. Furthermore, as he was still the second heir, everyone treated both brothers with the courtesy reserved for the monarch. Charles had been in several near misses during his training course and in traffic. Anything could still happen that might require the 'understudy' to step in.

His money-conscious parents knew better. They already worried about how he was going to support himself. Their second son had grown accustomed to very much but would inherit very little. The Queen knew from the constant struggles of her own sister Margaret how wretched and precarious the position of being second was. Andrew had picked up the privilege of free air travel on his eighteenth, but the queen reduced his £20,000 state stipend to an allowance of £600 and invested the yearly balance as a nest egg for the moment of reckoning in his future.

She also tried hard to create a public role for him for which, like his father before him, he was not naturally suited. Andrew possessed that disregard for the sensitivities of people in a vulnerable position that Prince Philip had and he would best his father. Later, on official duty for the Queen—a visit to Lockerbie, where eleven people had died on the ground when Pan Am Flight 103 crashed on the town in December 1988—he told the grieving locals that the disaster had been 'much worse' for the Americans and said that it had 'only been a matter of time' before a plane fell out of the sky. All his mother said in private about the PR debacle was, 'I wish I had gone.'

He was no better with royal employees. Royal bodyguard Ken Wharfe said he was once moved from a window seat on a plane from Balmoral because he was obstructing Andrew's view. 'His manners,' Wharfe said, 'are just awful.'

An aide said: 'I've seen him treat his staff in a shocking, appalling way. He's been incredibly rude to his personal protection officers, literally throwing things on the ground and demanding they "fucking pick them up". No social graces at all. Sure, if you're a lady with blonde hair and big boobs, then I bet he is utterly charming.'

After the glamorous trips to Canada as a senior royal (and a year later there were also the Commonwealth Games he attended with his parents), his time at Gordonstoun was drawing to a close. The Canadian interlude that had mellowed him was rapidly a distant memory. The structure of his life as a royal in Britain reasserted itself with a vengeance.

Andrew liked the idea of going to Cambridge for a spell before enlisting in the navy. Charles had gone to Trinity, Cambridge's grandest college, and for Andrew Clare College was mooted before the news was witheringly shot down. Clare College's admissions tutor said, 'We're probably among the most stringent colleges as far as academic qualifications are concerned.' Instead of a relaxed spell in Cambridge, Andrew opted to join the navy as a pilot straightaway. It was, he said later, a 'logical choice' as it offered the 'greatest intellectual challenge' in the military. The courtiers at the palace who massaged the process clearly understood the prince's intellectual capabilities and towering self-regard well.

To an extent Andrew understood that he was more limited than Charles, who was naturally curious, and while not over-confident, at ease with whom he was. 'I become bored with being myself and like taking on other roles', Andrew recognised, 'I make a comedian of myself'. In the end Andrew put in some effort for three A-levels, rugby, hockey, shopping and going out, and left Gordonstoun under somewhat of a cloud after his detective reported some of the boys (Andrew was not one of them) for smoking cannabis.

4

'MUMMY'S BOY'

The Queen and Prince Philip realised that they had made a mistake with their first two children, Charles and Anne. In the gloomy aftermath of wartime austerity and rationing, which lasted until 1954, they had gone along with regular news items about Charles's and Anne's growing-up. For Charles, in particular, the public spectacle turned into a feeding frenzy as he grew older. He was stalked by journalists and members of the public alike wherever he went once he stepped outside palace gates.

With Andrew his parents decided to try and make a clean start and were at pains to avoid a media circus. While there was not much chance of weaning the public off of its obsession with royal children, they were determined to shield Andrew as much as possible from the public eye until he came of age. The palace dialled down the tap of photo opportunities to a mere trickle and any contact with the outside world was considered a threat to his privacy. When Andrew joined the Marylebone Boy Scouts, he didn't go to them. Instead the cubs came to him at the palace like Moses to the mountain. Likewise, for soccer practice he was secretly taken to a Guards' field where hand-picked team members met him. His and Edward's other outside activities were enacted as covert operations, too. Andrew's very first public appearances took place around his eighteenth in Canada, to ease him into being a professional royal. But the first ones in Britain only started piecemeal after his twenty-first birthday.

By this time, the British public had only seen photographs of him with an occasional write-up of a few lines. His parents only shared the most basic information on him. Nonetheless his adolescent pictures made a phenomenal impression. From a chubby child with big teeth and a slightly toothy grin, he had turned into young adult who was not only the tallest of his family but also the one who had inherited his father's striking good looks as a young man and the self-assured demeanour. He looked like the archetype of a prince.

Another cautiously controlled publicity step came after his eighteenth. Accompanying them on a trip to the 1979 Commonwealth Conference in Lusaka, he was for the first time made officially part of the coverage for the British press pack that followed in his parents' wake. The press was avidly hunting for gaffes from Philip and were obviously curious whether Andrew was cut from the same cloth. They followed him closely wherever he went and particularly when he was entertained by bare-breasted dancing girls in Botswana. But he gave no interviews. Apart from walking into a goat shed and being taken for a paparazzo, there were no real mis-steps to speak of.

However, there was an unprompted and popular response from the public at large to the handsome prince of the kind that Prince Charles had never received. There was Andymania. In Dar-es-Salaam, a group of British wives unfurled a banner saying: 'Hi Andy, come and have coffee'. When he visited Blantyre in Malawi, a man bet his wife £5 that she would not dare ask Andrew for a dance. 'The next thing I knew I was in his arms, looking up into his eyes, such fabulous blue eyes', she swooned about the royal heartthrob.

As being a royal pin-up was not really a gainful occupation, however, a career as pilot beckoned. Andrew, aged fifteen, had already earned his wings as a glider pilot at Gordonstoun, and had joined Charles on a parachute-jumping course. Now, he joined the navy after his A-levels. Prince Philip's favourite son, however, was given a far less stringent ride compared to the heavy lifting expected of Charles during his five-year stint in the Royal Navy. Andrew was accepted after an aptitude test to see whether he could become a trainee pilot. On September 13, 1979, he followed in the footsteps of his elder brother and went to the Royal Naval College in Dartmouth.

As always, he was treated unlike anyone else. Andrew's first day set the tone when he had lunch with the head of the college, Captain Nicholas Hunt. He also pulled up in his new Escort RS 2000 while cars were banned for other recruits during the first four training weeks. The college claimed, 'Once this small official ceremony is over the Prince will be treated like any other midshipman'.

But the other cadets soon resented his privileges. He was bombastic and brash. Also, he was well ahead of his fellow midshipmen. He already had his pilot's licence, had parachuted, canoed in the Arctic, and he didn't let his less fortunate peers forget it. He also, as always, had his own police escort.

In his diaries, Andrew nonetheless notes that he 'fell out of my hammock with the help of someone else and ended up with a black eye.' He understood the reason perfectly well. 'He played the big "I am the Prince" routine all the time and seemed rather arrogant,' said one cadet.

Andrew's nickname in the navy was to be 'H' as the abbreviation of His Royal Highness.

Dartmouth, Andrew parking his Ford Escort

The wife of one of the instructors said: 'Prince Charles is still remembered with tremendous affection, but Andrew isn't popular with either the staff or his fellow cadets. His brother was a great practical joker, but Andrew walks away from anything like that. He never lets you forget who he is.'

The higher ranks were also left somewhat underwhelmed. 'Andrew is very likeable, but he's very conscious of being a royal,' said one senior officer. 'He's a bit of a mummy's boy. You could never say that about Charles. Charles would never need encouragement to join in the fun. And he certainly wouldn't talk about girl conquests.'

The Dartmouth naval college had caught the palace's paranoia of the press. They were anxious that the prince should avoid press photographers at all times. At the beginning of a charity event, the prince raced out of the college's gates with the paparazzi soon in hot pursuit.

'I remember we were reversing up narrow lanes at forty miles an hour and doing handbrake turns around corners to shake them off,' Andrew said. He was not at all put out as his brother would be. It was both a confirmation of his importance and a game of cat and mouse—'It was great fun but they were very persistent.' The charity event turned out to be an excuse for sailors to have a rowdy night out.

On Andrew's first 'run ashore', the press was waiting outside the naval college's gates in Dartmouth to take pictures. In the end they were waiting in vain because he had been put on the duty roster so that he could leave unobserved at a later time.

Sometimes the press's persistence paid off, however. One of the paparazzi managed to get a picture of a sheepish Andrew with naval-architecture student Kirsty Robertson having a drink together in a remote pub before the landlord set the dogs on the hacks.

While at the naval college, Andrew was given a quick preparatory course in legal and political matters should he ever become king. Andrew was still second in line to the throne, Charles was still single and Diana not yet on the scene as the Prince of Wales's fiancée. In fact, Andrew and Diana spent time together while Charles went skiing in Klosters with Diana's sister.

Andrew sat in on a murder trial at the Old Bailey and Prime Minister Margaret Thatcher made time available to receive him at 10 Downing Street. Later, he would also become a Councillor of State, replacing the Duke of

Gloucester, so that he could handle state papers in the absence of the Queen when he reached the age of twenty one. For good measure, the prince also received his green beret in the same year after completing a short version of the Royal Marines training course.

Andrew's flight training progressed from a de Havilland Chipmunk and an RAF Bulldog to—after passing out—a Gazelle helicopter and finally a Sea King helicopter. At Dartmouth he had been given special treatment, and his pilot training in the navy turned out to be none too different.

Although he enjoyed being a pilot and had an aptitude for it, his schoolroom discipline amounted to what he could get away with, and his nickname among classmates was 'Golden Eagle' on account of dropping clangers when questioned by his instructors. He had two private Gazelle helicopters for his training sessions and the resentment was rife among his peers.

'Andrew is a bit toffee-nosed,' said one. 'He doesn't behave like anybody else. He wants his own way and when he is around, you have to bow and scrape.'

'Even when he drives round the base in his car, you have to salute that. I mean, fancy saluting a flipping car.'

The tack on his first tour of duty on a battleship, the aircraft carrier HMS Hermes, was different, however, from what he had grown used to thus far.

Introduced to the captain of the HMS Hermes aircraft carrier that September he said casually: 'Hi, I'm Prince Andrew, but you can call me Andrew'. The captain replied: 'And you can call me Sir.'

His brother Charles had also served on board the Hermes and the inevitable comparison was made. In contrast to his witty older brother, Andrew was found to be wanting. 'He was very conscious of being a royal', the crew complained like the prince's fellow students in college.

The navy brass wasn't going to babysit the young adult on behalf of the palace.

The young prince, sexually frustrated by the tour of duty on board the aircraft carrier, immediately hit the headlines on shore leave in Florida, having been photographed in Trader Jon's Club Pigalle in Pensacola, ogling topless go-go dancers. Club owner Martin Weissman said: 'We were amazed when he came to see us, but he seemed to have a wonderful time looking at our pretty girls.'

'It was a real treat having the prince here,' said Weissman's wife. 'But Lord knows what his mother would have thought.'

One of the topless dancers, Lindy Lynn, said: 'He couldn't keep his eyes off us. Now I know where he get his Randy Andy nickname.' She later renamed her act the 'Randy Andy Eye Popper'.

Another topless dancer, Sonia Larren, said: 'He was a real prince charming. I didn't feel embarrassed at all. But I would imagine that the Queen would not be amused.'

The Royal Navy weren't particularly bothered about it themselves. 'When sailors go on the town, it's only natural they want a bit of fun.'

The impact on the US media, however, was electric. The switchboard at the US Navy base in Pensacola was, paradoxically perhaps, overwhelmed by southern belles asking for the English prince under its Dial-a-Sailor scheme—'that English Prince Andy or whatever he's called'. If his eye was caught by strippers, American women of other walks of life may have assumed they could well be in with a chance. A supposedly secret visit to the wholesome Disney World to shake hands with Mickey Mouse further rocketed his transatlantic fame.

On the last stretch of his navy training, Andrew did try his double best to impress his father with his grades. Passing out as sub-lieutenant, the prince received best pilot award from the proud Duke of Edinburgh (though not the one for character and leadership). His mother smiled, equally delighted with the result. A commission as a Sea King pilot on light-aircraft carrier HMS Invincible followed.

Keen to exploit the prince's growing sex appeal for The Firm, the palace decided to cooperate with a book on the photogenic young adult destined to hit the bookshelves around his twenty-first birthday. Within a year another three books were to follow in its wake, amplifying the message Buckingham Palace sought to broadcast.

All the personal information on Andrew that had hitherto been carefully screened from the public eye was suddenly spilled. It was somewhat of a gamble after two decades of virtual radio silence. But the Queen was proud of Andrew and clearly wanted the public to see what they, his parents saw, and make her second son a popular fixture of the monarchy.

The intimate but not totally endearing details of his childhood and youth were prefaced by the biographers with epithets such as 'Andrew has almost devastating good looks'; 'cool'; 'great'; 'dishy'; 'super'; 'hunky'; 'Andrew has developed into a strapping young man'; 'To go with his seventy-two inches, Andrew has a thirty-two-inch waist, measures thirty-nine inches around the chest and is the possessor of what his tailor calls "good shoulders"'; 'Andrew seems to have a natural aptitude for nearly every kind of sporting activity he undertakes'. The writer mentioned sports 'from croquet to water-skiing'.

The adulatory comparisons didn't stop there. 'It is almost as if Darwin's theory of natural selection had worked to perfection, packaging the best genes from both sides of the family tree', one over-the-top writer purred, 'Mums wish they had a son like him'. One of the covers trumpeted, 'The Warrior Prince'.

The books firmly put the media spotlight on the young second heir to the throne, who was already struggling with the self-inflated view he had of himself because he was the Queen's and his father's favourite. Whatever the personal rivalry between him and Charles, and however much his parents wanted to indulge their wilful second son, the rules of the monarchy were clear. The oldest takes all. Andrew's position as the spare was, despite the glittering trappings of his life and the adoration of his parents, anomalous and precarious.

Then fate intervened. Out of the blue, Britain was under attack. On 2 April 1982, a month and half after the prince's twenty-second birthday, Argentina invaded the Falkland Islands. The HMS Invincible immediately set sail as one of the first ships of Britain's South Atlantic Task Force tasked to repel the Argentine forces occupying Britain's two dependent territories in the South Atlantic.

There was some muttering in Margaret Thatcher's government that Andrew should not sail and should be given a desk job so as not to mark the HMS Invincible as an Argentinian target. But the Queen made clear through her press office that 'he is a serving officer and there is no question in her mind that he should go.' In any case, the two aircraft carriers of the Task Force would be a prime target for the Argentinians regardless of the prince's presence. Without them the convoy of the Task Force would be sitting ducks for the Argentine air force, ready to be picked off one by one.

Luckily the Falklands War ended quickly and well for Britain in a matter of ten weeks, and in the ensuing euphoria the palace must have believed it had won the top prize in the lottery.

Here was the second-in-line to the throne, a youthful modern-day hero, who had accepted the life-and-death risks of combat. He had more or less followed in the footsteps of Prince Philip, King George VI and Lord Mountbatten, who before him had attained that distinction. 'More or less', because their wartime service happened when the future of the nation was at stake as opposed to that of an island with under two thousand people and over four hundred thousand sheep.

The palace didn't resist riding the Falklands frenzy and pressed the second-in-line's profile as a royal superman hard. The stars seemed to have lined up for the monarchy and the prince. For the first time, five reporters had been embedded among British troops during wartime. They were allowed to travel on board Andrew's ship the HMS Invincible. In as far a wartime role can ever be out of harm's way, it was one of the safest places in the fleet for civilians. One of the strict conditions was that they must not approach the prince.

Andrew, however, didn't think the press a nuisance the way Charles did. Unlike him, he had grown up with both paparazzi and the IRA after him. The former seemed manageable and by far the lesser of two evils. At the aircraft carrier's bar, after a few days of giving them sideways glances, the prince himself made a point of befriending the members of the press after the first week of sailing. His opening words were, 'It's about time we introduced ourselves'.

From thereon he sought them out whenever he wasn't co-piloting his Sea King helicopter (up to ten were stationed on the Invincible), overrunning the reporters with ideas, laughing, debating and dining with them as they were working. A.J. McIlroy, the *Telegraph*'s reporter, would later write, 'We knew we had earned the prince's confidence'. In fact, the *Daily Star*'s reporter complained that the prince's cosying up to them was becoming irritating. 'It was difficult to get the prince off the press's back as he wandered into the makeshift press office.'

Andrew knew that he was safe for the duration of the war. Everything the reporters wrote would be severely censored by the ship's communication room, the captain, or the Ministry of Defence, before it was sent on to the newspapers' foreign desks in London. The embedded war correspondents themselves didn't even know what was and wasn't printed until after the war was over and they were back home. He gossiped with the journalists over diner, 'Charles and I have even compiled a hit list of Fleet Street reporters'—the ones they didn't like.

The prince seemed to grow most attached to the *Telegraph*'s reporter, to whom he confided his longing for news from home. 'Apart from the unnecessary observations about love and affection family, particularly for his grandmother, the Queen Mother, there are many human things the prince would say about home and family in innocent conversation that I would never dream of making public.'

Although Andrew's squadron was the loudest in the wardroom, none of the pressmen ever saw him smoke or with a drink stronger than Coca Cola for the duration of the war. However you could always tell when Andrew was present from his enormous guffaws of laughter. One movie night in the wardroom, however, he walked out of The Rose, Bette Midler's portrayal of a singer struggling with addiction and life in general, saying, 'silly cow'.

Five days after the surrender of the Argentinian troops on 14 June 1982, the palace set up an official, exclusive first interview with the *Express* with a true but lavish angle. The headlines were 'My War' and 'I Was a Decoy for an Exocet.'

In the interview Andrew described his role in protecting the HMS Invincible from Exocet rockets as part of the Sea Kings' team. 'The helicopter is supposed to hover near the rear of the carrier, presenting a large radar target to attract the missile. So when the missile is coming at you, you rise quickly above 27 feet and it flies harmlessly underneath—in theory. But on the day the Sheffield was hit [4 May 1982], one Exocet was seen to fly over the mast of a ship—that's well over 27 feet'.

Merely being on board the HMS Invincible was hairy enough for the thousand men on board. 'When you are in your anti-flash gear and are told to hit the deck because the ship is under attack, there is nothing worse. You can only lie there and wait and hope. It's a most lonely feeling.'

Weeks later, on 25 May, an Argentinian Exocet sunk a military-stores ship, the Atlantic Conveyor, that was adrift in a violent storm with twenty foot waves. Argentina didn't have many Exocets, but it had picked that day to launch one at the Invincible. The hovering Sea Kings had diverted it, but the missile struck the unfortunate supply ship instead. The Sea King co-piloted by the prince rescued eight crew as more Argentinian shells came close.

'I was airborne when the Atlantic Conveyor was hit. We saw the odd 4.5-inch shell come pretty close to us and I saw the Invincible fire her missiles', the prince said.

'Normally, I would say it looked very spectacular but from where I was it was very frightening.'

It was not the only danger the Sea King was in. British Sea Wolf defence missiles were being fired back at the Argentines. 'Sea Wolves locked on to our helicopter three times while we were hovering.'

'It is not much fun having one of those fellows pick you out as a target. It was probably my most frightening moment of my war.' The prince added that it got the adrenaline racing, 'It really makes the hair stand up on the back of your head'.

Separately, the military made one of the conveyor's survivors available for press interview—'Prince Andrew Hailed as Falklands Hero', UPI headlined the piece that rounded off the PR the army sought for the prince.

'He and the rest of the helicopter crew did a great job', merchant seaman Michael Chapman praised the team. About the prince he said, 'He was very cool, just like the rest of the helicopter crew. He asked me how many more men were on the life raft.'

'We tried to thank the crew afterwards, but I never got to see the prince again… It would be nice if I could buy them a pint (of beer) to say thanks one day.'

Four days after the surrender, during a televised interview with the BBC in Port Stanley, the prince set forth his opinion on the war, 'Military speaking, I've been, I suppose, shocked and yet proud. I have been shocked at what has happened, at the way the ships were taken out. It is a really nasty… when you think that a small missile of perhaps eighteen feet long can do that much damage.'

Like the photogenic Trimmer in Evelyn Waugh's *Sword of Honour* trilogy, Andrew was pushed as one of the war's heroes for media stories. He was the navy's shorthand for the bravery of the troops who had vanquished the enemy and suffered the consequences of combat, as well as the beaming, fresh face of the Falklands War's successful ending. And why not? Like his fellow servicemen in the war, Andrew clearly executed his military duties with dedication and honour.

Nonetheless, the palace's move was a stretch of the circumstances given the fact that Andrew's peers in the rescue were given little recognition during the interview by either the interviewer or the interviewee. Royal stardust glittered brightly.

Whoever had authorised making Andrew the media magnet overlooked the fact that Trimmer could stand for the army's Ritchy-Hooks (Trimmer's Jack-Reacher-style brigadier) fighting in the thick of it because the former hairdresser would eventually sink away from the public consciousness never to be heard from again. But Andrew was different. Scrutiny of the prince would continue for as long as he lived because of his family name. Even though he had served well and with skill—unlike Trimmer—suddenly the height from which he could fall was that much higher.

While palace officials clearly failed to see this, or did see it but underestimated it, it had not escaped the attention of the writer of the 'The Warrior Prince'. He had future-proofed his gushing claim that Prince Andrew packaged the best of the Windsor genes for when the Falklands euphoria was but a faint memory.

His adulatory words were sandwiched with distinctly double-edged praise for the prince's sense of self. Andrew, the writer said, was 'the most exciting and dynamic young prince' since, he continued, 'the late Duke of Windsor was a youthful Prince of Wales in the distant 1920s.' He added for good measure, '"Divine" was the label given to the young Duke of Windsor by the flappers of the 1920s. Yesterday's "divine" has become today's "cute" where Andrew is concerned'.

The comparison couldn't have been more grating in view of the abdication crisis Edward VIII. Given the bad odour the duke was in with his immediate family when he resigned as king to marry the twice-divorced American Wallis Simpson, these words must have stung the older royals and courtiers. The same writer added, 'he is his father all over again.'

The twenty-two-year-old sub-lieutenant was insouciant like Trimmer during the TV interview in Port Stanley. Flanked by his squadron's commanding officer, the dashingly-dressed Andrew told the reporter breezily about himself,

'I came here this afternoon to pick up air stores for the Invincible and I happened to be passing through the HQ here and they said that there was a telephone on board the [HMS Sir Bedivere]. So I happened to grab a vehicle who[se driver] very kindly took me down there and got a hold of the telephone and I said, "Any chance of getting hold of Buckingham Palace?" And they said, "Oh of course." So we pick up the telephone just like dialling a number from London to London.'

The Marisat satellite-telephone communications system on board the Sir Bedivere was a ray of light for the troops. As soon as she had entered Port Stanley, soldiers on free-time from the battle and their daily duties to patrol the island began to queue up outside the ship's communication cubicle to say that they were all right in brief time-rationed calls. During the fighting there had been no mail or other way of communicating. It was the only way the troops had to dispel fears at home in Britain they might be injured or, worse, be among the war's casualties.

Excitedly, the prince told the camera for a clip that would go round the world what happened after he was given the phone ahead of the line of waiting men for a fifteen-minute phone call home: 'the line was clearer than it is from London to Edinburgh. I mean, really it is absolutely amazing.' Without guile the prince described the reception his whim got at Buckingham Palace: 'I surprised everyone I can tell you'.

'Yes, she was in', the sub-lieutenant radiated when the BBC reporter queried whether the Queen was at home. The *Telegraph* reporter also noted the evident joy of Andrew's after speaking to his mum.

'Luckily. She was in, it was about the right time in the evening. Yes she had… er… She was quite surprised to hear from me.'

His mum, Britain's commander-in-chief, would be briefed regularly on her son, unlike common soldiers. The Queen didn't miss a beat and smoothly covered over her son's gaffe. She had immediately brought things back to the subject at hand.

'But she did ask', the prince continued with a more serious tone, 'she did say, that if I saw anyone here, particularly on the ships, to pass on her very best and how very proud she is of everybody and… er… the magnificent work that is being done down here by not only the army but also the navy'.

Shaking his head, the junior co-pilot ended his train of thoughts by dividing the glory for those who had fought: 'Significantly, this has been a naval operation with the support of the Royal Airforce and of course with the army coming in now.' As an engine drowned out the sound, he breezily looked at his watch and interrupted his cogitation with a laugh and said, 'That is my helicopter flying over at the moment. I think it is almost time that I should go.' With his commanding officer now standing almost shoulder to shoulder, the prince concluded, 'Never mind, someone is telling me it is time to go.'

Nonetheless, after the TV interview followed a tour for the prince of Port Stanley in a field car captured from the Argentinians. The day after the surrender, Associated Press had released a news report that Prince Charles was hoping to make a 'lightning' visit to the Falklands. But Buckingham Palace had clearly overruled the heir to the throne and plumped for Andrew to do the honours for the monarch. Charles's staff then scrambled to deny his intention to visit, saying that his supposed intention to visit was no more than loose gossip. The sub-lieutenant was the winner in this competition with his older brother.

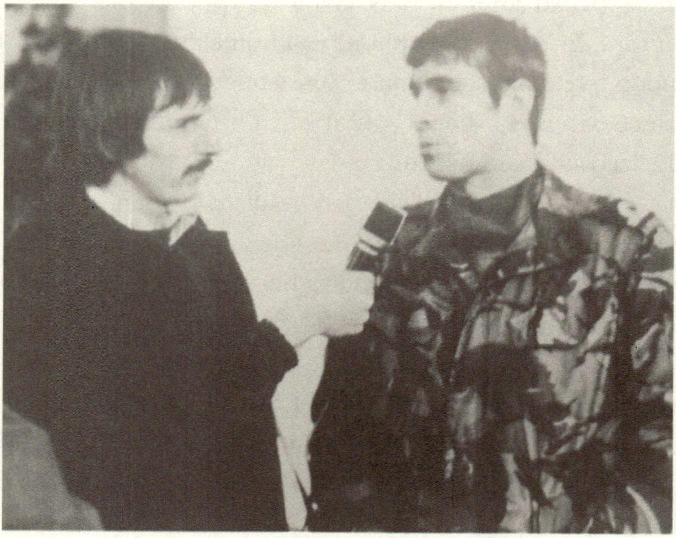

Andrew interviewed in Port Stanley

Standing in for his mother, as he first had as a seventeen year old in Canada, the twenty two year old Andrew got out of the requisitioned car during the tour and walked around, talked to the locals and posed for photographs as he shook hands and passed on the Queen's message to them: 'I am proud of you'. He also visited Government House to meet with marines commander Major-General Moore, who had received the surrender of the Argentine forces.

Visiting a commanding general was thoroughly anomalous for a mere sub-lieutenant and underlined Andrew's exceptional treatment that day. The press duly followed in his wake and observed him standing confidently and smiling in his green flying uniform when he was recognised by two local girls.

For the record Andrew said, 'It's the first time I've been in Port Stanley, though I have seen pictures of the place.' His impressions of the location over whose possession 255 service men died was that, 'It's smaller than I imagined. It is rather a nice little town, but muddier than I expected. I am only sad that I had to visit in these circumstances. But at least there is peace now and you can start thinking about the future.' He also added what else was on his mind, quipping, 'It is a perfect place to bring my bride on honeymoon.'

Thankfully, it didn't really matter whether the prince gaffed or not. Everything was seen through the rose-tinted glasses of victory.

Initial media speculation at the beginning of the war was that the prince was being kept out of harm's way during the hostilities. In another statement ten days before the surrender the palace clarified that the sub-lieutenant 'had been involved in many operations' and was doing sorties 'round the clock'. Apart from rescue missions, the day-to-day tasks of the squadron of the Invincible's Sea Kings was to ensure safe passage ahead and to do the milk run, getting supplies to the ship. This itself was not without risk due to the Falklands' atrocious weather. The first casualty witnessed by the HMS Invincible was the result of a Sea King that ditched with loss of life on 24 April because of the weather. Prince Andrew was the co-pilot on the helicopter sent out to rescue the sole survivor.

John Witherow, the embedded reporter for *The Times*, said that they were told by the navy, 'As far as we are concerned he is like everyone else. He is just another officer.'

Having observed the interactions on board and in the wardroom, he wrote in *The Winter War*, 'It became apparent over a period of time that this was true'. Piloting in the South Atlantic was as almost as dangerous as being an 'Exocet decoy'. Twenty helicopters were lost, including four Sea Kings that ditched.

Had Andrew grown up after the Falklands War? When asked during his HMS Invincible watch, he said, 'It was an experience but I would not say I would not have missed it.' He also added, 'If I had the choice, I would not want to go through it again.'

'If you've been through those sorts of experiences you understand the frailty of life. And it's not particularly nice being shot at and I can attest to that', Andrew wrote later in life, 'It was dirty; it was exhausting; it was monotonous; people really bled and death might be a consequence'. A few times he thought he wouldn't come back alive. He said, 'One was being shot at, one was being missed by a missile which didn't actually really arrive because it already hit somebody and the other one was trying to identify a ship at night.'

It would take the prince forty more years to mention the physiological effect of these experiences on him during the notorious TV interview with BBC Newsnight covering Jeffrey Epstein. The prince said that he 'had suffered what I would describe as an overdose of adrenaline in the Falklands War when I was shot at, and I simply—it was almost impossible for me to sweat.' The prince would add that 'there is a medical condition' that labelled his predicament. Medical experts, however, were at a loss to explain the condition that defied medical precedent and military experts were equally puzzled.

At the same time as the startling announcement regarding his inability to sweat, the prince announced that he would once again sweat like normal people. He told the BBC that, after forty years of suffering the condition, he was suddenly making a swift recovery. 'It's only because I have done a number of things in the recent past that I am starting to be able to do that again', the prince said, leaving it for another time to talk about the advice he had followed to achieve this result.

Putting his own war contribution in perspective to the one by his fellow soldiers in the Task Force, he told reporters in 1982, 'I didn't do a great deal. I have been at sea. But we did do quite a lot of flying the last month and a half, when it really got intensive. We have done our little bit and the lads have done extremely well.'

After being baptised by war conditions, he better understood, he said, 'courage, sacrifice and camaraderie'.

His cautious words notwithstanding, on the thirtieth anniversary of the war the prince, conceded that at the time he fully shared Britain's elation about the victory.

'I have to say that afterwards I thought I was completely invincible and if anybody wanted to do it again, absolutely bring it on.'

Perhaps, the navy had placed the young prince under strict orders not to sound triumphant and instead to stick closely to a press briefing about the sacrifices of war. Either way, John Witherow of *The Times* observed that, 'It almost seemed as if a different character had emerged. He was more articulate and less self-conscious than before, perhaps the endless flying, the responsibility and the danger had matured him beyond his years.'

Within hours of being in sight of Britain, Andrew's life reverted back to the normal. The HMS Invincible was boarded by his valet, who arrived to pack the prince's belongings, and by two detectives to accompany him from his first step on shore.

He had certainly developed a taste for publicity. Andrew bounded down the gangplank after his parents with a single red rose clenched between his teeth. It was given to him by a little girl for 'his lady' and he presented it to his mother. For the first time, Charles admitted he was envious of his younger brother for having been 'tested' by war time.

Unlike the snarky comments before the war, Andrew's squadron peers didn't talk behind his back—except for comments made by two of his fellow pilots. One said that the prince was less standoffish to them compared to training college. The other said that Andrew got somewhat irritated if there was no story or photograph about 'Randy Andy', because he liked appearing in the press.

Years later it would become known that Argentina's leader General Galtieri had mooted withdrawing Argentinian troops from the island before the arrival of Britain's Task Force. The withdrawal would look like a magnanimous gesture of peace and allow him to force a diplomatic solution. Prince Andrew's presence on board the HMS Invincible, it was said, was one of the reasons that changed his mind. Instead Galtieri opted for a full-blown war.

After the Exocet attack on the HMS Sheffield killed twenty troops, the general's spokesperson would say, 'the Invincible is our priority target. It is a symbol.' During the war the Argentinian press agency would go as far as distributing fake pictures showing that the aircraft carrier was sinking and that the prince was hurt in order to boost morale at home and to distress the Queen.

5

GIRLS, GIRLS, GIRLS

While the British Task Force returned home almost immediately, the HMS Invincible stayed on in the Falklands and so did Andrew. It meant that he missed the christening of his nephew Prince William, who was born seven days after the surrender. Even though Charles and Diana delayed the christening in the hope he would be there, Andrew was still not back by the time the ceremony took place in Buckingham Palace on 4 August.

The birth of his nephew was the silent pivot of Andrew's early life. It meant there was virtually no chance left he would ever become king. As Charles's male heir William became second in line to the throne, moving Andrew to the third place in the pecking order, lengthening the odds beyond any plausible chance. Like so many princesses and princes before him, his function had become merely decorative. He was no longer special, but one of many.

This fact hadn't escaped his peers in the navy. A fellow officer was quick to rib the prince in the wardroom, 'Congratulations on your demotion, "H".' Andrew may not have realised it fully at the time, but he was now in suspended animation as far as the palace was concerned. In monarchical terms, the twenty two year old had crested. It was ironic that it happened in the year in which he had finally bested Charles's popularity. The limelight would henceforth solely be fixed on his older brother's family.

Quite likely, the Ministry of Defence thought that it was time to draw a clear line under the sub-lieutenant's special treatment in Port Stanley and before. When quizzed about Andrew's absence at his nephew's christening, the ministry said the ship would stay in the Falklands until September and confirmed that the prince had not made a request to be relieved of duty either. None in the ranks on board the ship would expect to be given leave for family reasons and it would be bad form to ask for it merely on account of having been born with the title 'prince'. The palace appeared to accept the ministry's point and said, 'He went out as a serving officer and he will want to come back with the ship's company.'

The new treatment must have been a disappointment for Andrew. In 1981, when the prince first came on board the HMS Invincible there was the navy's equivalent of a red carpet. He was made very visible to the other crew of a thousand servicemen. He made a guest appearance on the ship's TV station and plans were afoot to give him his own show to host on board, A Dose of Andrews.

Unprompted, the prince himself suggested that he would be the mystery guest on the aircraft carrier's version of What's My Line?, which the ship's TV officer accepted from the second-in-line-to-the-throne. The crew could phone in and ask questions, but no one guessed who Andrew was. There was, of course, also the advantage of royal patronage. He invited his entire helicopter squadron to dinner 'at his place', Buckingham Palace, before they sailed for the Falklands. He was doubtless the only one of the crew to do so.

When the Invincible crossed the equator on April 16 as it headed for the Falklands, Andrew had tried to run from Neptune during the crossing-the-line ceremony for novices. Having been given a golden crown to wear, and a stencil with the words 'H—The Real Prince', the Queen's second heir was hauled before the king of the sea in front of all the crew including—from the bridge—the captain. Andrew's crime? 'Getting on camera so 'your mum will see you on television.' Roaring with laughter he denied it, and was doused in red gunge and dunked three times in an inflatable pool.

It was a mild, media-friendly show—Andrew had actually already crossed the equator on the way to Lusaka with his parents the year before. The treatment of some of the reporters on board was a lot harsher. The faces of those who had written critical tabloid pieces on soldiers were covered in something foul-smelling.

Back in Britain, the royal family's popularity was running miles high after the fairy-tale wedding of Charles and Diana in 1981 and the birth of a male heir a year later. The euphoria was further inflated by early success in the World Cup. And now there was a warrior prince returning from the country's Falklands victory.

Despite his demotion in the monarchy, Andrew's star was rising, propelled by luck and the concerted efforts of his parents. Even before the Falklands he was regularly listed as one of the world's most eligible bachelors. After Andrew's ogling of Florida strippers had put him on the map in the US, the American Bachelor Women's Society selected him alongside John Travolta, Warren Beatty, John McEnroe and Woody Allen as their favourite. The society's president, Rhonda Shear, put none too fine a point on it: 'He's much better looking than Prince Charles.' America's mass-market *People* magazine also regularly put him in their list of the top ten best-looking men.

In Britain, the first stories about earthy, curvaceous, model girlfriends had started appearing from his time at Dartmouth's naval college. His HRH title was dubbed to stand for 'His Royal Heartthrob'. A headline in the *Express* ran, 'His dates are legion, showing a preference for stunning models rather than dukes' daughters—looks before lineage.' The press liked this common touch.

As at Gordonstoun, it was a revolving door of beautiful girlfriends. After his four-week course with the Royal Marines, the prince was seen with nineteen-year-old beauty queen Carolyn Seaward, then Miss UK and runner-up to Miss World. They had a candle-lit dinner together in Buckingham Palace. But eyes were everywhere. A footman spotted her leaving early one morning.

'Prince Andrew was very charming, witty and amusing,' she told the newspapers. 'After dinner we just relaxed, listened to music and chatted.'

Asked if they had kissed, she said: 'That's a question I'm not answering, but I did tell my mum afterwards.'

Buckingham Palace was more tight-lipped. 'We are not prepared to confirm, deny or comment on such a story,' a PR spokesman said. Andrew must have been annoyed. In the royal game of hide-and-seek with the media, the press had scored a goal.

Seaward was next seen with tennis player Ilie Nastase, who had just split from his wife Dominique and she went on to become a Bond girl, while Andrew was spotted approaching a pretty blonde during Cowes Week on the Isle of Wight.

'He really laid on the chat for a good half-an-hour,' the blonde said. 'Then he realised I was married and toned down the yo-ho-ho stuff. He certainly likes to flirt with the girls. He knows he's good looking, but he's not conceited. He listens to what you have to say. He's interested in what you are and who you are. I suppose that's the secret of his chatting-up technique. He's genuinely interested in you as a person. He's a bit of the wholesome boy-next-door type. Really sweet but very fanciable and lots of fun. He likes to laugh as much as anyone.'

The prince turned up at the Ritz for Princess Margaret's fiftieth birthday party with twenty-two-year-old Gemma Curry. Her father had taught Andrew to fly at RAF Leeming. The relationship foundered when he was sent to the Royal Navy air station at Culdrose in Cornwall to learn how to fly helicopters.

Gemma was replaced by her cousin, twenty-two-year-old cover girl Kim Deas, who dined alone with Andrew at Windsor Castle. She was also with him at his belated twenty-first birthday party at Windsor, along with cousin Gemma and other previous favourites of Andrew's.

It was a sumptuous ball under a dramatic canopy of laser beams, but it was also a shared birthday ball with his father, who celebrated his sixtieth that year. Prince Philip, too, was clearly keen to support the Queen's desire to create a prominent place for their second son. There couldn't have been a greater symbol of the strained family dynamics around Andrew than the party.

The shared birthday ball was held on Philip's birthday. But Andrew's twenty first in February that year had received no attention at all—he merely dined at Windsor with his mother and father.

All decks were cleared by the palace that month for the engagement announcement of Charles to Diana on 24 February, days after Andrew's birthday, following Charles's proposal on 4 February. Andrew had clearly been told not to appear in public and upstage the heir to the throne, as there were no photos of Andrew that month, which must have been somewhat galling to him.

It was also cruel, the way life at court can be, as Charles's marriage marked the beginning of the end of Andrew's position in the palace hierarchy. In February he was literally sidelined by the marriage, despite his parents' concerted efforts on behalf of their second son. Ironically, the public celebration of Andrew's own sixtieth birthday in 2020 would also be cancelled by the Queen on account of The Firm's image—This time as a result of Andrew's entanglement in the Epstein Affair. After forty years, the prince was as insignificant as he was as a twenty one year old.

DJ Kenny Everett and Elton John provided the music for more than six hundred invitees at the princes' ball, doubtless a case of the Duke of Edinburgh humouring his son and giving him full reign over the party. The extended royal family were there and of course Diana, but also Margaret Thatcher. Old flame Sandi Jones from his time in Canada was in attendance and Andrew had invited his pals from the navy's pilot-training course.

It was an odd, slightly mismatched affair. Elton John called it the 'world's quietest disco with the music turned down about as low as you could get without switching it off', because they didn't want to upset the Queen. It didn't prevent Elton from dancing with the Queen—who clutched her handbag on the dance floor—and Margaret though. He could hear his own feet moving across the floor, well over the music. Everett was playing an exotic selection, from waltzes to disco. Meanwhile, a laser beam pulsated to the low-sounding beat.

Prince Andrew himself made his first public speech that year as the guest of honour at the century dinner of the Varsity rugby match between Oxford and Cambridge. Most of the audience was drunk and the atmosphere boisterous. But they appreciated his joke about a cannibal father and son who see a stunning girl walk by in the jungle.

'Look at her father. Why don't we take her home for dinner?' to which the father responded, 'I have a better idea—why don't we take her home and eat your mother?'

Might he have told this Les Dawson joke in earshot of his parents? Probably. The Queen and Prince Philip would have smiled as Andrew started giggling uncontrollably as he was about to reach the crass punch line sacrificing his mother for dinner.

The prince seemed to like jokes plain and simple. A year later, on the HMS Invincible, red with excitement, he told A.J. McIlroy, the embedded reporter for the *Telegraph*, in the wardroom that he had perfect prank for the *Sun*'s war reporter.

'Just tell him I want to play him at snooker and that he will find me at the ship's gyro-stabilised snooker table. It's remarkable. However much Invincible heels, the table stays level and the balls don't roll around.'

McIlroy duly paddled off, but the *Sun*'s reporter didn't fall for the hoary navy joke. Back in the wardroom, Andrew, helpless with laughter, told the other pressmen, 'I hope his newspaper doesn't print that story.' 'It's the oldest joke in the navy. I should know, I fell for it hook, line and sinker, soon after I walked in.'

The embedded reporter of the *Daily Star*, noted disapprovingly that Andrew liked playing the 'court jester', food fights and all, and was 'almost childish'. For royals this perpetual state of adolescence wasn't that unusual, however. George V and Queen Mary were supposed to be 'lethal' with after-dinner water siphons at the palace. For those forever waited on by staff, messy antics were an entertaining anachronism.

After the twenty-first birthday ball, rumours circulated that Kim Deas had jilted Andrew when she flew to New York on a modelling assignment. Countering comments that he was a male chauvinist pig after he got her to wash his car at Buckingham Palace, she said: 'He isn't at all. He's a lovely man.'

'I don't want to say anything bad about him because he's still my friend. People think that because he's so good-looking he's not a nice person. But he's extremely sensitive and kind. He certainly doesn't live up to his nickname of Randy Andy at all. He's simply a good friend.'

Pressed on the details of their split-up, she repeated what seemed to be becoming a refrain: a twenty year old trapped at the centre of a solitary world.

She said, 'I went to Buckingham Palace to see him and found him on his own watching television. He was happy that I was going to New York for the first time because it was something he couldn't do. He doesn't put on the prince bit at all although I'm sure he wouldn't like me to say it. He's just a very nice young man under a lot of social pressure.'

A month later Andrew was best man at Charles's wedding and encouraged his brother—who gave in after much hesitation—to kiss Diana on the balcony of Buckingham Palace in front of 750 million people watching. He stuck a piece of carton on the married couple's Landau as they drove off, plastering 'Just Married' on it with lipstick. It was a great hit with the media around the world.

Even the Falklands War didn't stop news about the prince's love life. While he was at sea, the story of a candlelit supper at Buckingham Palace with topless model Joanne Latham came out in the press. In fact it had never happened. Joanne later admitted she had made the whole thing up. Andrew didn't mind at all.

Then, while the HMS Invincible was still patrolling the Falklands after six months without shore leave, a 'concert party' including three young female dancers was flown out to the ship to entertain the restless soldiers. Gazing into the eyes of curvy Carole St James, the prince passionately sang along to 'You Made Me Love You'.

Dressed in bikinis, she and her friend Carol Hungerford made a beeline for the prince, who they treated as the VIP at the concert. Sitting side by side, his arm around their waists, Prince Andrew gave them a squeeze as a shipmate bellowed, 'Andrew's pulling again'.

Carole said, 'He gave us a squeeze and a lovely cuddle', and 'Randy Andy' head-lined pictures soon found their way to the front pages in Britain.

It was an off-beat prelude to the full-blown 'Andymania' that was now raging back home. It was the popularity the palace was aiming for.

Almost half a century later, the behaviour of the crowds at the prince's second public speech in Britain, after the Oxford one, is somewhat unimaginable. The warm regard for the prince, then, was as omnipresent as it was for Diana, Charles's young and attractive bride. Andrew could do no wrong in the eyes of the public.

It was a wintry November day when the prince drove up in a Rolls Royce to switch on the Regent Street lights from what was then the Jaeger store. Housewives and young girls lined the street and roared, wailed and chanted, 'We want Andy'.

The prince waved, grinned and spoke a few prepared words for the cameras to uncontrollable cheers from the onlookers. As he waited before going to the reception inside, he chatted amiably with the Jaeger shop girls asking them for instruction on 'separates' and whether they had been trained in first aid.

The police, with linked arms, could by now barely contain the growing, tightly-packed crowds. Girls fainted and had to be lifted overhead as people shouted, 'More more', whenever a shadow darkened the curtains of the store. The behaviour was as if a pop star had landed.

Looking worried, Andrew finally left as the crowds surged forward and sent police helmets rolling. Store manager Mike Morton summed it up well:

'It's absolutely amazing. I've not seen anything like this since the days of Beatlemania'. Diana had switched on the lights the year before, but Andrew's crowds and popularity easily beat hers.

Prince Andrew switching on the Regent Street Christmas lights

It was at the height of his popularity that he first met Ghislaine Maxwell, Robert Maxwell's youngest daughter. She was studying at Balliol, Oxford University, and was one year younger than the prince. She lived with her father who was at the height of his power as a press baron, taking on Rupert Murdoch's newspapers and publishing companies for dominance. One friend recalled she was 'very flirtatious, sexy'; 'very jolly' remembered Andrew Yates, a former school friend and editor at the *Daily Mail.* Another university friend said, 'She was really, really good fun. She was a laugh'. Her father was not well-liked, though. The friend said he 'was a complete cunt. We'd go to Headington Hill Hall and have lunch; there'd be two Filipinos behind his chair, piling up the food for him.'

Ghislaine and the prince weren't romantically linked at this time. Girls were throwing themselves at the young officer, but the prince was in love. Also, Maxwell belonged to a group of socialites who aimed to marry the sons of rich magnates rather than aristocrats with titles but no money.

It didn't take long before this relationship with American starlet Koo Stark made headlines. They had met at Tramp before the Falklands War. Like textbook hooray-henries, Andrew and his friends had been making a racket on the dance floor when she came over and asked them to pipe the volume down.

'Stop being so boring,' said Andrew. 'We're having a great time, come and join us.'

They fell into conversation, danced, Andrew bought a bottle of champagne, and they were both swept off their feet. It was the beginning of what was thought to be his first real love affair. The revolving door had come to a stop. He visited her basement flat in Chester Square, which she shared with former New York gossip writer Liz Salamon.

Before the Falklands, they had managed to keep their relationship secret, agreeing not even to tell their parents. When Koo's father, Hollywood producer Wilbur Stark, flew over to the UK while Andrew was in the South Atlantic, she told him: 'Daddy, I'm going out with a really nice guy. He's very special to me.' But she did not mention his name.

Andrew wrote to her while he was away during the Falklands War. She sent pictures—one in a skin-tight outfit, another in a black T-shirt with the words 'Weird Fantasy' on the front. He secreted them away in his navy locker, but he was also writing to Carolyn Seaward at the time.

Naturally given the prince's Randy Andy nickname the newspapers made great play of Koo's film career, which began in 1976 with The Awakening of Emily, in which she masturbates on camera. It was never established whether Andrew had enjoyed her play Emily or any of her other movies, but he was clearly not a puritan.

'A prim and proper teacher is introduced to the wonders of hot, sweaty, nasty sex', is how IMDb describes the plot of Emily, a film directed by Etonian Henry Herbert, the Earl of Pembroke and Montgomery. Made ten years after the 1967 summer of love, it was typical of the burgeoning genre of soft porn liberation spewed out to capitalise on it. It was written and funded by 'Anthony Morris', a pseudonym of novice producer Christopher Neame's. He had graduated from traditional Christopher Lee Dracula films to overseeing the less staid Blood from the Mummy's Tomb, featuring a surprisingly young female pharaoh clad in an ancient Egyptian bikini made of very few beads.

'I felt very vulnerable,' Koo said about her role in Emily. 'The masturbation scene was very difficult because in my personal experience it has never done anything for me. Emily was supposed to be seventeen, had not made love to any man before, and what she was doing was just giving herself innocent pleasure. It was not the sort of masturbation where she was imagining a man making love.'

There was also a lesbian shower scene with actress Ina Skriver.

'We were not given any direction at all,' grumbled Koo about the Etonian's languid style as director.

'But by the time we came to shoot, it was running very late and people were arriving on the set at Shepperton for the end-of-picture party. I looked around and suddenly thought: 'Hell, I'm naked and in front of all these people too.' I got them cleared off immediately. These people were staring and making me feel terrible. By this time tension was really high. Ina got into the shower and gave me a really hard back massage. When I was kissing her body I had to close by eyes because of the water and I could only tell where I was by touching her breast or around her waist. It was only afterwards that the strain hit me mentally. I felt so drained I could hardly stand.'

The film earned Koo the title of the British answer to Emmanuelle, an earlier sex-lib off-shoot that gained world notoriety and a massive box office. Koo had taken the role of Emily after talking to novelist Graham Greene, who worked with her the year before. That year, apart from meeting Greene, Koo had landed her first lead role in The Adolescents, an art film with Anthony Andrews. She played a shy public-school girl targeted by Andrews. After falling in love with him, she has sex with him and he takes naked pictures of her for a Danish porn magazine. Andrews gained more lasting critical acclaim as Jeremy Irons's love interest Sebastian in Brideshead Revisited not long after.

Cruel Passions followed Emily. It was a film based on one of the Marquis de Sade's most notorious novels. Koo played Justine who wants to remain virginal and virtuous. But when she refuses to pleasure some nuns she is thrown out of her orphanage and falls into a life of debauchery, torture, whipping, sadism and slavery. Sodomised by Lord Carlisle, she is savaged by dogs and raped by two grave robbers. Simone de Beauvoir rated de Sade's novel.

Koo also appeared on TV in The Blue Film, yet another work that featured explicit sex scenes, and that had to be put on late at night as a result.

'I was with an actor who had what I would call a physical reaction to my body,' she said. 'He and I were chatting for about fifteen minutes lying a couple of feet apart in bed waiting for all the lighting men to get things together to shoot the scene. As soon as our bodies touched I thought "Oh dear" and got out of bed right away. The director gave him a couple of minutes to cool off. He was very embarrassed.'

The media attention to her career as a starlet in erotic films did not simplify her budding relationship with Andrew.

'I never wanted to do an erotic film,' she reasoned, 'but it's all that's being produced.'

She hated the atmosphere in the studio. 'I hate jokes about nudity on set,' she said. 'Some technicians try it on and make cracks, attempting to be ultra-casual. That I can't stand nor that sort of man either. In fact I hate men who are crude about sex. It is a subject which should be treated with sensitivity and love.'

Nor did she think she was cut out for her acting career.

'I feel very insecure at times,' she said. 'I hate my bottom. It looks so fat and I have a thing about it.'

What did she like in Andrew? 'I particularly like strong hands. They should be delicate yet strong. A man with sensitive hands is often sensitive about other things as well.' She reckoned her ideal partner should be knowledgeable about films as well. Andrew must have fallen in this category as well.

In 1982, Andrew invited Koo to Balmoral where she appeared in an extremely short gold ra-ra skirt. According to royal biographer Lady Colin Campbell, the Queen was 'much taken with the elegant, intelligent, and discreet Koo'.

Princess Margaret lent the young lovers her holiday home, Les Jolies Eaux, on the Caribbean island of Mustique. Prince Philip, however, advised him against taking Stark to the island, for it would only land him in bad press. Andrew took no notice.

Before they flew off, they went to see The Pirates of Penzance in Drury Lane, with Liz Salamon and other friends providing false leads as to who Andrew was seeing. This led some on Fleet Street to think that he was back to dating Kim Deas again.

Koo and Andrew secretly checked in to the flight to Antigua as Mr and Mrs Cambridge. By chance a *Daily Express* photographer, Steve Wood, was also on board. He was having a Caribbean holiday with his girlfriend. Andrew's bodyguard approached them and told him that he was not to take any pictures. Wood had no inkling that Andrew was on the flight and naturally assumed that the royal passenger was Princess Margaret.

Andrew disappeared onto the flight deck while Koo hid under an airline blanket. However, Wood's girlfriend spotted them at Antigua airport. So, while they were sunning themselves on Mustique, the story broke around the world.

Even Koo's Spanish-born cleaning lady in London made the headlines when she told a reporter: 'I saw the *principe* leave two or three times at about nine in the morning. He always looked rather tired.'

The paparazzi soon tracked the couple down. They hired boats to get out to the island, but its wealthy inhabitants, who were used to having celebrities such as Mick Jagger and Raquel Welch to stay, closed ranks. Local girls told reporters, 'We're all jealous of Koo… He's a lot better looking than Prince Charles.' And the local steel band composed the Randy Andy Mambo in his honour. Unobserved, Andrew got hold of a live lobster and tried to shove it down Koo's bikini, to the hilarity of his friends.

To thwart the paparazzi, the phone lines to the outside world were cut off and the island's three taxis were barred from carrying journalists. So the press pack travelled on foot while Andrew and Koo rode in a Land Rover.

Two photographers were arrested on the grounds of Princess Margaret's villa and were locked up in the island's only cell—a bare room next to the local church—where they were entertained by a temperance sect singing gospel songs and served lobster provided by generous colleagues. The two photographers somehow managed to take the only picture of Andrew standing on his aunt's balcony, proving that he was on the island.

The prince then evaded the press, leaving Mustique by commandeering the plane hired by a photographer from the *Daily Star*, while Koo and her friends took an early-morning flight to St Lucia. She then flew to Miami, where she went into hiding. Reunited with the press pack on a British Airways flight to Heathrow, Andrew turned around and chatted happily in the first-class cabin to the men with whom he had duelled over the past week. As a public secret, he bought a big bottle of Chanel N° 5, Koo's favourite perfume—in duty free.

Despite the intensifying interest of the press, Andrew and Koo managed to spend a weekend together at Floors Castle in Scotland. She was also seen visiting his rooms in Buckingham Palace. But rumours that she would spend New Year's Eve with him at Sandringham proved false. Instead she went skiing in St Moritz.

While shopping for the trip, she was approached by a young woman who said, 'Marry Andrew and to hell with the consequences.' Koo replied that she was in love with Andrew and Andrew loved her.

But it was not to be. Others in the palace found the relationship inappropriate and they broke up in 1983.

The exchange with the young women duly found its way into the papers, as did the fact that Liz Salamon was looking for a bid of £20,000 for pictures of the Mustique trip, which Andrew foiled by offering to develop everyone's camera film. Koo was reportedly offered £1 million to tell all about her romance with Andrew, but turned it down. Though Andrew may have been her Achilles heel, it suggested that the Queen was indeed a fine judge of character.

6

WHEN ANDREW MET FERGIE

Once again unattached, the prince turned to Katie Rabett. But the relationship foundered when nude pictures of her appeared in the tabloids. At twenty-three he had a brief fling with topless model Vicki Hodge when his ship, HMS Invincible, docked in Barbados, where she had a holiday home. She tried to put reporters off the scent by having him pose with her friend Tracy Lamb.

In the end, the press cut to the chase. Hodge took £40,000 from the *News of the World* for explicit details of their romps on a beach holiday they had enjoyed, including details of 'love among the scented flowers'. The story was accompanied by a photograph of Andrew standing naked in the surf, swinging his swimming trunks over his head.

Vicki said she had discovered why his previous affairs had been so brief. His strong, sensitive hands notwithstanding, the prince finished far too quickly. She took him under her wings to slow things down, telling him to distract himself by counting—later complaining that he put her off by counting aloud. Nevertheless, she claimed to have converted Randy Andy from a sprinter into a marathon lover.

The palace were more sanguine about Sarah Ferguson—aka 'Fergie'—the former live-in lover of racing driver Paddy McNally and daughter of Prince Charles's polo manager Major Ron Ferguson. She, Diana and Andrew had known each other as children. However, they met again in 1985 at a party held at Windsor Castle, during Royal Ascot week, a race meeting held nearby. He was then twenty-five; she was twenty-six. Within a week, they had become romantically attached.

It seems that Princess Diana engineered the match. She and Andrew were very fond of each other and hung out together before she and Charles started dating. Perhaps Andrew even had a hand in the latter. She wasn't Andrew's type, which doubtless helped their friendship, and had never had a boyfriend before. She was very loyal. To his delight, Diana wrote to Andrew frequently during the Falklands War with family gossip. He told his fellow officers that there were only four women in his life—his grandmother, his mother, his sister Anne and his sister-in-law Diana.

Diana understood that Andrew needed to be nudged in the right direction to pause the revolving door. More than ever before, girls coming after him as bees to honey following the Falklands. It was part of the perks of the job, as one of the books observed, 'Throughout the ages, delectable young ladies have never been slow to hurl themselves at royal princes. Even royal princes whose physical appearance was nothing to write home about.' Edward VIII had affairs with married women who could be counted on to be discreet to entertain himself. The social rules had changed in half a century, but Andrew tended to get distracted by the latest curvaceous figure that crossed his path.

Andrew invited Sarah to Sandringham, the first girlfriend he had taken there since Koo Stark. His relationship with Fergie was once again hampered by his duties as pilot on the HMS Brazen as he was constantly at sea. This was despite the fact that he was the only one on board with a private phone, which made him popular with his fellow officers who said he was a lot of fun to be with. But in February 1986, he was on shore leave and they were staying at Floors Castle in Scotland for his birthday when he dropped to his knees and said: 'Miss Ferguson, will you marry me?'

'Certainly, sir, I will,' she replied, adding: 'If you wake up and change your mind in the morning, I'll quite understand.'

By 4 March, Andrew was back in his quarters in Buckingham Palace when he called Garrard's, the royal jewellers, and asked them to bring a selection of suitable engagement rings. Although Fergie found several she liked, he was not satisfied with what he saw and produced drawings of what he wanted. The workshops at Garrard's then set about making an eighteen-carat white and gold ring with a Burma ruby surrounded by ten drop-diamonds. It was ready in a week. She wore it for the first time on 17 March, the day the engagement was announced.

They had already been seen in public a week earlier at the Royal Opera House in Covent Garden to see the Royal Ballet's production of Frankenstein, the Modern Prometheus. Afterwards they headed off in different directions.

On 15 March, they had been to Windsor to see the Queen. When they got her permission to marry, they toasted the occasion with champagne. When Fergie went back to her job at a publishing house the following Monday, she was accompanied by two uniformed policemen and two plain-clothed officers to see her through the press cordon that had assembled outside her office.

They did a television interview sitting side by side in his study, where she showed off the ring.

'It had to be something red,' said Fergie, being a red-head. 'I wanted a ruby—well, I didn't want a ruby, I'm very lucky to have it.'

'We came to the conclusion that red was probably the best colour for Sarah,' Andrew chipped in. Afterward they kissed on the back lawn of the palace for the photographers.

They were to be married by the Archbishop of Canterbury in Westminster Abbey on 23 July. Unfortunately, Andrew's ship HMS Brazen would be in the Middle East then and his fellow officers would not be able to form a guard of honour. He would also be stood down from his duties as a helicopter pilot on HMS Brazen and was sent to Greenwich Royal Naval College to study economics and defence policy in preparation for a promotion.

On 21 April, Fergie undertook her first royal engagement. She joined the royal family for a service of thanksgiving at St George's Chapel in Windsor. Afterwards they drove to London, where six thousand children waited outside Buckingham Palace to sing 'Happy Birthday' and wave daffodils. Fergie joined the Queen, the Queen Mother, the Prince and Princess of Wales, Prince Philip, and Prince Edward on the balcony.

Not unlike the Wills-Kate and Meghan-Harry quartet, it was a publicity master stroke. Together they were not only stratospherically popular around the globe and in Britain—a future king, a hero prince and two photogenic young women—Diana and Fergie genuinely liked each other and were friends from well before. Diana looked better on a picture, but Fergie was more fun. Diana helped her create a wardrobe for her new role and the duo also tried to raid Andrew's stag night at Aubrey House in Holland Park. With comedienne

Pamela Stephenson, they dressed up as policewomen (a criminal offence), but were foiled by the press men waiting outside. Inside Elton John sang, Billy Connolly told jokes and four young ladies provided 'bachelor entertainment'. At the wedding's thank you party, Fergie urged everyone to jump in Windsor Castle's pool and persuaded Diana to do the cancan.

Fergie's father Major Ronald Ferguson hosted a dinner and dance in a large marquee at Smith's Lawn, the headquarters of the Guards Polo Club. He also paid for his daughter's wedding dress, a creation in ivory duchess satin designed by Lindka Cierach and adorned with silk flowers. Heavy beadworks incorporated various symbols including hearts representing romance, anchors and waves representing Prince Andrew's navy background, and bumblebees and thistles, which were taken from Sarah Ferguson's family heraldry. It had a seventeen-foot train with the initials A and S intertwined in silver beads. The bodice was boned to give her a slim waist. She said she lost twenty-six pounds to fit into it.

On the eve of the wedding, the couple were interviewed again on British television. Andy and Fergie both loved appearing on TV. It was a medium where they thought they could do no wrong. They discussed why they had decided to keep the traditional 'obey' in the service, though Fergie pointed out: 'I am not a person to obey meekly.'

She was also shown displaying her new wardrobe. It was said that she had spent more on clothes in the last six months that she had in the previous twenty-five years. And she shrugged off criticism of her fuller figure.

'I do not diet,' she said. 'I do not have a problem. A woman should have a trim waist, a good 'up top' and enough down the bottom—a good womanly figure. I dress for Andrew and only for Andrew. I am not a great clothes horse.'

As for having a fully-fledged royal wedding: 'I'm so excited. Fantastic! The more the merrier—more carriages, more pomp. Wonderful, I love it.'

Unlike when Charles and Diana married, Andrew and Sarah's wedding day was not to be a public holiday, but many people took the day off work anyway—such was their overwhelming popularity. Again security was tight with the SAS on the rooftops and armed detectives dressed as coachmen riding on the backs of the carriages. Five miles of sewers under Westminster had been checked.

The world wanted to know every single detail. Fergie spent the night at

Clarence House. At 9am, her wedding dress arrived, along with hair stylist Denise McAdam, makeup artist Teresa Fairminer, and manicurist Beverley Nathan. At 10, an announcement was posted on the railings of Buckingham Park saying that the Queen had conferred on Andrew the title Duke of York—a title very dear to her as it had been her father's before he became king. She also made him Earl of Inverness, and Baron Killyleagh—a Scottish, and a Northern-Irish title.

Andrew and Fergie engaged.

The Queen enjoys conferring titles on the family. To mark the death of the Queen Mother in 2002, it was suggested that Prince Philip be elevated to become knight of the Royal Victorian Order. Philip rejected the offer, saying it was 'an order for servants'. However, in 2003, Prince Andrew was raised to Knight Commander of the Royal Victorian Order. Then, in a private ceremony at Buckingham Palace in 2011, the Queen invested her favourite son as a Knight Grand Cross of the Royal Victorian Order, the highest rank of the order, to add to his glittering array of honours and medals before the two of them settled down for tea. But in 2011 the background was somewhat less festive as the Epstein scandal unspun.

Some 1,800 wedding guests arrived at Westminster Abbey. Among them were show business favourites Billy Connolly, Pamela Stephenson, Elton John, Michael Caine, David Frost and Anthony Andrews, along with Margaret and Denis Thatcher and other leading politicians and their partners.

At 11am, the royal family began leaving the palace in horse-drawn carriages. A minute or so before 11.15am Fergie descended the grand staircase at Clarence House to be greeted by her father, who was wearing a morning suit rather than a military uniform. Both had to wipe away a tear before they climbed aboard the 1881 Glass Coach, which left the black gates of Clarence House at a brisk trot. They were escorted by mounted policemen and six Life Guards from her father's regiment.

The Glass Coach had arrived at the Abbey at 11.20am. Designer Lindka Cierach had been whisked by car from Clarence House to arrange the skirt and train as Fergie got out. Four page boys in sailor suits held the hands of the four bridesmaids in ivory frocks with flowers in their hair and carrying floral hoops. The trumpeters of the Royal Marines sounded a fanfare and the organist struck up Edward Elgar's 'Imperial March' as the bride and her father began their walk up the aisle.

The vows exchanged, the rings in place, and the register signed, the couple made their way back to Buckingham Palace, where they thrilled the crowd by a kiss on the balcony. After a traditional wedding breakfast for 120 guests at Buckingham Palace, the newlyweds and some three hundred guests moved to a party at Claridge's hotel. The newlyweds set off for Heathrow Airport in an open carriage. The royal jet then flew them to the Azores, where they spent their five-day honeymoon on board the royal yacht Britannia.

Their marriage was passionate at first and their very public displays of affection sometimes embarrassed friends. On one occasion, the prince even pulled royal rank and interrupted a naval exercise so that he could spend two hours with Fergie in a cabin on a support ship. This was not a privilege extended to other seamen. The excuse—seasickness.

But Fergie soon tired of Andrew. In the case of Diana and Charles, it was the disagreements over how William and Harry should be raised that gnawed at their union before the reappearance of Camilla Parker-Bowles as a mistress. But in the case of Andrew and Fergie it was marital relations, or rather the absence of it. Andrew was always away on duty, and she spent her first pregnancy alone at home. Like his father, Andrew led a sailor's life in the navy, but Fergie was not the Queen or his commander in chief.

In 1990, the duchess complained that they had only spent forty-two nights a year together during their four years of marriage. To make matters worse, when the duke was home he devoted most of his energy to playing golf. Meanwhile she put on weight, causing the press to dub her the Duchess of Pork. (She later capitalised on the name by becoming the US spokesperson for Weight Watchers International.) The *Daily Mail* commented: 'She gives the impression of a council estate girl in the typing pool who's married the boss's son and is exploiting it for all she can get.'

Bored, Fergie began gallivanting round London clubs with the newly liberated Princess Diana and jetting off on endless holidays at the taxpayers' expense. She also shredded all of Prince Andrew's love letters, giving as reason that they might be stolen. She was criticised for having too many holidays and accepting too many free gifts, which earned her the nickname 'Freeloading Fergie'. In response, she complained that her allowance from Andrew would not cover first-class air travel. She demanded payment for interviews and asked designers to give her free clothes. Furthermore, she only attended 108 official engagements in 1991, compared to Princess Anne's 768.

In the meantime, Major Ron had found himself the subject of some embarrassing photographs taken at the Wigmore Club, a London massage parlour where sexual services were also provided. These snapshots heralded a veritable deluge of incriminating pictures, which were to haunt the royal family throughout the year.

In January 1992, 120 photographs were found by a cleaner in the London flat of Texan playboy Steve Wyatt. They showed the American and Fergie on holiday together, sunning themselves by the pool. She had also introduced him to the Iraqi oil minister at a Buckingham Palace reception, furthering his business interests.

Although the pictures seemed innocent enough, there was something in the complex relationship between Andrew, Fergie and Wyatt, that led the prince to ask for a divorce and to turn for succour to his former lover Koo Stark. Another old flame, thirty-eight-year-old divorcée Jane Roxburghe, also provided a shoulder for him to cry on.

The Queen ordered Fergie to stop seeing Wyatt, but the newspapers reported that she secretly visited his flat on at least two more occasions. The announcement that the Yorks had separated was made on 19 March 1992.

To escape from the growing scandal, Fergie headed out to Florida, where she stayed with a notorious womaniser, sixty-six-year-old Robert Forman, who prided himself on going out with girls young enough to be his granddaughters.

Then she went for a holiday in the Far East with her financial adviser Johnny Bryan, who was later despatched back to Britain to find out what sort of divorce settlement the duchess could expect. Unless a satisfactory figure could be arrived at, there was always the threat that the Duchess of York might publish her memoirs, which, at a conservative estimate, could be worth £4 million.

It was at this sensitive juncture that details of Major Ron's affair with a glamorous thirty-three-year-old horsewoman, Lesley Player, were serialised in the Sunday papers. To put the icing on the cake, Fergie was photographed topless in the south of France, with her children and two male bodyguards looking on. And who should be with her—kissing, cuddling, tucking her hair behind her ears, rubbing suntan lotion into her naked back and sucking her toes—but the same financial adviser who was negotiating her divorce, Johnny Bryan. The divorce was finalised in 1996. Just before the divorce, and supposedly off the record, Lord Charteris, the Queen's former private secretary, told the *Spectator* that Fergie was a 'vulgarian... vulgar, vulgar, vulgar'.

The Queen, however, seemed to tolerate the shipwreck of her second son's marriage. One Sunday around the time of the divorce, she told the Duke of Edinburgh that she had invited Fergie round to Windsor Castle. The Duke said, 'I can't face that. I am having tea in my study.' Edward, who was also there, said, 'I can't face it either. I will have tea with my father.' Princess Margaret, despite her share of peccadilloes was no different. 'Poor Andrew. Thank goodness, he's got rid of that dreadful woman', she said to a companion on a drive through Oxfordshire.

Fergie knew the Queen was 'furious' about what was going on. 'Her anger wounded me to the core,' she said, 'the more so because I knew it was justified. I had violated her trust.' 'I'd betrayed the bond that we'd built ever since she had invited me to Royal Ascot in 1985 as one of the younger people she enjoyed having about', the duchess observed.

The Queen remained supportive however when Fergie published her memoir, called *My Story*. 'Better now than in five years time when everything is quiet and it's all dragged up again', she said to one of her confidants.

By now not much was left of the carefully construed image of Andrew as the hero prince that she and Prince Philip had so assiduously promoted, though Andrew could still claim to be the playboy prince and Andy Randy without anyone raising an objection. Many more unflattering sobriquets lay in store in the years of news reporting ahead.

Old flame Kim Deas accompanied him on a trip to the US, where his behaviour was so bad he was dubbed the Duke of Yob by the British press. The American media called it 'the most unpleasant royal visit since they burned the White House in 1812'.

The dynamic royal quartet of yore had disintegrated, too, and was no more than a dysfunctional nightmare. The role in The Firm that Andrew's parents had so proudly created for their favourite son was well beyond any hope of repair.

That Christmas, Prince Charles was sinking fast in the public opinion polls because of his continuing association with Camilla Parker-Bowles and he began to suspect that his younger brothers Andrew and Edward were plotting against him. In a massive own goal—one not unlike Andrew's Newsnight interview decades later—Charles had in a TV interview admitted to being unfaithful to an audience of 25 million people.

It didn't help that the Queen and the Prince did not rate Charles's handling of his marriage crisis. After Diana said in an interview on Panorama that she did not think Charles would be king, he convinced himself that Diana and Fergie had plans to replace him as heir and announce that, on the Queen's death or abdication, Andrew would be regent until William was eighteen.

'Andrew wanted to be me,' Charles bitterly told his private secretary Mark Bolland. 'I should have let him work with me.'

It would never have been a success. An incident at Cowes, back in the summer of 1979, illustrated the way the two royals rubbed along from an early age. The thirty-year-old Charles tried to teach his nineteen-year-old brother how to windsurf by barking instructions at him, Prince Philip style. Andrew took his revenge with a speedboat, creating waves and destabilising the heir to the throne while he was enjoying some windsurfing on his own. The two seemed to have a Batman-Robin-like relationship, with Charles as the overachieving older brother to whom Andrew looked up and had to play second fiddle.

Despite the public rivalry between the brothers, John Witherow, while on the HMS Invincible during the Falklands War, had remarked on the extent to which Andrew seemed to present himself as a copy of Charles: 'His voice and mannerisms were strikingly similar to those of Prince Charles.'

As a sub-lieutenant, Andrew seemed very aware of the impression he would make on others. It struck Witherow that he 'was always amazingly smartly dressed. His clothes seemed that bit crisper than the rest of the officers', and his hair was always so well cut that the journalists on board the HMS Invincible speculated whether there was a barber on board, by royal appointment. Andrew had always been very controlled about his appearance. While his peers dressed outrageously, from jockstraps to feather boas, during their Dartmouth graduation parade in naval college, the prince donned his pyjamas. The Queen was not best pleased if a royal wasn't smartly dressed.

Charles struck back at the perceived plot against him, trying to remove Andrew's daughters Beatrice and Eugenie from the royal payroll. But Andrew made efforts to keep his daughters close to the Queen to ensure their future as fully paid-up members of the family. He also wanted Beatrice and Eugenie to retain the rank of working royals and to have round-the-clock security costing £250,000 each.

Andrew complained to senior palace personnel how he and other minor royals were being pushed aside. He thought it was an insult that his daughters were discouraged from carrying out royal duties even though they were the only two 'blood princesses' of their generation—a rarefied argument about lineage at best that he thought should matter to others, too. In response to the news, the palace released a public statement by the prince that said, 'As a father, my wish for my daughters is for them to be modern working young women.'

Charles then saw to it that Andrew and Edward were excluded from a lunch for seven hundred people celebrating the Queen's Diamond Jubilee. Nor were they seen on the balcony of Buckingham Palace afterwards. Andrew saw this as a demotion, even though his chances of ever succeeding his mother had been infinitesimal for more than a decade.

Although divorced, Andrew and Fergie continued to live in Sunninghill

Park, the two-storey fifty-room red brick mansion built by the Yorks in Berkshire with a staff of eleven. It was mocked as 'Southyork' after 'Southfork', the Texan oil tycoon's estate in the 1980s soap opera Dallas. The estate had been given to the couple as a wedding present by the Queen and the couple expected equipment suppliers to furnish the kitchen and bathroom free of charge. Notable was a giant marble bathtub that the builders dubbed HMS Fergie.

Andrew lived there with her until 2004, when they both moved into the palatial Royal Lodge in Windsor, a forty-room Georgian property originally designed by John Nash and with immaculate gardens looked after by a head gardener, a private chapel set in 98 acres and eight cottages for staff.

Stuffed with priceless antiques, this had been one of the Queen Mother's grace-and-favour country estates and was where she died in March 2002. It was then leased to Andrew for seventy-five years for a lump sum of £1 million, or £250 a week, from the Crown Estates. He promised to renovate the building, which he did for £7.5 million, installing a swimming pool and a driving range.

It was not very clear where all that money came from as the interest on the principal alone dwarfed his navy pension and the allowance from his mother. It was either the Bank of Mum or he had been extremely lucky since he left the navy and had been given an unpaid diplomatic role. Fergie moved out of Royal Lodge in 2006. She rented Dolphin House, just next door to Royal Lodge. The following year, there was a fire at Dolphin House and Fergie moved back into Royal Lodge with her former husband. 'I'm in and out all the time and he's in and out all the time', she said airily on radio in 2016.

After several years on the market, Sunninghill Park was sold in 2011 for £15 million—£3 million over the asking price—to a Kazakh billionaire called Timur Kulibayev, though by then it was almost derelict. The oligarch sat on the expensive ruin for another eight years before demolishing it, and then sat on the empty site for another three years. The prince said the deal had been negotiated by the Queen's financial adviser and that 'any suggestion otherwise is completely false.'

In fact, Amanda Thirsk, the prince's private secretary (who was also to negotiate the disastrous 2019 BBC Newsnight interview for the prince) was involved, offering the billionaire buyer a referral to Andrew's interior designer at Royal Lodge, discussing the possibility of having armed guards, as well as negotiating for three acres of adjoining fields at close to a peppercorn rent from the Crown Estate—which would have had to turf a farmer off them—almost doubling the size of the five-acre estate for a few thousand pounds a year.

Clearly there was something fishy about the deal and it attracted the interest of prosecutors in Italy and Switzerland.

'We cannot be clearer that there is no question of the Duke of York having benefited from his position as special representative in his sale of the property,' the prince's spokesman said. 'Any suggestion that he has abused his public position is completely untrue. The sale was a straight commercial transaction.'

As always, Buckingham Palace rallied to the defence of the beleaguered prince, issuing a statement saying: 'There was never any impropriety on the part of the Duke of York, any suggestions of which are false.'

7

'NEVER HEARD OF YOU'

After the separation from Fergie, Andrew lost his interest to be at sea and was free to plot his own course in the bedroom. His naval career, slightly lack-lustre when compared to his father's, peaked in 1993 when he was made lieutenant-commander in charge of a minesweeper, the HMS Cottesmore. It was the largest ship in the navy built out of glass-reinforced plastic. After a year and a half he returned to a final spell in the navy as an active pilot. Based out of Portland, he could indulge in his real passion, flying.

In the year his divorce from Fergie became final, a job came up for him as staff officer at the Ministry of Defence in the Directorate of Naval Operations. His brief was 'Naval Diplomacy with the Rest of the World'. He agreed to be 'headhunted' for the job, he told the *Financial Times*.

In the Spring of 2001, he told the Ministry of Defence's in-house journal, *Focus*, that the work there had proved a strain.

'It got a little bit wearing at times,' he said. 'It became very evident in the summer of last year that I was doing too much. I was feeling tired. No, no, no, it was just doing little things, you're not always on peak performance. But that's the way the cookie crumbles and you just get on with it.'

The difficult summer he was referring to was 2000. In June that year the prince, Fergie and the children, vacationed at the Bahamas estate of Peter Nygard, the fashion tycoon who would twenty years later be accused of sexual assault by a total of 46 women, including one who was fourteen at the time. Leading up to the year of 2000 when the duke did too much, Fergie met

Jeffrey Epstein in 1998 with the two princesses, and in January 1999 Andrew flew on Epstein's gulfstream to his private island Little Saint James in the Caribbean.

In March 2001, the duke left the Ministry of Defence job he had been headhunted for, and the prince came off the active list in June. But after that Andrew still managed to get promoted by dint of reaching a number of birthdays. Three years later Lieutenant-Commander York was made an honorary captain. On his fiftieth birthday in 2010, he was promoted to rear admiral and made a vice admiral five years later.

Meanwhile he was appointed as Special Representative for International Trade and Investment, taking the role from the Duke of Kent, his mother's cousin, after being given a tongue-lashing by Prince Philip for being 'selfish and lazy'. His mother gave him £249,000 a year and there was the £20,000-a-year pension from the navy. This position was itself unpaid, but it did offer plenty of other opportunities.

Epstein's 'Orgy Island' Little Saint James

When ashore Andrew still lived with Fergie and his daughters. On his fortieth birthday, 19 February 2000, they caused outrage when they pulled up at the Millennium Wheel in their official Jaguar and jumped the queue, forcing others to wait in the cold for an extra hour.

'I can't believe they have made us all wait this long just so Andy and Fergie could get a free ride,' said Derek Brown, who had brought his family up from Reading. 'We were all ready to go up at twelve, but then, after we made some inquiries, we were told we could be almost an hour late.'

Another would-be rider was more forthright, shouting: 'You lot are nothing but freeloaders.' Despite the boos, they smiled and waved at the crowd.

Five of Andrew's former girlfriends turned out for the birthday party Fergie put on for him. Le Caprice restaurant was not available that day for a booking so the staff at St James's Palace was prevailed upon for a suite of state apartments for the night to lay on a lavish dinner. The table was decked with elaborate candlesticks, flowers, silver cutlery and china with the royal crest and the meal was served by liveried footmen.

Andrew's name meanwhile was soon linked to that of twenty-three-year-old French professional golfer Audrey Raimbault, whom he sneaked into Buckingham Palace for a tour of his private quarters. She also stayed at Windsor on at least two occasions. Next came blonde Australian PR girl Emma Gigs, who was thirty-three. Ever conscious of his public image, in July 2001, he was said to be madly in love with twenty-four-year-old PR girl Caroline Stanbury.

Andrew's old friend Ghislaine Maxwell was never far away. The couple had been spotted dining together in New York in April 2000, causing some newspapers to speculate that they were dating. They were seen together some twelve times around that time. Confusingly, there was also continued talk that Andrew and Fergie would remarry.

In an interview in *Tatler* magazine in May 2000, the navy Commander confided in its editor Geordie Greig: 'I don't rule remarriage out.' Fergie added: 'I simply say, if it should happen, great. It is not in, nor is it ruled out.'

In a rare moment of introspection he admitted that he knew what his reputation was like, which, Greig recorded, was as a 'cack-handed, blonde dating oaf'. The prince was 'sensitive to the nuances of the way he has been portrayed'. He blamed himself for missing 'the cries for help' from Fergie until it was too late to save the marriage. Following the interview, the duke went on a trip with supermodel Elle Macpherson. And, before the interview was even published, he was seen out with supermodel Christy Turlington.

Then there was model-turned-TV presenter Catrina Skepper, PR executive Aurelia Cecil, South African former burger-bar waitress turned model Heather Mann who was invited to the Queen Mother's hundredth birthday party at Windsor, former Miss USA Julie Hayek whom he dined with *à deux* in Manhattan, and former *Playboy* model Denise Martell. Even American rock star Courtney Love claimed that Andrew came knocking at her door at one in the morning 'to look for chicks'.

Just months before Giuffre alleged to have met Andrew in London, the prince dated the striking twenty-eight-year-old lingerie designer Caprice Bourret. He took her twice to Buckingham Palace, where she sat on the Queen's throne and she spotted a bowl she liked. She asked Andrew whether she could nick it for her mum and he let her.

The status of these very public dates was not entirely clear. Were they extensions of 'Andy's Harem', pretty girls to be seen with?

Caprice said the dates remained 'platonic' and she ended them when the press were starting to link her and Andrew. She set him up with Martell, who first met him for dinner on 2 November in Beverly Hills and for two consecutive nights. She told the UK press that on one of these the prince, in his boxer shorts, tucked her in.

It was even suggested that Fergie was a matchmaker introducing her ex-husband to some non-threatening girls. In 1998, when Andrew's relationship with Aurelia Cecil was getting serious, it was Fergie who introduced him to Heather Mann and the relationship with Cecil petered out. The only real threat was businesswoman Amanda Staveley, whom Prince Philip thought was the ideal choice to be the next duchess. He had always vehemently opposed Andrew's remarriage to Fergie. In 2004, Andrew was to propose to her, but Staveley turned him down.

'If I married him all my independence would have disappeared,' she said. Having the ex-wife live almost next door and drop in on the children all the time might, if anything, have created a triangular relationship rather than a marriage and one can see Staveley's dilemma. Was Andrew really that into her? Would he take a new union seriously enough to upend the comfort of his existing routines? She married someone else and went on to amass a fortune of over a hundred million with a reputation as the go-to fixer for Middle Eastern sheikhs buying football clubs.

Despite the arm candy, Andrew did not think his new-found millionaire playboy lifestyle left him out of touch as he was leaving service as a navy officer.

Looking trim, handsome and fit, the forty-year-old Andrew also told Geordie Greig at the *Tatler* in 2000: 'I am a good deal more down-to-earth than people would expect of a member of the royal family. The ivory tower is not a syndrome from which I suffer.'

Andrew in Phuket, Thailand, January 2001

The prince, in fact, thought he was ready for something new. 'It has taken me a long time to realise there are only 24 hours in the day and that there is more to life than slaving away', he confided to Greig, who, while sitting in on the prince's daily life, recorded a dizzying number of projects and fundraisers that were resolved by Andrew asking his staff to reserve state rooms in one of the Queen's palaces for an event. In his retirement interview to the army's *Focus* magazine a few months later the duke added: 'My life is a great deal more ordinary than perhaps is portrayed in the media. And that's about it, really. There's a great deal more normality in my life than people first imagine.'

Months later, before the meetings that Giuffre alleged happened but Andrew categorically denied took place, the navy Commander was seen with Ghislaine Maxwell and billionaire Jeffrey Epstein and Victoria's Secret model Heidi Klum at her 'Pimps and Hookers' Halloween party in an upscale New York nightclub. He was seen near a prostitute and other seedy characters. He was then photographed beside a topless waitress at a Chinese New Year reception. The *Daily Mail* later reported that he had befriended a drug dealer in Los Angeles.

On Boxing Day 2000, Andrew flew to Thailand to stay at the luxurious Amanpuri hotel in Phuket, at the invitation of a friend. The Phuket party included Madonna's record producer, an actor who was a former punk, models, a fashion designer, as well as David Tang, and a twenty-two-year-old pop singer whose ex-fiancé had been arrested for robbery. In private, Fergie and the Queen were reported to be dismayed that Andrew had spent the New Year's holidays away from his children and instead partied with people from tinsel town.

At the Amanpuri, Andrew splashed around on the beach with a beautiful blonde. He also left his security detail behind to board a yacht moored in front of the hotel and was photographed surrounded by a bevy of topless beauties. Andrew made no excuses for his presence, saying: 'I was just reading my book. I wasn't really aware of what everyone else was doing.'

He toured Phuket's red light district of Patong with a police bodyguard in tow. It was like his first Florida trip on leave as a twenty-year old navy serviceman. In one go-go bar—bearing the motto 'good food, cold drinks, hot girls'—he danced with half-naked young women. A regular said: 'You certainly wouldn't get a member of the Thai royal family in a place like this. The area is very raunchy and many of the girls are prostitutes.'

Another bar offered: 'Patong's hottest girls. Number one for adult entertainment.' There was a bar above, under the same management, that promised: 'Topless girls upstairs.'

It was alleged that the prince set up the company Naples Gold with one of his Phuket friends, using the pseudonym Andrew Inverness after one of his lesser-known titles—the Scottish one of Earl of Inverness. His job title was 'professional consultant' and the date of birth on the company's records was as 19 February 1960, the same as Andrew's. A creditor of the luxury ski company Descent International was one 'Andrew Inverness, care of Buckingham Palace'. When the company collapsed in 2009, a spokesperson for the liquidators told reporters: 'We understand that to be Prince Andrew.'

On the day Andrew left the glamorous revellers, Jude Law's then-wife arrived and together with supermodel Kate Moss, whose stellar modelling and fashion career would later be curtailed by cocaine use, waved him goodbye. For the next few years, the press would hound the prince as he was going out to exclusive night clubs and parties in order to find out whether he looked sweaty and out of sorts.

New Hollywood A-listers would present themselves. Actor George Hamilton introduced Andrew to his former daughter-in-law Angie Everhart who had appeared in several *Sports Illustrated* swimsuit issues and posed nude for *Playboy*. Since breaking up with his son, Ashley, Angie had dated a string of famous men including Prince Albert of Monaco, Kevin Costner, Sylvester Stallone and Joe Pesci, whom she was briefly engaged to. Angie recalled that Hamilton had called her one day and asked her if she'd like to have dinner with a prince.

'George told me, "He likes redheads and he has a wish list of girls he'd like to meet while he's in town—and you're on it",' she said.

Angie took the possibility of becoming the next Duchess of York seriously.

'I'd have been a bit more popular than the last American, that Duchess of Windsor. But I was already divorced when we met,' she later told the *Mail on Sunday*. 'Maybe things would be different now that everyone has accepted Charles's divorce. But when I first met Andrew I don't think it would have been acceptable.' Angie also later had a run in with Harvey Weinstein, who, she claimed, masturbated in front of her.

Andrew's name was also linked with socialite Goga Ashkenazi, who was photographed with Andrew in 2007 having lunch at Ascot just three days after the birth of her son. She also had an affair with Italian tycoon Flavio Briatore. Goga said: 'It is every girl's dream to have a prince on one arm and a billionaire on the other.'

Royal watcher Margaret Holder said: 'The playboy image is not one Prince Andrew discourages. He's been seen many times on these party yachts and he thinks it enhances his reputation. Attracting luscious young ladies makes him feel young.' By 2010, she reckoned he had been through about fifteen girlfriends since his divorce.

However, former BBC royal correspondent Jennie Bond remained more sceptical. She repeated the refrain the Gordonstoun girls—both those inside and outside 'Andy's Harem'—rehearsed about Andrew while he was a school boy.

'It is rather difficult to know whether the girls he's seen with are serious consorts or not,' Bond said. 'There is definitely a huge advantage in being seen with the prince. And there's no getting away from the fact that Prince Andrew is a great catch, except of course he still lives with his ex-wife in Windsor Great Park.'

It was meanwhile reported by *The Times* that Andrew looks out of sorts at parties unless there was a girl fawning over him. Also, he didn't seem to have tinkered much with his image problem as an oaf.

'[He is] pretty base in terms of women,' a woman told the paper. "He is a boobs-and-bum man. There is nothing sophisticated about it. One minute you're having your bum pinched, and the next minute he is reminding you he is Your Royal Highness.'

A woman who met him at a jet-set party in St Tropez complained: 'He doesn't have much conversation other than himself.'

'He's everything people tell you,' another said. 'Boorish, interrupts you and laughs at his own jokes.'

Andrew's first year as an official trade envoy for the government after leaving the navy had not gone well. Aides at the palace were understood to have been furious about the bare-breasted women scandal and other raunchy details from the Phuket trip as they overshadowed the official news of his recent appointment. Later in his first year on the job, the prince was in Los Angeles for an official visit when he tucked *Playboy* model Martell in at night in boxer shorts.

'Prince Andrew is keen to bang the drum for British exports,' a palace spokesman had said when the prince's posting was announced.

'Heaven help Britain's exporters,' an editorial in *The Sunday Times* responded.

Some doubts were even expressed in the palace. One courtier said: 'If he goes off to America to promote business, people will worry about what he is doing in his time off. Will he be heading off with Ghislaine Maxwell to a nightclub? The trouble with Andrew is that his private life will, willy-nilly, intrude into his public role.'

Within months of his appointment as the special representative for British trade and investment, Andrew had attracted complaints. Too often, the Foreign Office's protocol department said that he refused to stick to the agreed itinerary and 'left a trail of glass in his wake'.

'Andrew's relations around the world are dicey,' commented one official at the weekly heads of department meeting, 'He's showing bad judgement about people. He's rude, lashes out to lay down the law, and it's so difficult to sell him.'

Complaints from British embassies about Andrew were not to be made in writing. Diplomats had been warned by the Foreign Office not to include adverse comments in their dispatches. Anything unfavourable was conveyed by telephone. These included comments about Andrew.

The public became aware that 'Air Miles Andy' refused to fly on commercial airlines after the government published a list of his destinations, which were a golf tournament, a football match, and social visits to beautiful girlfriends across the globe. Despite being pampered with private jets, he remained rude and arrogant. Typical behaviour of his was overheard in an early-morning exchange in his £13-million ski chalet in Verbier.

A young guest was making his breakfast tea when Andrew suddenly appeared.

'Andrew, would you like a cup?' asked the guest politely.

'I'm Prince Andrew to you,' snapped the host, and walked off.

Initially, the Foreign Office relied on Andrew's private secretary to ask him to behave better. She failed. Following complaints from embassies in the Middle East and Latin America, senior officials met to discuss 'the Andrew problem'. The Queen needed to be told. She prevaricated and suggested that Prince Philip be consulted. He was annoyed, and advised that Andrew be officially told to 'sharpen up his act or lose his job'. An official met Andrew and issued an appropriate warning.

In 2003, it was reported that Andrew spent £325,000 on flights. That included £2,939 on a helicopter he used to make a 120-mile round trip to Oxford, and RAF planes to fly him to St Andrews for two golfing jaunts.

Most trips were to places that had golf courses. A trip to the US took in the Masters golf tournament. In 2004, he was criticised for taking an RAF jet to Northern Ireland, where he played a round of golf before turning up to a royal garden party late. He also attended other sporting events. A 2004 trip to Bahrain coincided with the Formula One grand prix. The *Mail on Sunday* noted: 'If Prince Andrew does not swiftly learn the limits of public patience, he will endanger not just his own position, but that of the monarchy as a whole.'

Ian Davidson, Labour MP for Glasgow Pollok that time, complained about Andrew's travel costs, saying: 'There is a question mark over what are genuine royal duties which the public should pay for. I'm not entirely clear what benefit the public get from him being the captain of one of the most exclusive clubs in the world. Second, there is a question about whether there is due economy when travel plans are being made.'

In 2005, the National Audit Office investigated forty-one of his journeys, including a £3,000 bill for a helicopter to a business lunch in Oxford, when the train would have cost £97, and three trips to golfing events as part of his captaincy of the Royal and Ancient Golf Club of St Andrews at a cost of some £32,000. Once it cost £4,645 for him to take an RAF jet to the course in Fife so he could finish eighteen holes. Taxpayers forked out £681 to fly him thirty-five miles to baby-product giant Johnson & Johnson in High Wycombe. And it was £3,600 for a RAF jet to take him to a military base ninety miles away in Somerset last June.

Ian Davidson MP, member of the Public Accounts Committee, said: 'The idea that because train journeys were unreliable, he therefore got an helicopter is outrageous. This option is not open to many of us and this junior member of the royal family appears to regard the public purse as a bottomless pit to be drawn on as and when he wishes. He pays little regard to economy when choosing how to travel.'

The Audit Office report said that the previous year the prince's flights, most of them paid for by the taxpayer, had cost £565,000.

'In terms of the return on investment to the UK,' Andrew said, 'I would suggest that £500,000 is cheap at the price.'

The NAO exonerated him because no rules on royal travel had been broken. Andrew was unapologetic, saying later: 'I could have worse tags than "Air Miles Andy", although I don't know what they are.' He had gained the soubriquet for using planes and helicopters when he could have travelled by car or train. In spite of the criticism the costs were not coming down. *The Sunday Times* reported in July 2008 that for 'the Duke of York's public role… he last year received £436,000 to cover his expenses.'

In 2008, Prince Andrew travelled to the US in a private jet costing a whopping £100,000. Later that year his trip to China and the Far East cost taxpayers £30,000 for transport and accommodation. In January 2009, a visit to Switzerland cost £21,700 in hotel, travel and other overheads. All his travels in 2009 cost the taxpayers £140,000. The following year he was severely chastised for using the Queen's helicopter on a 146-mile trip hopping around official engagements which were in the same area. The same year, he flew from Windsor to Kent for a party at a golf course where he was patron. The bill was picked up by the Treasury.

Andrew once again defended himself, saying: 'The helicopter is very often the most efficient way of packing in as many engagements as we can. It enables us to see more people all over the country, do more things and get better value for time and money out of my role as Special Representative.' However, he conceded that 'he couldn't expect the British people to accept his explanation because he also used the helicopter and other means of travel looking for the finest golf courses.'

But the expenses continued. On 8 March 2011, the *Daily Telegraph* reported: 'In 2010, the Prince spent £620,000 as a trade envoy, including £154,000 on hotels, food and hospitality and £465,000 on travel.'

Abroad he travelled with a team of at least six equerries and private secretaries—including a valet with an ironing board so that he could have perfect creases in his trousers. Visiting Bahrain he sent ahead instructions that the water should be served at room temperature. The deputy head of the mission there, Simon Wilson, said his behaviour was 'boorish' and 'rude', and he regarded himself as an expert on every matter. Wilson said that Andrew was 'more commonly known among the British diplomatic community in the Gulf as HBH: His Buffoon Highness. This nickname stemmed from his childish obsession with doing exactly the opposite of what had been agreed in pre-visit meetings with his staff.'

Sir Ivor Richards, the ambassador to Italy, who hosted Andrew's visit there, said 'his kind of diplomacy is not mine, in the sense that it has not always led to improved relations with the people he is supposed to be schmoozing.' He described Andrew as 'brusque to the point of rudeness'. At a party, Andrew dismissed the head of a well-known fashion house with the words: 'Never heard of you.'

Tatania Gfoeller, Washington's ambassador to Kyrgyzstan, recorded how, speaking at a business event, Andrew called the UK's Serious Fraud Office 'idiots' for investigating bribery claims around an arms deal in Saudi Arabia and accused *Guardian* journalists of 'poking their noses everywhere' for reporting on the deal.

Sunninghill Park's rear facade

'The problem with Andrew,' a senior Buckingham Palace official had already said in 2001, 'is that his mouth engages before his brain does.'

The duke's jaunts around the world allowed him to collect a wide circle of dubious acquaintances, including one-time Libya dictator Colonel Gaddafi and his son Saif al-Islam, once a promoter of eco-tourism but later wanted by the International Criminal Court for crimes against humanity. Then there was Sakher el-Materi, the son-in-law of the deposed Tunisian president Zine al-

Abidine Ben Ali, whom Andrew entertained at Buckingham Palace three months before the regime collapsed. He went into exile in the Seychelles and was sentenced to sixteen years after being tried in absentia for corruption. A trip to see the president of Azerbaijan led to the headline 'The Duke and the Despot', while a skiing trip with convicted Libyan gun runner Tarek Kaituni led to 'Prince Takes Holiday with Gun Smuggler'. Andrew was also said to have accepted a £20,000 gold necklace for Beatrice. In February 2011, during the Libyan Civil War, Andrew's questionable connections there led UK shadow justice minister Chris Bryant to doubt the duke's suitability to be trade envoy.

Andrew carried on regardless. He went goose-shooting with Nursultan Nazarbayev, the president of Kazakhstan and the longest serving non-royal leader in the world, in office from 1990 to 2019. No election was judged free and fair since the country gained independence from the Soviet Union. In April 2015, Nazarbayev was re-elected with almost ninety-eight per cent of the vote, as he ran virtually unopposed. Nazarbayev has been accused of human rights abuses by several international organisations.

It was the son-in-law of his fellow goose-shooter, Timur Kulibayev, who bought Andrew's house for £3 million above the asking price. The prince remained tight with the Kulibayevs and in 2011 personally tried to get his mother's bankers to fly out and meet them as prospective private-banking clients. It didn't work. In the words of a senior banker at Coutts this was because they 'are the sort of people we generally don't touch with a bargepole.' In a statement about the duke's leaked email (sent as 'The Duke'), the palace suggested Andrew was trying to increase Britain's prosperity.

Certainly Andrew thought he was above the rules that apply to others. In 2002 he told a police officer who pulled him over for speeding that he was in a hurry—to get to a golf tournament, as it turned out—and drove off before he could be given a ticket. Three years later there was a stand-off at Melbourne Airport in Australia when he refused to subject himself to a routine security screening before boarding a flight to New Zealand. 'Who does he think he is?' one member of the airport security team said. 'What a pompous prick.'

He caused a diplomatic incident when he publicly criticised George W Bush's White House for failing to listen more to the advice of the British government over the post-war strategy for Iraq. 'It is frankly embarrassing,' the *Guardian* said, 'that Britain should be represented in any capacity by such a halfwit.'

In the last year of his trade role he clocked up 77,000 air miles. The year after, 2012, it was 93,500. The next year taxpayers funded a trip to New York for a series of official engagements that coincided with his daughter Princess Eugenie move to the city. The timing, the palace insisted, was a coincidence.

In 2010, he was photographed on a 154-foot yacht off the coast of Sardinia with a twenty-five-year-old bikini-wearing beauty rubbing sun cream on him. She was the half-Spanish, half-Filipino model Alexandra Escat, who was half the prince's age.

She later recounted how she fetched Andrew some sunscreen and was taken aback when he asked her to apply it for him. 'This is somebody I have barely met and he's royal. I mean, that's just weird, right?'

Royal sources initially claimed that the pair were just friends and that Escat was married to another guest on the yacht. In fact, she was single. He was photographed kissing her hand and they were later seen jetting off together.

Throughout this playboy time of rubbing shoulders with the rich and infamous—and, in some cases, corrupt—Andrew knew Epstein.

Just a week after the December 2010 photo of Andrew and Epstein stroll in Central Park appeared in the papers, Andrew's press secretary, Ed Perkins, got a phone call from Sian James, an assistant editor at the *Mail on Sunday*, who told him that they had obtained an interview with Virginia Giuffre.

She said on the call that Virginia Giuffre alleged that Epstein had turned her into an underage prostitute and had taken her to London, at age seventeen, to have sex with Prince Andrew. The paper had also got hold of the picture of Andrew with his arm around Giuffre's bare midriff. Also in the picture was Ghislaine Maxwell.

Andrew denied everything, but—despite receiving a defamation warning from the palace's lawyers after the prince had sworn to his parents nothing untoward had ever happened—the paper published the photograph of him and Giuffre anyway, though not the story behind it.

It revealed the first link between the duke and the Epstein scandal, suggesting that the prince, Maxwell, and Giuffre, had been together in London at the same time. Epstein, it was alleged, had taken the picture.

As William would marry Kate a month later, the palace was keen to deflect attention firmly away from the brewing scandal and quickly organised that Andrew would receive the Knight Grand Cross of the Royal Victorian Order, the highest grade, from the Queen for 'personal service' to show Buckingham Palace was closing ranks behind her second son.

Andrew texted Goga Ashkenazi, Timur Kulibayev's mistress, 'Have you seen the papers?', and told her he was 'very, very upset' about the way he came off in them.

Andrew was already embroiled in another scandal at the time. His lodger, the cash-strapped Fergie, had been caught offering access to Andrew for £500,000 by an undercover reporter for the *News of the World* posing as a businessman. The meeting had been secretly filmed in May 2010.

'If you want to meet him in your business, look after me, and he'll look after you. You'll get it back tenfold,' Fergie could be heard saying on the video. 'That opens up everything you would ever wish for. And I can open any door you want. And I will for you.' A one per cent commission would also be payable on any deals struck.

She walked away from the meeting with a briefcase carrying a large cash down payment. She was forced to return this and move out of Royal Lodge, later telling Oprah Winfrey that she had been drinking before the meeting and that 'I was in the gutter at the moment'.

In her apology, Fergie denied that Andrew had any knowledge of the bribe and said he 'was not aware or involved in any of the discussions that occurred'. However, in the tape she told her would-be benefactor that Prince Andrew 'knows that he's had to underwrite me up to now because I've got no money'.

She was thought to be anywhere from £2 million to £5 million in debt, owing £200,000 to a firm of London solicitors in unpaid legal fees.

Chris Bryant, who was a Foreign Office Minister at the time Andrew held his trade envoy role, demanded a parliamentary inquiry into the prince's business behaviour.

'It all just stinks,' said Bryant. 'I don't think he has ever been able to draw a distinction between his own personal interest and the national interest. It's morally offensive. He clearly was never fit to hold that office. Either the Foreign Affairs Committee or the Public Accounts Committee should launch an inquiry into this.'

He told the *Daily Mirror*: 'It should look at the evident conflict of interest when he was travelling at great expense to the taxpayer as a trade envoy but actively pursuing his own financial interests and those of his mates.'

Even after Andrew resigned as Britain's trade envoy, other public duties continued. In 2013, he was elected a royal fellow of the Royal Society, but Britain's pre-eminent scientific institution faced unprecedented dissent from members over the move, with one professor describing the duke as an 'unsavoury character'. To add insult to injury, the prince had no background in science.

Norman Baker, a former MP who published a damning book about royal finances in 2019, told the *Daily Mail*: 'This is outrageous behaviour by Prince Andrew. Any Minister who behaved in this way would be summarily sacked. Even an MP who behaved in this way would face questions from the Commons Standards Committee. We have all had enough of Prince Andrew. He should have his HRH designation removed. As far as I am concerned he should be persona non grata and not be seen in any way to represent this country.'

8

WHO WAS JEFFREY EPSTEIN?

Prince Andrew was born in the Belgian Room of Buckingham Palace on 19 February 1960 to a Germanic family, while Jeffrey Epstein was born in Brooklyn on 20 January 1953 to a family of Jewish immigrants who had escaped the Holocaust. He was brought up in the quiet, lower middle-class district of Sea Gate on Coney Island. His father worked in the parks department. His mother was a school aide. So how did he become filthy rich?

Educated in the local schools, Epstein was bright and particularly gifted in maths. He graduated from high school two years early in 1969 and went to the prestigious Cooper Union College in lower Manhattan to study advanced maths and made extra money by tutoring classmates. Suddenly in 1971, he dropped out and moved to New York University's Courant Institute of Mathematical Sciences to study the mathematics of heart physiology, but dropped out again in 1974 without graduating. Nevertheless, he got a job as a maths and science teacher at Manhattan's distinguished Dalton School while Rupert Murdoch's daughter Prudence was a pupil.

Another student recalled the special attention Epstein paid to the girls at the school. Scott Spiser told the *New York Times*: 'I can remember thinking at the time, "This is wrong." He was much more present amongst the students, specifically the girl students, during non-teaching hours… It was kind of inappropriate.'

Epstein was sacked by the school in 1976. However, he had impressed one student's father who was a Wall Street broker, and who got Epstein a job with the investment bank and brokerage firm Bear Stearns. He quickly rose through the ranks, handling multi-million-dollar clients. One of his specialties was hiding the money of dodgy dictators. Soon he became the toast of lower Manhattan, riding around Donald Trump-style in a chauffeur-driven limo with a beautiful woman on each arm.

Interviewed for *Vanity Fair*, he became friendly with contributing editor and author Jesse Kornbluth, who remained in the dark about where his enormous wealth had come from and jokingly compared Epstein to Bernie Madoff—who years later was sentenced to 150 years for running a Ponzi scheme that netted $65 billion. They fell out after Epstein phoned Kornbluth's fiancée the night before the wedding and said: 'Since you're going to be married tomorrow, this is your last night of freedom. Why don't you come over and sleep with me?' Later he phoned other women, purporting to be Kornbluth.

In 1981, Epstein was caught on insider trading and lost his job at Bear Stearns. He set up on his own, taking on controversial clients such as Saudi arms dealer Adnan Khashoggi. Together they pulled off a global arms deal that included selling AWACS (Airborne Warning and Control System) planes. According to the Defense Intelligence Agency, Khashoggi was one of the biggest drug traffickers in the 1980s and 1990s. He also worked for the CIA, and Epstein boasted that he was a CIA agent too. Indeed, he had connections. He rented an upmarket Manhattan apartment from the State Department at $15,000 a month. After Epstein was arrested in 2008, he had his Bentley armour-plated, afraid that someone was going to try to kill him. People connected to him then began to die mysterious deaths. When he died, the FBI discovered that he had an Austrian passport under a fake name giving his country of residence as Saudi Arabia.

Epstein was also friends with Crown Prince Mohammed bin Salman, the *de facto* ruler of Saudi Arabia and the man who in 2018 was responsible, according to the CIA, for the brutal assassination of former Saudi courtier Jamal Khashoggi. Showing a full-length photo of bin Salman in the same year, the billionaire bragged to the *New York Times* that the Saudi ruler often visited his New York home and that they spoke frequently.

Two days before Trump's election as president, Epstein's jet flew to Riyadh and back on the day of the election. It was unclear why, but MBS was desperate to buy technology for a Saudi nuclear bomb and, after the frosty relations with Obama, he reckoned that the vain Donald Trump, who had been keen to open hotels in Saudi Arabia, would be his mark. Three weeks later MBS's right-hand man Khalid al-Falih flew to New York to meet with Jared Kushner, fully briefed on how to charm the make-shift Trump transition team. The Yorks also had an MBS connection. Almost exactly a year after Jamal Khashoggi had been cut into sixteen pieces by Saudi officials, Fergie accepted an invitation from MBS's office to speak as a 'resilient philanthropeneur' at a youth forum in Riyadh, meanwhile promoting her line of 'room infusers, flavoured teas and jewellery'.

Epstein was also involved in laundering money and, in the late 1980s and early 1990s, worked for the Tower Financial Corporation. It was another Ponzi scheme. His boss Steven Hoffenberg was sentenced to twenty years, fined $1 million and ordered to make $463 million restitution. Mysteriously Epstein was not indicted and walked away with millions.

Throughout these dubious dealings, Epstein kept one legitimate client, Les Wexner, founder and CEO of The Limited, the company that owned the lingerie empire Victoria's Secret. They became firm friends. In 1989 Epstein acquired from Wexner the townhouse on East 71st Street that he had bought for $13.2 million and had completely renovated. The following year, Epstein bought his house on El Brillo Way in West Palm Beach for $2.5 million, just a mile and a half from Donald Trump's estate at Mar-a-Lago. Then in 1991, Wexner gave Epstein full power of attorney over his business affairs.

It was in 1991 that British media tycoon Robert Maxwell disappeared after embezzling hundreds of millions of pounds from his company's pension fund and his business empire was about to collapse. It has never been determined whether he simply fell overboard, committed suicide or was murdered. Maxwell had been working for Mossad, according to Pulitzer-Prize-winning author Seymour Hersh, and a lot of his early money was made by publishing material from behind the Iron Curtain. Martin Dillion, author of *Robert Maxwell, Israel's Superspy*, believes that Ghislaine was also on Mossad's payroll. Some of Robert Maxwell's correspondence and files were stored in Epstein's Florida home.

Ari Ben-Menashe, a former Israeli spy and alleged 'handler' of Robert Maxwell, said of Epstein: '[Robert] Maxwell introduced him to us, and he wanted us to accept him as part of our group.'

He also said that Epstein started dating Ghislaine in the late 1980s and had met her through her father. The young couple had then been recruited by Israeli intelligence. Ben-Menashe told journalist James Robertson: 'Epstein was the simple idiot who was going around providing girls to all kinds of politicians in the United

States. See, fucking around is not a crime. It could be embarrassing, but it's not a crime. But fucking a fourteen-year-old girl is a crime. And he was taking photos of politicians fucking fourteen-year-old girls—if you want to get it straight. They would just blackmail people, they would just blackmail people like that.' It was a straightforward honey trap.

After Epstein died, a man using the pseudonym Patrick Kessler said he had years' worth of communications, financial records and video footage from Epstein's hidden cameras. Kessler claimed to have footage of prominent men, including Prince Andrew and several billionaires. He claimed to have been hired by Epstein in 2012 to set up his digital archive on encrypted servers. With Epstein dead, Kessler said, he had unfettered access to the material.

He approached the Manhattan lawyers Stanley Pottinger and David Boies, a famous litigator known for his work in support of gay rights, as well as Al Gore in the Supreme Court election battle against George W Bush, and latterly infamous for representing the disgraced Hollywood producer Harvey Weinstein. Kessler showed the two lawyers grainy footage on his phone of two people having sex. The veteran attorneys' instinct was to believe Kessler.

'I have to evaluate people for my day job, and he seemed too genuine to be a fake, and I very much want him to be real,' Boies told the *New York Times*. However, he changed his mind after the archive did not show up.

'I think that he was a fraudster who was just trying to set things up,' said Boies. Whether or not a real Epstein archive exists remains unknown.

Robert Maxwell and Donald Trump knew each other. Both men had bought their yachts from the Khashoggi family and both named them after their daughters. Both Robert and Ghislaine Maxwell also had connections to the Clintons. At one time, Trump and the Clintons were also friendly. They were guests at his wedding to Melania in 2005 and he supported Hillary when she ran for the nomination in 2008.

When Robert Maxwell died in 1991, Ghislaine moved to New York. A trust set up by her father guaranteed her $100,000 a year for the rest of her life. It became clear to those who knew them that she and Epstein were tight. Her sister Isabel thought that Ghislaine was in love with Epstein and wanted to marry him. She helped him throw lavish dinner parties with exclusive guest lists that read like a *Who's Who* of the rich and famous, one of whom was Kevin Spacey, whose acting career was curtailed by allegations of paedophilia.

Many of these famous guests were also frequent fliers on Epstein's private jet, Lolita Express, named for the 1955 novel *Lolita* about a middle-aged literature professor who is obsessed with a twelve-year-old girl, and becomes sexually involved with her after becoming her stepfather. Also on board was Epstein's personal massage therapist Chauntae Davies, who said: 'On almost every trip that I did go on, there were young girls around.'

The director of Santa Fe airport, near the 10,000-acre Zorro Ranch in New Mexico that Epstein purchased in 1993, was told that Epstein flew in prostitutes, some of whom looked suspiciously young. Epstein's chauffeurs also worried that some of their young female passengers were underage. The girls were often accompanied by Ghislaine Maxwell, while Epstein would travel in another car. They were often nervous, but Maxwell reassured them, telling them that, when it was over, they would be very happy and be returned home. The drivers would tell themselves that the girls might be his nieces—though no one had that many nieces. When they took them to his home, they would only be there for two or three hours.

Epstein's Zorro Ranch, New Mexico

Among the people Epstein and Maxwell cultivated was Prince Andrew's ex-wife. She called Epstein regularly and he provided her with cash. Epstein found in Andrew a kindred spirit. Epstein was delighted to be invited to the Dance of the Decades at Windsor Castle in 2000.

A friend who knew them both well said, 'Jeffrey had Andrew put on a pair of sweatpants for the first time in his life. He had him wear blue jeans for the first time. It was Jeffrey who taught Andrew how to relax.' It wasn't quite accurate as Andrew had previously dressed down as a seventeen year old during his year abroad from Gordonstoun in Canada. Relieved from palace pressures in Canada and treated like an exotic celebrity, he'd loved being carefree. But the prince had buttoned-up again in the navy. It seemed that Epstein renewed Andrew's more playful side. The men partied together again at Heidi Klum's 'Pimps and Hookers' Halloween party in New York. They visited Sandringham that December.

In Spring 2006, Andrew flew out to Epstein's Zorro Ranch in New Mexico, where the poolroom was decorated with a striking portrait of Maxwell, next to the communal shower and hot tub.

'There was this huge painting of Ghislaine naked with her legs open, six foot by six foot,' a member of staff said. 'She was on a chair, leaning back, with her legs open. You could see everything. She would definitely have posed for that.'

There were pictures of Andrew and Ghislaine. On that occasion Epstein had a beautiful young woman with him. While the others went out, she stayed at home with Andrew.

'We had all these different teas that you could pick,' said Deidre Stratton, one of the staff at the Zorro Ranch charged with recruiting young massage therapists. 'She asked me to find one that would make him more horny, that he hadn't been interested in her. I'm guessing because she understood her job was to entertain him.'

Stratton thought that Epstein had the woman on a retainer.

'She knew what her job would be,' she said. 'Should be, you know, to make these people happy.'

Asked why Epstein would set Prince Andrew up with a stranger, Stratton said: 'I have read where the island was set up with cameras where Jeffrey could tape these men with their underage people and use it as blackmail. I mean, that's the oldest game in the book, isn't it?'

Hidden from his friends, Epstein continued his career as a sexual predator until March 2005 when a woman called the Palm Beach police department, saying her fourteen-year-old stepdaughter had been lured to Epstein's mansion and given $300 to strip to her underwear and give him a massage. Palm Beach Police Officer Michele Pagan persuaded the woman to bring her stepdaughter down to be interviewed. The local Florida lawyer who was to represent the fourteen year old and twenty others, Bradley Edwards, would later write a book, *Relentless Pursuit*, about his decade-long legal fight to bring the billionaire's exploitation of minors to justice.

The girl said a friend of a friend told her she could make hundreds of dollars in one hour, just for massaging some middle-aged guy's feet. Lots of other girls had been doing it, some three times a week. She claimed she had been driven to the mansion on El Brillo Way, where a female staffer escorted her up a pink-carpeted staircase, then into a room with a massage table, an armoire topped with sex toys and a photo of a little girl pulling her underwear off. Epstein entered the room wearing only a towel.

'He took off the towel,' she said. 'He was a really built guy. But his wee-wee was very tiny.'

She said Epstein got on the table and barked orders at her. She told police she was alone in the room with him and terrified. Pagan wrote a incident report, saying: 'She removed her pants, leaving her thong panties on. She straddled his back, whereby her exposed buttocks were touching Epstein's exposed buttocks. Epstein then turned to his side and started to rub his penis in an up-and-down motion. Epstein pulled out a purple vibrator and began to massage Mary's vaginal area.' She said he ejaculated and wiped himself with the towel.

Palm Beach assigned six detectives to the investigation. They conducted a 'trash pull' of Epstein's garbage, sifting through paper with phone numbers, used condoms, toothbrushes, worn underwear. In one pull, police found a piece of paper with Mary's phone number on it, along with the number of the person who recruited her. In another, they found an Amazon delivery slip dated 4 September 2005 for several suspicious books—*Slavecraft: Roadmaps for Erotic Servitude*, *Training with Miss Abernathy: A Workbook for Erotic Slaves* and *SM 101: A Realistic Introduction.*

On 11 September 2005, detectives got another break. Another girl told Detective Joe Recarey that she had been going to Epstein's house since she was sixteen. Alison had been working at the Wellington Green Mall, saving up for a trip to Maine, when a friend told her: 'You can get a plane ticket in two hours… We can go give this guy a massage and he'll pay $200,' according to her statement to the police.

She told Recarey that she visited Epstein hundreds of times. She said he had bought her a new 2005 Dodge Neon, plane tickets, and gave her spending money. He even asked her to come and live with him full time as his 'sex slave'. During her time with him, she said Epstein slowly escalated his sexual demands. Despite Alison's insistence that they never had intercourse, she alleged, 'This one time… he bent me over the table and put himself in me. Without my permission.'

But she was in abject fear of him and would not accuse him of rape.

'Before I say anything else… um, is there a possibility that I'm gonna have to go to court or anything?' she asked.

'I mean, what he did to you is a crime,' said Recarey. 'I'm not gonna lie to you.'

'Would you consider it rape, what he did?' she asked.

'If he put himself inside you without permission… That, that is a crime,' Recarey said. 'That is a crime.'

'I don't want my family to find out about this,' the girl said. 'Cause Jeffrey's gonna get me. You guys realise that, right?… I'm not safe now. I'm not safe.'

'Why do you say you're not safe?' Recarey asked. 'Has he said he's hurt people before?'

'Well, I've heard him make threats to people on the telephone, yeah. Of course.'

'"You're gonna die? You're gonna break your legs?" Or…'

'All of the above!' the girl said. She also said that Epstein got so violent with her that he ripped out her hair and threw her around.

'I mean,' she said, 'there's been nights that I walked out of there barely able to walk, um, from him being so rough.'

Over the next year, the police tracked down thirty-four other girls who had experienced something similar.

One said: 'Every girl that meets Jeffrey starts off with giving him a massage. The more you do with him, the more you make. Basically, if you take off your clothes, you're gonna make more. If you let him do things to you, you're gonna make more… touch you in inappropriate places… He uses his hands, and I wouldn't really call it a vibrator, I guess like a massager. I did it naked, but I wouldn't let him touch me or anything like that. My friend told me that she knew a girl that slept with him and made $1,000.

'So after that he's like, "You know what? I'll pay you $200 for every girl that you bring to me. I don't want you to massage me anymore, just bring girls to me." So for every girl that I brought to Jeffrey, I would make $200.'

All of them were under eighteen, the age of consent in Florida.

'He told me the younger the better. I tried to bring him a woman who was twenty-three and he didn't really like it….'

Sixteen-year-old Marjorie Hernandez was in class when the girl sitting next to her passed her a note asking if she wanted to make some extra money for Christmas. All she had to do was massage old guys and not tell anyone about it. The classmate took her to Epstein's house. A woman took her to a massage room. Epstein appeared wearing only a towel. He lay down on his stomach and told her to massage his feet, then his calves, while he made a business call.

When he got off the phone, he began to ask her about her sex life, then persuaded her to strip to her panties and bra, which he then unfastened and tried to pleasure her.

'He knew that I was uncomfortable,' she said. 'He continued anyways. He was really going to town on himself. He kept going and then at one point he just, I guess finished and he jumped up, wrapped his towel around him.'

He thanked her, saying he would like to see her again and gave her $200. She cried all the way home. A year later, she got a visit from the police.

Another girl said: 'About five minutes into it he took the towel off and started pleasing himself, which I was very uncomfortable with. Like I wanted to leave right when I got there. I'm sorry, I don't like thinking back on it, it was so… When he started pleasing himself he got up and went over to a drawer and he pulled out this vibrator thing and then he pulled down my panties—it was like this stick with a knob on it. He didn't like stick it inside me but he put it on me. He just got up and walked out. He's like, "OK you can put your clothes on," and he closed the door. After he walked out and when I went out, I went downstairs and he was down there and there were like other girls there. I guess they stayed there or something.'

Detective Recarey interviewed Epstein's former house manager of eleven years Juan Alessi. In his probable-cause affidavit Recarey said: 'Alessi stated Epstein receives three massages a day… towards the end of his employment, the masseuses… appeared to be 16 or 17 years of age at the most… [Alessi] would have to wash off a massager/vibrator and a long rubber penis, which were in the sink after the massage.' Another house manager, Alfredo Rodriguez, told Recarey that very young girls were giving Epstein massages at least twice a day, and in one instance, Epstein had Rodriguez deliver one dozen roses to Mary at her high school.

When the police eventually raided Epstein's mansion, they found pictures of naked girls, X-rated videotapes, sex toys, massage tables and hidden cameras, some of which had been removed, leaving their cables hanging. It seemed that Epstein had been tipped off. The police were also keen to examine Epstein's body. Victims said that his penis was 'egg-shaped' or like a 'teardrop'—thick towards the base, thinner towards the head.

In May 2006, Florida police charged Epstein with multiple counts of unlawful sex acts with a minor. But it didn't prevent Epstein from partying with real royalty and movie royalty. A few weeks after the charges he was photographed dressed in white as a navy SEAL, together with Ghislaine Maxwell and Harvey Weinstein, at Princess Beatrice's glamorous eighteenth-birthday fancy dress ball at Windsor Castle. It was reported by the press that Prince Andrew had put Epstein on the guest list.

To deal with the Florida sex charges Epstein had a powerful defence team including Ken Starr—whose investigation into the Clinton administration led to the president's historic impeachment trial—and Alan Dershowitz, the Harvard law professor who had defended OJ Simpson.

The police then found details of their case had been leaked, so the Palm Beach police handed the case over to the FBI. This put the prosecution in the hands of United States Attorney Alex Acosta, who drew up a fifty-three-page indictment. According to the *Miami Herald*'s Julie Brown, in October 2007, Acosta had a secret meeting with one of Epstein's attorneys over breakfast in the Marriott in West Palm Beach. They agreed that Epstein would plead guilty to minor felony state charges of procuring a person under eighteen for prostitution and register as a sex offender. Interestingly, any possible co-conspirators would be immune to further charges as well.

The deal would mean that Epstein would only serve just under thirteen months in prison and then ten months on probation. Brokered without the knowledge of Epstein's victims, it meant that four women subsequently named as Epstein's alleged accomplices—Nadia Marcinkova, who would later be described as his 'Yugoslavian sex slave', Sarah Kellen, Adriana Ross and Lesley Groff—were not charged. The immunity also extended to Ghislaine Maxwell, though she was not named in that case. However, her name was written on message pads, flight manifests and other documents found by the police in Epstein's home.

It was only later, with Virginia Giuffre's accusations in 2015, that she became publicly associated with Epstein's crimes.

The excuse for this sweetheart deal, Epstein's establishment lawyers insisted, was that he had been unaware of the girls' ages. Epstein told the *New York Times* that he had replaced them with a full-time male masseur and, when he went to jail in Miami, he set his email to auto-reply that he was 'on vacation'. No further investigations were made in New York, New Mexico or the Virgin Islands. The case was confined to south Florida.

Instead of being sent to a federal penitentiary, Epstein was given a private wing at the Palm Beach County Stockade Facility and had his own personal security guards. He paid $128,000 to the Palm Beach County Sheriff's Office for the privilege. The cell door was left open and he was given 'liberal access' to a room with a television. It was argued that these arrangements were made for Epstein because he may otherwise have been victimised by other inmates.

After just three months, he was granted work release that allowed him out of jail for up to sixteen hours seven days a week at an office at the Florida Science Foundation, an organisation he had set up. He could also spend two of those hours at his Palm Beach home, where he had committed the original offences. Among those who visited him in jail were the two women accused of being co-conspirators—Sarah Kellen and Nadia Marcinkova, who herself had been underage when she had got involved with Epstein. The *Miami Herald* discovered that, bizarrely, Epstein had bought two pairs of women's panties from the prison commissary. They were size five—too small for either Kellen or Marcinkova to wear.

According to the *Miami Herald*, Epstein had got off so lightly after Acosta had been told to back off because Epstein 'belonged to intelligence'. The Iraq War was still going on. Britain was the last member of the US-led coalition of the willing, and the Bush administration could not afford to alienate its only ally by dragging Prince Andrew's name through the mud, and clearly he had other influential friends who he may, or may not, have supplied girls to. As part of the deal, the agreed terms themselves were to be kept secret and Epstein had the money to pay off curious reporters. Even the victims and their attorneys were not told.

However, when no federal charges were pursued, victims began to file civil suits. The lawsuits involved Epstein being deposed. He would only answer the most trivial questions. Otherwise he would cite the Fifth Amendment, which allows witnesses to refuse to give answers to questions that might incriminate them. When asked to confirm the description of his genitalia, he walked out and had to be ordered by a judge to return.

The civil suits were settled for undisclosed sums. Some victims complained that they and their families had been threatened. However, two victims filed a lawsuit against the US government for failing to notify them of the plea deal—a violation of the 2004 US Crime Victims' Rights Act. In 2014, two more victims joined the suit. One of them was Virginia Giuffre, who had made allegations against Maxwell as well as Epstein, and for the first time Prince Andrew's name surfaced in the case.

After Epstein's arrest and conviction in 2008, most of his friends kept him at arm's length. However, Prince Andrew was guest of honour at a 'welcome home' party in Manhattan in 2010 after Epstein had completed his sentence. It was then that Epstein and the prince were photographed strolling together in Central Park, and Andrew was videoed saying goodbye to Katherine Keating at the door of Epstein's townhouse.

Epstein was unrepentant. 'I'm not a sexual predator, I'm an "offender",' he told the *New York Post* in 2011. 'It's the difference between a murderer and a person who steals a bagel.' Later some made the suggestion that Epstein had staged the walk in Central Park as part of either a blackmail or twisted rehabilitation campaign.

Meanwhile he sought to rebuild his reputation by cultivating new friends among the scientific community. Stephen Hawking visited Little Saint James. He was photographed with a young blonde with a ponytail. At the time, Ghislaine's sister Isabel was helping visual theorist Al Seckel organised a conference for Epstein on St Thomas and Little Saint James. He was accused of running off with $500,000. Soon after he died in a mysterious accident when his rental car drove over a cliff. A magazine article claimed he was trying to sell the correspondence and files of Robert Maxwell that were later found in Epstein's Florida home.

Other scientists were invited out to the Zorro Ranch. Some of them were Nobel Prize winners. The locals remained suspicious about the secrecy that surrounded the goings on at the ranch. There had already been a Repository for Germinal Choice, a sperm bank in California for the seed of Nobel laureates. However, Epstein's plan was to improve the human stock using exclusively his own sperm. He planned a baby farm where he would impregnate some twenty women. And when he died he wanted his head and penis preserved cryogenically.

With his new circle of high-powered friends, it seemed as if the world had forgotten about his past misdemeanours. In December 2018, he thought he was finally in the clear when he paid off Bradley Edwards representing three final victims. This cost him $5.5 million, but there would be no trial and the deal ensured the women's silence. However, after ten years, Bradley's lawsuit on behalf of the three women against the US government over the non-disclosure of the plea bargain that meant Epstein and any possible co-conspirators would not be prosecuted was suddenly back in play.

In February 2019, US District Judge Kenneth A. Marra for the Southern District of Florida ruled that the United States government had indeed broken the law by allowing Epstein's victims to believe that a federal prosecution was still a possibility. They had been told to be 'patient'. What's more, Epstein and his co-conspirators had transported his victims between states and internationally for the purpose of sex. This was a contravention of the 1910 Mann Act.

On 6 July 2019, federal agents were waiting on the tarmac when the billionaire's private jet, the Lolita Express, landed at Teterboro Airport in New Jersey. He was handcuffed and taken into custody. Meanwhile G-men were crowbarring the heavy oak front doors of his Manhattan townhouse to search the place.

Two days later, with Epstein secured behind bars, the FBI and Geoffrey Berman, the US Attorney for the Southern District of New York, held a joint press conference announcing that Jeffrey Epstein had been indicted for sex trafficking and appealing for other victims to come forward. US District Judge Richard Berman said that indictments from the 2008 sexual abuse case had been unsealed. A reporter asked that, if Epstein had a non-prosecution agreement in Florida, how would federal prosecutors bring new charges?

'Jeffrey Epstein entered into a non-prosecution agreement with the Southern District of Florida,' Judge Berman explained. 'The Southern District of New York is not bound by that agreement and is not a signatory to that agreement.' The same rule would apply to Epstein's possible co-conspirators.

Epstein was being held in the Metropolitan Correctional Center in Lower Manhattan, a high-security facility that had held Mexican drugs baron Joaquín 'El Chapo' Guzmán and Mafia boss John Gotti. He was held in a cell on the ninth floor, which housed violent inmates and new arrivals who require protective custody. Prisoners were only allowed out of their rat- and roach-infested cells for thirty minutes a day.

On 8 July, Epstein appeared in court and pleaded not guilty. He and his attorneys discussed the possibility of making bail at a bail hearing on the 12th. His attorney Martin Weinberg argued that the allegations against him had taken place before 2005. Clearly his thirteen months in jail had taught him a lesson. He had not offended since then and he was no longer a threat to young girls. Weinberg then suggested that the judge set Epstein's bail at $100 million. Judge Berman wanted to review the evidence before he made a decision.

However in a new lawsuit filed on 16 July, Kaitlyn 'Doe' said that Epstein had continued to commit sexual offences while on work release from his 2008 sentence. She claimed that he had sex with her, aged eighteen, repeatedly in the offices of the Florida Science Foundation—the entity Epstein funded to sit out his Florida sentence.

According to Kaitlyn's lawsuit, when she had met Epstein in 2006, he had promised to help her cure an eating disorder, but instead groomed her to perform sex acts in a massage room at his Manhattan mansion. She was seventeen at the time, and a virgin. He then had her flown to his luxury compound in the US Virgin Islands, where he coerced her into sex, she said. That led to months of sex acts, while he promising to pay for expensive surgery she required.

Later in October 2008, when Epstein was serving his sentence in Palm Beach County, he got her to fly to Florida, where he promised her a job at his foundation. But she did not do any foundation work there. Instead, Epstein again coerced her into sex acts—sometimes alone, sometimes with another young woman. This took place when the Palm Beach Sheriff's Office was supposed to be keeping him under close surveillance, the suit said.

Kaitlyn said Epstein continued having sex with her until 2014. The lawsuit alleged he also coerced her into marrying another woman, one of his associates, so she could get her green card to stay in the US.

The following day Judge Berman denied Epstein's application for bail. He was to stay in jail until the trial date, which was set for June 2020, the judge said.

On the night of 23 July, Epstein's cellmate—a former cop charged with the murder of four men—called for help. Epstein was found motionless on the floor. It was thought he was dead. The guards, who had little time for Epstein, dragged his body out. However, he revived. There were questions as to whether he was a victim of foul play or suicide. He was transferred to solitary confinement in the suicide prevention wing. To get himself out of there, he blamed his cell mate for his injuries.

He was taken off suicide watch and returned to his cell. This was unusual as once on suicide watch, inmates usually remained on it until they left the facility. Ten days later Epstein signed a will assigning his $500-million-plus estate to a trust, protecting it from further claims by his victims. One of the executors was biotech Boris Nikolic, chief scientific advisor to Bill Gates. Though Gates denied any close personal friendship with Epstein, he had flown on the Lolita Express and had been photographed in Epstein's Manhattan home. There, he said, he met 'a very attractive Swedish woman and her daughter'. The woman, it seems, was former Miss Sweden Eva Andersson-Dublin. Documents taken from Epstein's home show that he had a thing for her fifteen-year-old daughter.

On 9 August, the papers from the Giuffre-Maxwell defamation case were unsealed. These contained Virginia Giuffre's allegations against Prince Andrew and other high rollers. That day Epstein's cellmate was moved out. The CCTV cameras outside his cell, it seems, were broken. That night the two prison guards who were supposed to look in on Epstein every half an hour fell asleep at exactly the same time and miraculously awoke again at the same time—at least according to the records, which they were later charged with falsifying. At 6.25am, they found Epstein with a sheet knotted around his neck. The other end was tied to the top bunk. His lifeless body was rushed to hospital where he was pronounced dead at 7.36am.

The results of the autopsy were withheld. It was only a week later that the chief medical examiner announced that Epstein had committed suicide. He had tied the sheet to the top bunk with the other end around his neck and fallen forward, hanging himself.

In the process he had broken several bones in his neck, including the hyoid, the U-shaped bone in the neck which supports the tongue. Breaking the hyoid occurs in twenty-seven per cent of suicides by hanging, but usually when there is a longer drop, applying more force. However, the hyoid is broken in fifty per cent of homicides by strangulation. While the medical report was not released, conspiracy theories abounded. Epstein's old friends Donald Trump and Bill Clinton accused each other of his murder. Others blamed Mossad, the CIA, MI6, the Saudis and MBS, Russia's FSB—pick your own culprit.

One of the most intriguing conspiracy theories comes from John Mark Dougan, a former Palm Beach County Deputy Sheriff, who fled to Russia where he was granted political asylum. He said that, while Epstein was on 'work release', the two deputies who were supposed to be watching him looked the other way when he brought underage girls into his office or his home.

Dougan reckoned that Epstein was murdered because the world's intelligence agencies could not afford for his blackmail DVDs to go public. These had disappeared after they had been seized by the Palm Beach County Sheriff's Office and the Palm Beach County State Attorney's Office. The police officer in charge of the case, Detective Joseph Recarey, had died suddenly, age fifty.

Fearing for his life, Dougan said, he had made off with some of the encrypted files. He believed that Epstein had been getting important people to have sex with underage girls so they could be blackmailed by Western intelligence agencies.

On 22 September 2019, the *Sunday Times* reported: 'British intelligence chiefs are concerned that Russia may have obtained *kompromat*, compromising material, on Prince Andrew over the Jeffrey Epstein scandal.'

After allegations about Prince Andrew surfaced, Dougan released a statement to clarify his position, saying: 'According to news reports, US intelligence agencies apparently analysed the files and communicated with British authorities. If Britain's secret intelligence service, commonly known as MI6, has concerns about any ties between Prince Andrew and Jeffrey Epstein, they got it from their Washington counterparts, not me.'

'I will not be divulging any of the information I may know of or possess, because the secrecy of the data I have access to ensures the safety of me and my loved ones. I hope the growing concerns and reports about Jeffrey Epstein's international sex-trafficking empire, and his relationship with the rich and powerful people like the Duke of York, will generate official and news media investigations which will uncover all the facts.'

Journalist Ron Chepesiuk said he had seen some random scenes from Dougan's files and vouched for their authenticity. Dougan, he said, was fearful of being gunned down by MI6. Apart from Al Seckel, who died in 2015, and Recarey, there have been other mysterious deaths in the case. Alan Ross, an attorney who represented one of Epstein's victims, died of a fast-acting cancer at the age of sixty-eight, as did Alfredo Rodriguez, the houseman who cleaned Epstein's sex toys, when he was just sixty. His widow said: 'He knew all about Prince Andrew.'

9

SEX SLAVES AND PURITANS

During much of the time Andrew was jaunting around the world as a UK's trade envoy, he was also stopping off to see Epstein and stay at his various homes. But then, apart from the meeting in December 2010, Andrew had broken off contact with him following his conviction in 2008. However, this did not leave Andrew in the clear. He had already been named in legal documents.

In 2011, the embarrassing headlines the allegations spawned and their impact on the prince's taxpayer-funded role as UK trade envoy were discussed at the highest levels of government in 10 Downing Street. Legal paperwork, held by lawyers in West Palm Beach acting for some of the fourteen girls who lodged suits against fifty-eight-year-old Epstein, also named Prince Andrew's close friend Ghislaine Maxwell, Epstein's girlfriend, as an abuser.

Maxwell strenuously denied all allegations against her, and continued to state they were all lies, but Epstein himself had already settled with twelve victims. Lawyers moved on to question two women said to be at the heart of his sex-trafficking operation—Sarah Kellen and Nadia Marcinkova, both in their twenties and given immunity from prosecution in the deal fixed by their former boss when he was jailed. Marcinkova was brought over from Slovakia by MC^2, a modelling agency run by Jean-Luc Brunel funded by Epstein ($E = MC^2$) and which was thought to have trafficked underage girls into the US.

On 24 March 2010, at the offices of Epstein's attorney Jack Goldberger in West Palm Beach attorney Spencer Kuvin, representing three of the victims, asked Kellen: 'Would you agree with me that you have been present where Jeffrey

Epstein and Prince Andrew have had sexual relations with underage girls?'

She replied: 'On the instruction of my lawyer, I must invoke my Fifth Amendment privilege.'

Then he asked: 'Would you agree with me that Prince Andrew and Jeffrey Epstein used to share underage girls for sexual relations?'

She gave the same reply. She even took the Fifth when asked if she knew who Prince Andrew was.

Three weeks later on 13 April, Marcinkova—described by lawyers as Epstein's 'bisexual sex slave'—was asked: 'Has Jeffrey Epstein also made you perform sexually on his friends?'

She replied curtly: 'Fifth.' She gave the same answer to 'Have you ever been made to perform sexually on Prince Andrew?' and 'Do you know Prince Andrew?'

There were further claims that Prince Andrew was a guest at Epstein's Florida home while naked pool parties were going on with hosts of young women frolicking in the water. The allegation was made by handyman and butler Juan Alessi, who spent eleven years working for Epstein. He said that Andrew was not naked himself and there was no suggestion any of the naked women were underage. However, he said Andrew had 'daily massages' when he visited the £4-million Palm Beach mansion. Was he happy after each session? he was asked.

'Wouldn't you be?' said Alessi.

Did he come out of the room with a smile on his face?

'Yes, of course!'

The mansion was already notorious from the 2008 investigation. Pictures of naked young girls adorned the walls. There were hidden cameras and private areas where the alleged abuse took place. Virginia Giuffre waived her right to anonymity in her court case to tell of the abuse she had suffered there.

It was then that she revealed, at seventeen, she had been flown to London at Epstein's expense to entertain Andrew, and the pair danced the night away at Tramp nightclub.

'After about an hour and a half we drove back to Ghislaine's,' she said. 'All of us went upstairs and I asked Jeffrey to snap a picture of me with the prince. I wanted something to show my mom. Ghislaine and Jeffrey left us after that, and later Andrew left. In the morning Ghislaine said, "You did well. He had fun." We flew straight back to the States.'

For this, Virginia was paid $15,000 dollars by Epstein.

'It was amazing money,' she said, 'more than I'd ever made on a trip with him before.'

Giuffre said that Maxwell had recruited her from Donald Trump's Mar-a-Lago Club in Palm Beach, where she was working at the time. Trump had bought the resort in 1985 to recreate under the Florida sun the infamous Manhattan Le Club, where, in Trump's own recollection, 'you were likely to see a wealthy seventy-five-year-old guy walk in with three blondes from Sweden'. For Mar-a-Lago, Trump insisted on a ratio of at least three females to two presumably older rich males as at Le Club. Maxwell had introduced Giuffre to Epstein and the two of them had groomed her, 'including lessons in Epstein's preferences during oral sex'.

In her deposition, Giuffre alleged that Maxwell was 'Epstein's primary manager' for the recruitment and training of girls Epstein paid for sexual services, and had participated in sexual abuse. As Epstein's 'sex slave' Virginia she had been forced to have sex with 'many other powerful men, including numerous prominent American politicians, powerful business executives, foreign presidents, a well-known prime minister, and other world leaders'.

'My whole life revolved around just pleasing these men and keeping Ghislaine and Jeffrey happy,' she claimed. 'Their whole entire lives revolved around sex.'

Suddenly under direct attack from Giuffre, Andrew got help from Koo Stark. She had never spoken about their relationship, but now she came to his rescue. She told the *Mail on Sunday*, 'That is why I have decided to reveal some details of my relationship with Andrew. My view is clear: I believe him to be a good man and I believe I can help rebut, with authority, the allegations against him.' She recalled the time when she dated him almost thirty years ago with fondness. He was 'a nice man, a tender, loving and caring normal boyfriend' and that he 'is a dear friend and godfather to my daughter. I've only known him to be honourable and honest, with Christian values.' She added, 'I couldn't shrug off Virginia Roberts' assassination of his character any more than he has been able to'.

Maxwell didn't shrug off Giuffre but called her a liar. In her 2015 deposition, when she was asked if she knew whether Epstein had sexually abused minors, Maxwell said in a sweeping statement: 'I can only testify to what I know. I know that Virginia is a liar and I know what she testified is a lie. I can only categorically deny everything she has said.' Under her married name Giuffre, Virginia Roberts sued for defamation. The case was settled in May 2017 with Giuffre being paid millions. The court papers were sealed as part of the settlement, however.

When they were unsealed the day before Epstein died, it turned out they included a deposition in which Virginia said that she had been lent out to numerous important men for sex.

'Donald Trump was also a good friend of Jeffrey's,' she said in testimony. 'He didn't partake in any sex with any of us but he flirted with me. He'd laugh and tell Jeffrey, "You've got the life".'

Giuffre's lawyer Bradley Edwards said that he asked Donald Trump on several occasions about Epstein. After being subpoenaed by Edwards in 2009, Trump told him that Epstein wasn't 'secretive' at Mar-a-Lago—Epstein seemed to fit the three-females-to-two-males profile at the club where Giuffre first met its guest Ghislaine Maxwell. Trump also observed, Bradley reported, 'he always saw Epstein around younger girls, but to his knowledge, none were underage'. But when reminded whether he had once expelled Epstein from Mar-a-Lago for taking home a fifteen-year-old (this girl was not a worker like Giuffre, but the daughter of a Mar-a-Lago member), Trump paused and conceded that something like that happened but could not remember the details. Later, in 2019, Edwards wrote in his book he would see a video from 1992 that suggested Trump and Epstein may at one point have been closer friends than mere 'business associates' as Trump let on to him. But this fact didn't matter to his investigations.

The flight log of Epstein's private jet had also been admitted in evidence. It showed that both Donald Trump and Bill Clinton had been on board. With the court papers from the Giuffre-Maxwell case now in the public domain, there was now a media feeding frenzy. Donald Trump joined in. In typical form, Trump shared a tweet from conservative comedian Terrence Williams that linked Bill and Hillary Clinton to the death of Epstein. But the joke rebounded. As the sitting president, Donald Trump was the paymaster of the federal prison where Epstein died.

A forensic pathologist hired by family of Jeffrey Epstein said the autopsy 'points to homicide rather than suicide'. Dr Michael Baden told Fox & Friends that Epstein had been strangled. He cited the specific fractures on Epstein's neck, saying they are unusual in hangings by suicide and more common in death by strangulation. He also said there were haemorrhages in Epstein's eyes that were common in homicidal strangulation and uncommon, though not unheard of, in suicide hangings.

Giuffre also alleged that young children from poor families were brought in to be molested by Epstein. 'The worst one that I heard from his own mouth were these pretty twelve-year-old girls he had flown in for his birthday,' she said. The Daily Beast reported that there were three children, all aged twelve, who were flown in from France for the alleged sex abuse as part of the 'surprise birthday gift'.

As well as Giuffre's allegations, there was testimony from Johanna Sjoberg, alleging inappropriate sexual contact with Prince Andrew at Epstein's Manhattan mansion.

'I just remember someone suggesting a photo, and they told us to get on the couch,' Sjoberg testified at one hearing. 'And so Andrew and Virginia sat on the couch, and they put the puppet on her lap. And so I sat on Andrew's lap, and I believe on my own volition, and they took the puppet's hands and put it on Virginia's breast, and so Andrew put his on mine.'

Palm Beach County police logs from 2005 and 2006 included multiple interviews with girls who said they were recruited for Epstein by Haley Robson, a high school student at the time. According to a 2006 Palm Beach Police probable-cause affidavit for Epstein, Robson admitted to detectives she acted as one of his recruiters, although she was never arrested or charged in connection to him. She got a $200 referral fee. Some of the girls, she said, were as young as fourteen or fifteen.

The girls reported explicit encounters with Epstein where he would often fondle them and masturbate while they massaged him. They were told upfront that they would have to be, at the very least, topless—preferably naked. Epstein would be naked himself. Some encounters involved sex with him and another woman. Vibrators and other sex toys were involved. They were told that Epstein needed at least three orgasms a day.

Epstein was immensely wealthy, though no one knew where his money came from. He signed a will just two days before he died, ostensibly leaving an estate worth $577 million. He declared that his residences in New York, Palm Beach, New Mexico, Paris and two islands in the Virgin Islands were worth $180,603,063 and had $56 million in cash. His collection of planes, boats and cars were worth $18,551,700. The value of his art collection had yet to be determined.

Quoting someone close to the case, the *Daily Mirror* said: 'He used his wealth to buy buddies and then bestow his money on those he courted. Jeff knew his relationships with the rich and famous brought him protection. He kept a diary in meticulous detail in case he ever needed it.... One former congressman said there are a lot of people "breathing a huge sigh of relief" now Jeff is dead. They should hold their breath for a long time to come. It ain't over.' It was unclear what had happened to the remainder of Epstein's billion-dollar fortune.

Johanna Sjoberg

Epstein's death caused others problems, especially for his victims. A statement by one of the alleged victims released by counsel Lisa Bloom read: 'I will never have a sense of closure now, I'm angry as hell that the prison could've allowed this to happen. And that I, and his other victims will never see him face the consequences for his horrendous actions. I hope that whatever allowed this to happen and whoever allows this to happen also faces some time of consequence. You stole from us the huge piece of healing that we needed to move on with our lives.'

Some had faced a worse fate. Selby Patrick said told the *Daily Mirror* that her twin sister Skye had died of an overdose of heroin at the age of twenty nine after being recruited as a teenager for Epstein by Maxwell. She said that Skye had told her that she was so unnerved by Epstein's abuse that she once said: 'He scared the life out of me.'

Epstein sealed her fate. 'It was the money,' Selby said. 'She kept going back to his house, but all the cash did was provide Skye with cash for drink and then drugs. It was like he was handing her a death sentence.'

And she pointed the finger at Maxwell.

'It was Ghislaine, or Gillian as the girls knew her, who recruited Skye's friends into his world. One wanted to be a model, and Ghislaine made her believe they'd launch her to stardom if she did as she was told. It was the girl who took Skye to Epstein's house, saying they'd just be hanging out at a playboy's mansion,' Selby said. 'The life was hard to resist. Who wouldn't want to rub shoulders with royalty and live like a princess as Ghislaine did?… Skye always said Ghislaine was so sophisticated. You'd never think as a woman she was gonna hurt a young girl, but she was the one luring them into the trap.'

According to Selby, Skye was just sixteen when she first went to Epstein's Florida home. He offered her a massage and $300 to take off her top. He told her to take off her bra, then tried to rip it off. Selby said that whenever Skye or her pals visited Epstein's home, Maxwell was there 'trying to tell the girls what to do and making promises'. Skye and a friend who also visited the house got $50,000 each as a settlement from Epstein after his conviction in 2008. This was her downfall. Skye got hooked on heroin and was found dead in a motel in 2017, weeks before her thirtieth birthday, leaving a five-year-old son named Jayden who Selby was bringing up.

'Between Epstein and Ghislaine they created a life for her from which she could find no way back,' Selby said.

In fresh lawsuit filed, a woman identified as Lisa 'Doe' said she was an aspiring seventeen-year-old ballet dancer when Epstein lured her into his web. He said he could help her and 'was closely connected to many major dance companies in New York City and that he was close personal friends with some of the most influential names in dance'. In return, she should conduct private exercise classes for him at his home. This resulted in numerous 'massages' and consequential sexual abuse, the lawsuit said.

Lisa said that Epstein kept a stack of the book, *Massage for Dummies*, which he doled out to his victims. Lisa said he had her 'squeeze his nipples as hard as she could' and forcibly used a sex toy on her while he masturbated. The lawsuit went on to say: 'There were sexual acts in addition to those described above which acts are too graphic and perverted to detail in the complaint.'

Another lawsuit was filed by Priscilla 'Doe', who said she first met Epstein when she was twenty. He hired her for massages. During her numerous visits, he promised the young woman plenty of money to support her mother, and to boost her career as a dancer. Epstein had promised that he would not try to have sex with her, but then 'forced himself on [her] and took her virginity against her will and wishes,' according to the lawsuit. Maxwell gave her step-by-step instructions on how to properly pleasure Epstein, she said. She used her own hands 'to demonstrate how to pleasure Jeffrey Epstein manually so that plaintiff would know exactly how to make Jeffrey Epstein happy.' Maxwell also taught her the proper way to perform oral sex just the way he liked it, along with giving her graphic advice on stimulation and pressure.

On the Virgin Islands, he forced her to have sex with other men and held her prisoner by confiscating her passport. She said she was also made have sex with another woman while being choked by Epstein. Along with other young women, she was constantly on call to provide sexual services.

During his massages, Epstein often took calls from powerful people, sometimes speaking angrily to them. He boasted that 'he had the ability to cause serious harm to powerful people and anyone who did not cooperate with him'. Priscilla said Epstein could 'be on the verge of ejaculating and would stop in order to make a phone call, at times saying that nearing sexual climax evoked certain important thoughts in Jeffrey Epstein's mind'.

Epstein also bragged about his friendships with Donald Trump, Bill Clinton, Prince Andrew and the Sultan of Dubai—and that she was forced to serve as a waitress at a yacht party attended by director Woody Allen.

'This server's role was forced upon plaintiff in order to demean her, frighten her, and impress upon her the need for her to conceal the commercial sex trafficking enterprise he was running,' the lawsuit said.

For six years, she said, Epstein kept her as a sexual prisoner. 'During that time, Jeffrey Epstein controlled nearly every aspect of [her] life from the clothing and jewellery she was permitted to wear to the career path she was permitted to follow to the food she was allowed to consume,' the suit alleged.

Older allegations came to light. Baywatch babe Alicia Arden claimed that Epstein had groped her during what she believed was an audition for Victoria's Secret in 1997. Epstein was the mentee of Leslie Wexner, the company's owner. She said Epstein was evaluating—and criticising—her figure, when he said: 'Let me manhandle you for a second.' Then he began groping her buttocks.

'He was bigger than me. I felt like it could have been bad if I didn't leave,' she said. She complained to the police in Santa Monica, California. They interviewed Epstein but took the matter no further.

'If they would have taken me more seriously than they did, it could have helped all these girls,' Arden told Associated Press. 'It could have been stopped.'

Former model Amy McClure then said that Epstein had raped her in his Manhattan townhouse twenty-five years earlier in 1993. She had agreed to massage him. He asked her how old she was and when she said twenty one: 'He said something like, "You're too, you're too old. You're getting too old for this. What are you doing?"'

Then he threatened her.

'He said, "If you tell anybody anything, I'll crush whatever career you might have," or something like that. He was just so mean so quickly. It literally went from awkward to mean to rape so fast,' she told the *Sun*.

She said nothing at the time because she thought it would look like it was her fault.

'I felt nobody would believe me. I blamed myself for a lot of it. And I didn't know what anyone could do anyway. These people were from a different world—they were rich, untouchable.'

The unsealing of the Giuffre-Maxwell court papers brought to light more evidence against Prince Andrew. In a deposition to Virginia Giuffre's lawyers, pilot David Rodgers said that Andrew was on two flights on Epstein's private jet, heading for Florida and the Virgin Islands. He was also on the maiden flight of the Lolita Express—the Boeing 727 that replaced his Gulfstream. It had a bed on board which Epstein used for orgies. However, Rodgers did not allege any wrongdoing by Prince Andrew on the flights.

Despite the barrage of allegations the *New York Post* reported Prince Andrew had refused to cut his ties with Epstein. According to a 2011 report in *Vanity Fair*, an unidentified friend said: 'After Jeffrey was convicted, I phoned Andrew and told him, "You cannot have a relationship with Jeffrey. You can't do these things." And he said, "Stop giving me a hard time. You're such a puritan." From there, our conversation descended into a screaming match, and finally, Andrew said, "Leave me alone. Jeffrey's my friend. Being loyal to your friends is a virtue. And I'm going to be loyal to him." He does stupid things out of hubris, to show that he can do them.'

Andrew's mother, the Queen, likewise continued to show her loyalty to her son. She 'dotes on' him, the *Post* said, and 'excuses his every foible'. Though it tried to front it out, the royal family found itself in a perfect storm.

Virginia Giuffre went on NBC and said that Maxwell had recruited her from Mar-a-Largo when she was just fifteen. She was a vulnerable young woman. At the age of twelve, she said, she had been sexually abused by a close friend of the family. She developed an eating disorder, ran away from home and started living on the streets when she was thirteen.

'I was on the streets. I was picked up by a sixty-seven-year-old man who did exactly what Jeffrey did with me, abuse and violate my youthfulness,' she said. The man was Ron Eppinger, the boss of a modelling agency who was later convicted of trafficking young women into the country for the purposes of prostitution.

Giuffre said he got her hooked on opioids. At fourteen, Eppinger lent her to a wealthy client who abused her. Eventually the FBI raided Eppinger's home. He admitted to trafficking and money laundering. Her father rescued her and sent her on a drug-treatment programme, which was later revealed as a front for further physical and sexual abuse. With the help of her father and brother, she escaped.

Trying to get her life back on track she made it her ambition to become a massage therapist and managed to land a job at the spa at Trump's Mar-a-Lago Club. One day she said she was approached by a 'strikingly beautiful woman'. This was Ghislaine Maxwell. She told fifteen-year-old Virginia that she knew a wealthy man who was looking for a new masseuse.

Virginia's father Sky Roberts accompanied her on her first visit to Epstein's Florida home. He said Epstein 'seemed like a regular guy' and Virginia was keen to learn massage therapy. After Virginia's father had left, Maxwell took her to the master bathroom where Epstein was lying naked face down on a massage table. He needed a massage at least once a day, Maxwell said, according to Virginia.

Maxwell showed Virginia what to do. She started with Epstein's toes, then worked her way up. Then Epstein turned over. Maxwell took off her top and pressed her breasts against Epstein's chest. Maxwell then undressed the teenager. Virginia said she was too shocked to resist.

'I was asked to indulge Jeffrey in oral sex while Ghislaine caressed me from behind, cupping my small breasts and feeling me inside,' Virginia wrote later in her diary. 'I was inclined to scream out of humiliation for being so damned naïve.'

Things got worse: 'Jeffrey moaned out of delight and pulled up my chin to look at me then guided my hips to sit on top of him. He next forcibly entered me and used his hips to gratify his sexual needs. As soon as it was over, I quickly got dressed, and not sure how to keep my composure, just kept quiet. They both thanked me for a job well done as I had passed my trial.'

Virginia was paid $200 and given a lift home. The girl who had wanted to become a massage therapist now found that she was a prostitute. She kept quiet about what had happened to her because her complaint about abuse by a family friend and then the sex trafficker had caused such trouble. With those early experiences behind her, abuse by Epstein and Maxwell seemed quite mild. So when she was invited back to Epstein's mansion, she went.

Over the next few weeks, Virginia said, she was given training in how to be a sex slave.

'It was everything down to how to give a blow job, how to be quiet, be subservient, give Jeffrey what he wants,' she said. 'A lot of this training came from Ghislaine herself… and then there's Jeffrey who's telling you, "I want it this way, go slower".'

Maxwell denied all the allegations made against her.

Living with Epstein and Maxwell in Florida and New York, Virginia Giuffre said she was given training in S&M and the use of sex toys. She also had to have sex with other men and report back their specific requirements. In her court affidavit, she said: 'Epstein… got girls for [his] friends and acquaintances. Epstein specifically told me that the reason for him doing this was so that they would "owe him", they would "be in his pocket", and he would "have something on them." Afterwards she said he debriefed her so that he would possess "intimate and potentially embarrassing information" to blackmail friends into parking their money with him.

More recently, she said: 'Based on my knowledge of Epstein and his organisation, as well as discussions with the FBI, it is my belief that federal prosecutors likely possess videotapes and photographic images of me as an underage girl having sex with Epstein and some of his powerful friends…. I have asked the FBI to show me the video surveillance and other pictures of men that I believe they have in their possession. They said that I would have to go to the prosecutors to get them. But the prosecutors will not share anything with me.'

On her first assignment, she was to be sent to Little Saint James with 'a professor'. Soon she was making $400 an hour and taken on shopping sprees. She celebrated her sixteenth birthday on 'Orgy Island'.

'I mean, in some ways, we were a little fucked-up family,' Virginia later told the *Miami Herald.* 'It was, "Jeffrey needs to have sex at least seven times a day"… but in the meantime, we're gonna sit back and have some popcorn while you're giving a blowjob and watching Sex and the City. It was just a really screwed-up kind of little family unit.'

Virginia was sent out to recruit other girls, the younger the better, and showed them how to administer an erotic massage. There would be threesomes. She knew that everything they did was being filmed. Virginia also claimed that she indulged a number of celebrities on board the Lolita Express. Even Donald Trump made a showing.

'I didn't physically see him have sex with any of the girls,' she said. 'I can't say who he had sex with in his whole life or not, but I just know it wasn't with me when I was with other girls.'

Trump did not deny his connection to Epstein at the time. He told *New York* magazine for a profile of Epstein in 2002, 'He's a lot of fun to be with. It is even said that he likes beautiful women as much as I do, and many of them are on the younger side. No doubt about it—Jeffrey enjoys his social life.' However, in 2019, Trump backed off. 'I knew him like everybody in Palm Beach knew him…. I was not a fan.' They were seen together both in Florida and in Epstein's New York townhouse.

Just before her eighteenth birthday, Virginia Giuffre said she was taken to meet Prince Andrew.

'The first time in London, I was so young,' she told interviewer Samantha Guthrie. 'Ghislaine woke me up in the morning and she said, "You're gonna meet a prince today". I didn't know at that point that I was going to be trafficked to that prince….'

Maxwell said: 'You've got a big day. We've gotta go shopping. You need a dress because you're going to dance with a prince tonight.'

Later that day Andrew arrived at Maxwell's house with his police protection officers, and Virginia was introduced to him. Maxwell was alleged to have asked Andrew how old he thought Virginia was, and he correctly guessed seventeen. Maxwell joked that Epstein 'would soon have to trade her in' because she was getting too old for him.

The four went out to dinner, Virginia sitting between Epstein and the prince.

'Andrew was making eye contact with me at every chance and concentrating on my plunging V-neck top,' she told the *Mail on Sunday*. 'He didn't ask me anything about myself. I just sat there with a smile frozen on my lips. Ghislaine had whispered "The prince seems really interested in you".'

'We went on to Tramp. We were led into a VIP area and Andrew got me a cocktail from the bar, then he asked me to dance. He was the most hideous dancer I had ever seen. He was grabbing my hips and he was pouring with perspiration and he had this cheesy smile.

'I was used to being used for sex by men but it was not behaviour that I was used to in public, and not from a prince who had daughters. I felt everyone was watching us.'

Things got worse.

'We leave Club Tramp,' she said. 'And I hop in the car with Ghislaine and Jeffrey, and Ghislaine said, "He's coming back to the house. And I want you to do for him what you do for Epstein." I couldn't believe it.'

In the face of protests from the palace, Giuffre said: 'He denies that it ever happened. And he's going to keep denying that it ever happened. But he knows the truth. And I know the truth.'

After the four returned to Maxwell's townhouse, Virginia said that: 'All of us went upstairs and I asked Jeffrey to snap a picture of me with the prince. I wanted something to show my mom. Ghislaine and Jeffrey left us after that.'

In an interview with the *National Enquirer*, Virginia went further.

'He was groping me,' she said. 'He touched my breasts. He touched my ass. He was not my type, but I'd been trained not only to not show my emotions, but to do what was wanted. He started licking my toes, between my toes, the arches of my feet. He proceeded to make love to me…. He wasn't rude. It wasn't like rape, but it wasn't like love, either. It was more like, "I'm getting my business done".'

According to Giuffre, Andrew didn't use a condom during their encounter.

'Jeffrey knew I was on the pill,' she said.

To wrap up the night, Virginia said that she and Andrew took a bath together.

The next time she said she met the prince was on Easter 2001, when she was called in Florida and told she was needed at Epstein's New York mansion. When she arrived, she said, she was told, 'get ready, you are meeting someone in the library'.

'Andrew was sitting there in a big leather armchair behind which there was a desk covered with photos of girls and young women, including one of me,' she said. 'I was almost nude in the picture. I don't think Andrew could have missed seeing it when he walked in. Ghislaine had just given him a present, some kind of big blow-up toy that was his Spitting Image puppet. He was smiling ear to ear. He looked like a kid whose parents were taking him to Disney World.'

Clearly Andrew knew what he was in for.

'I took him upstairs to the "dungeon",' said Virginia. 'He was fondling me and we undressed and he lay on the table face down. I did my normal routine, which was to start with the feet, up the calves, tickling the thighs, up the buttocks, up the back. On this occasion I don't think I made it up to his shins when he flipped over. I was just another person he was bedding. He couldn't have cared less about me as a young woman.... He was being treated to sex for which someone else was paying. From the snickering noises he was making, he was really enjoying the whole thing, but I felt like a total prostitute. He never even said, "Did you enjoy it?" I was there for just one purpose.'

Later Virginia had a miscarriage. She hadn't even known she was pregnant, nor who the father was. By then she was moving out of Epstein's preferred age group, but there was another service she could provide. Virginia alleged that she was offered a house and $200,000 a month if she had a child.

Fearing that she would never escape Epstein's clutches, Virginia persuaded him to let her go to Thailand for proper training in massage. He agreed on one condition—that she bring him back a Thai girl. She went in the summer of 2002. In Thailand, she met Australian Robert Giuffre. They eloped and married in Australia. She remained there in peace until the FBI and then the Australian Federal Police got in touch in 2007.

10

NEMESIS

In July 2006, Jeffrey Epstein was invited to a masked ball at Windsor Castle to celebrate the eighteenth birthday of Princess Beatrice, Andrew's eldest daughter. This was month after the financier had been charged with solicitation of prostitution. Andrew said that he wasn't aware at the time the invitation was sent out of 'what was going on in the United States' and Epstein never mentioned it. However, the prince's long-term acquaintance Maxwell must have known. On 1 September 2006, the prince flew with Maxwell on Epstein's private plane from Luton to Edinburgh.

In 2000, Maxwell and Epstein as her plus one were on the guest list at Windsor for the fought-over Dance of the Decades, which celebrated Andrew's fortieth, Charles's fiftieth, Margaret's seventieth, and William's eighteenth birthdays. Maxwell accompanied Andrew to private parties and celebrity functions both in the UK and in the US that year. Epstein described her as his best friend. They were photographed together at the wedding of the prince's former girlfriend, Aurelia Cecil, near Salisbury in Wiltshire in September 2000. In December 2000, the prince threw a surprise birthday party for Maxwell at Sandringham, the Queen's estate in Norfolk. Epstein was among the guests. Andrew described this as a 'straightforward shooting weekend'. Prince Andrew and Maxwell went on a number of trips together visiting Florida and Thailand in January 2001 and Epstein had joined them on five such occasions over the previous twelve months.

A video showing the October 2005 police raid on Epstein's Palm Beach home surfaced in August 2018. It showed several massage tables and dozens of close-up photographs of scantily clad girls. One full-frontal photo showed Ghislaine Maxwell stretched out naked on a beach. Several more innocuous photos in public areas of the home showed Maxwell and Epstein together in public, including one where they appear to be standing at the White House press podium. Others featured Epstein shaking hands with world leaders including Fidel Castro and Pope John Paul II. However, one showed a girl who appeared to be around the age of six bending over in a tiny dress with her backside exposed. The image was considered so explicit that authorities blurred it out in the footage.

The hallway was decorated with a mix of nude photographs and pieces of artwork. A black-and-white portrait of Maxwell hung above the toilet opposite a photo of a young naked girl with her back to the camera, running her hands through her hair. On one edge of the yard was a workout room and office space with another cache of photos featuring young women, some of them naked.

A police report on the raid said they seized 'sex aids, videos, a school transcript, four massage tables and soap-on-a-rope… alongside some of the framed photos of naked girls.' There were also hidden cameras Epstein allegedly used to tape his famous friends in sex acts with underage girls for blackmail purposes.

According to the affidavit and application for a search warrant, in March 2005 the original complainant, a fourteen-year-old girl, told a detective that a woman who worked for Epstein brought her to his Palm Beach home in February and told her to come upstairs. The victim recalled there was a large picture of a naked woman in the room. There were also numerous photographs of naked women on a shelf.

'According to the victim, the woman led her to a room that had a massage table in it,' court documents said. The woman later took out lotions and left the room. Epstein later walked in wearing only a towel and told the girl to strip. She allegedly told detectives: 'He was stern when he told her to take off her clothes.'

According to the affidavit, Epstein then instructed her to give him a massage while he was naked and allegedly touched himself. Epstein paid the victim $300 cash, the court documents said.

Detectives also interviewed the woman who brought the teenager to Epstein's home. She told them that she was seventeen when she met Epstein through a friend who asked her if she wanted to make money. The woman told police she was brought to the house and was led upstairs by another woman who set up the massage table and took out oils. When the woman left, Epstein walked in wearing only a towel. Soon he was naked.

The affidavit continued: 'He explained, I know you're not comfortable, but I'll pay you if you bring some girls. He told her the younger the better.'

The woman subsequently told investigators that she brought at least six girls to Epstein's Palm Beach home. They were all between fourteen and sixteen. She said she had once tried to bring a woman in her twenties, but Epstein said she was too old.

This material had been used in the 2008 prosecution of Epstein but was suppressed until 2018 when the *Miami Herald* published a report on the plea deal he had struck with the prosecutor. The authorities then began to re-examine the evidence, which led to Epstein's final arrest and suicide.

The death of Epstein prompted more victims to come forward. One was Jennifer Araoz, who was an aspiring fifteen-year-old actress when she was raped in Epstein's New York mansion.

'He robbed me of my dreams,' she said. 'He robbed me of my chance to pursue a career I always adored. He stole my chance at really feeling love because I was so scared to trust anyone for so many years that I had such severe anxiety. I didn't want to leave my house, let alone my bed.'

She filed a lawsuit against Ghislaine Maxwell, alleging: 'Maxwell participated with and assisted Epstein in maintaining and protecting his sex trafficking ring, ensuring that approximately three girls a day were made available to him.'

British actress and former *Playboy* model Anouska De Georgiou also said she had been sexually abused by Epstein as a teenager.

'I was a victim, but I will not remain a victim and be silent for one more day,' she said. 'Although I think it's tragic when anybody dies before their time, I'm extremely relieved that Jeffrey Epstein will not be in a position to hurt any more children or any more women.'

Another teenage victim, Courtney Wild from Florida, said Epstein was a 'coward' for robbing his victims of their day in court. At times crying and holding each other for support, the three women addressed a special hearing convened on 27 November by District Judge Richard Berman, who presided over the case after federal prosecutors had Epstein arrested on sex-trafficking charges against dozens of women. The *New York Post* said that Epstein had plied them with drugs.

Another victim said: 'When I was fifteen years old, I flew on Jeffrey Epstein's plane to Zorro Ranch, where I was sexually molested by him for many hours.

What I remember most vividly was him explaining to me how beneficial the experience was for me and how much he was helping me to grow. I remember feeling so small and powerless, especially after he positioned me by laying me on his floor so that I was confronted by all the framed photographs on his dresser of him smiling with wealthy celebrities and politicians.'

There were inducements and threats. One girl said: 'He promised me that he would write me a letter of recommendation for Harvard if I got the grades and scores needed for admission. His word was worth a lot, he assured me, as he was in the midst of funding and leading Harvard's studies on the human brain, and the president was his friend. I had never even kissed a boy before I met him, and never throughout the horrific abuse did Jeffrey Epstein kiss me even once. When he stole my virginity, he washed my entire body compulsively in the shower and then told me, "If you're not a virgin, I will kill you." And then I wasn't a virgin anymore.'

When Chauntae Davies was first introduced to Epstein on Little Saint James, she said she tried to leave when he took his robe off, but found the door locked.

'I began my massage, trying not to let him smell my fear and obvious discomfort, but before I knew what was happening, he grabbed onto my wrist and tugged me towards the bed,' she said. 'I tried to pull away, but he was unbuttoning my shorts and pulling my body onto his already naked body faster than I could think. I was searching for words but all I could say was, "No, please stop," but that just seemed to excite him more. I ran off, my feet bloody from the rocks on the island. I cried myself to sleep that night.'

She later became a hostess and masseuse on board the Lolita Express.

On 6 July 2019, the day Epstein was arrested a second time, the FBI raided his townhouse on the Upper East Side of Manhattan.

They found a safe hidden behind a bookcase with the oil painting in its centre. Depicting a woman cupping an exposed breast, the painting covering the safe was Femme Fatale by Kees van Dongen, purchased for $6 million in 1990. Inside the safe were hundreds of CDs and DVDs containing thousands of photos and videos of a sexual nature, showing young girls naked or partially naked, sometimes with much older men.

There were other oddities about the townhouse, such as a painting of Bill Clinton in a blue dress and high heels. In a hidden room were blown-up photographs of women's bodies with their face and head cropped out of the picture. In a dark hallway was a large photograph of Epstein carrying a four- or five-year-old blonde girl on his shoulders.

That same day, agents landed on Little Saint James Island. Photographs of topless girls covered the walls of his mansion there. There were hidden cameras there too. The FBI suspected that they had been used in blackmail. Was this the source of his wealth they wondered.

The torrent of fresh allegations was unstoppable. Already a convicted sex offender, Epstein had clearly practised abuse on an industrial—one might almost say unmissable—scale. This new evidence made all the allegations by the victims seem highly credible. Epstein's suicide could be seen as a tacit admission of guilt. And it could hardly be denied that Andrew knew him well. Their friendship was a matter of public record.

In December 2010, after Epstein had been released from prison, Andrew flew to New York to stay with Epstein. They were photographed together in Central Park. After several days of newspaper reports on the Epstein connection in the spring of 2011, Prince Andrew was hit with a further blow when Sarah Ferguson admitted having accepted £15,000 from Epstein to help pay off her debts. It was the straw that broke the camel's back and Andrew was forced to quit his job as UK trade envoy.

Ironically, a year before fatefully staying and partying at the paedophile's Manhattan mansion, Andrew had finally made a half-way decent impression in the press. In an October 2009 interview with the *Financial Times* at Cipriani's on Fifth Avenue—eleven blocks away from Epstein, who had been released from custody in Florida two months before and was now under probationary house arrest in his New York mansion.

The duke came across as a committed if eccentric cheerleader of British businesses abroad—despite lecturing his host Andrew Edgecliffe-Johnson, a distinguished *Financial Times* editor, in some detail on the basics of the business world.

There were no snarky comments about people with expense accounts ('tabloid needling'), as it was not the sort of thing the paper's readers enjoyed. The prince explained ingenuously that 'the Queen funds out of her personal pocket the cost of my office' and that royals 'do not get an expense account anyway'. He only got reimbursed, he said, after his accounts had been audited. The wafer thin distinction was left as it was and, anyway, it seemed as if the prince's work for Britain was a free lunch.

Epstein's desk in New York

In town to meet financial firms and regulators—the duke conceded that his royal presence would make a 'minute' dent in a place like Manhattan—he boasted nonetheless that he was very busy working royal magic on Britain's behalf while tackling a teetotal dinner and giving measured, business-like answers. In 2008 he had 628 engagements, twice the number in 2005.

The prince saw himself as a kind of professional door opener for British enterprises abroad in a variation on the more traditional royal role as a ribbon cutter at home. Meeting business people after leaving the navy, the duke came to realise that 'business was the engine room of prosperity'. He spear-headed efforts of blue-chip companies such as BP, Rio Tinto, Lloyds of London, Rolls Royce, particularly in competition with the world's hegemon—the United States.

Andrew observed, 'We've got to fight clever. All right? So it's the art of being clever'.

It was only a year after the financial crisis and the world was still reeling while bankers and politicians stood in very bad odour. Royals were different, 'We are still trusted, as it were, above and beyond governments.'

There was also a good reason for cosying up to dodgy regimes around the world. Britain as a nation might have rocky relationships, but the prince could be a beaming friendly face. A few minutes with the new Russian president were invaluable in preparing Dmitry Medvedev for the G20 summit in London that year. 'He's a young man with no experience of that sort of environment... The ability to walk through the door and see a smiling face he knew made all the difference.' The prince was a door opener and a greeter. He quickly killed the idea that a book of his favourite nautical metaphors might be worth publishing as a business book. He recommended reading Sun Zu's *The Art of War* instead.

Andrew saw himself as 'self-employed' and added 'I don't work for anybody'. As for his political masters at the Foreign Office and Board of Trade, the duke observed, 'My corporate memory is now, as it were, slightly greater than theirs. So continuity is one thing I bring to this.' And with a swipe at the carping of permanent staff at the departments he said, 'Unfortunately, officers have initiative'. He explained he had 'taken the agenda that was given and developed it beyond what was originally envisaged or we ever considered appropriate.'

Why did he bother with a job for no pay? Bursting out laughing the duke said, 'That is because of who I am and that is because of the life of the family within which I've been brought up. So to me this state of affairs is not extraordinary. To anybody else who looks in, they think I'm bloody mad! But that's what we do.'

A year after the interview Andrew made the decision to stay at Epstein's mansion. Three months later, the public found out about that decision and that the prince had been a guest for days and partied at the paedophile's mansion. In a matter of hours, the credit the duke had built up was gone and his public career looked ready for the guillotine. Andrew should probably have taken the hint and fallen on his sword, but instead Prime Minister David Cameron offered him a reprieve to soldier on.

There was another murky detail about to come out of the New York mansion's woodwork, however. A few days after Andrew's visit, the billionaire secretly paid £15,000 as a first instalment to the personal assistant of the duke's ex-wife's. The ex-employee was owed a total of £78,000 in backpay, but the duchess had no money as she had racked up debts of up to £5 million and was unable to obtain credit from anyone.

When it also became public that Epstein had taken on paying off her debt of £78,000 and that Fergie had spent nine months haggling over it with the sex offender—who was then in part still on probationary house arrest—she put the final nail in the coffin of Andrew's unpaid self-employment.

The duchess said in a public statement: 'I personally, on behalf of myself, deeply regret that Jeffrey Epstein became involved in any way with me. I abhor paedophilia and any sexual abuse of children and know that this was a gigantic error of judgement on my behalf. I am just so contrite I cannot say. Whenever I can I will repay the money and will have nothing ever to do with Jeffrey Epstein ever again.'

She also conceded that it was her ex-husband and his palace office of four who had been very helpful in reducing her overall debt burden, though she was adamant Andrew had not been involved in Epstein's paying off her debt to her assistant.

A decade before sitting down with the *Financial Times* Andrew had told *Tatler*—months before leaving the navy and the alleged sexual encounters with Giuffre in March 2001—that life was not about 'making a nonsense of it. Both Sarah and I are determined not make a nonsense of it again and, as individuals, we are making a better fist of things than as a couple.'

Two decades after the prince's plan not to make a nonsense of his life outside the navy, the BBC's Panorama was to interview Virginia Giuffre in the aftermath of Epstein's death. Buckingham Palace decided to steal a march on her, and cleared Andrew's interview with Newsnight so that it would air first, before Giuffre's. Perhaps the palace and the duke had thought to take a leaf out of Sun Tzu's advice on fighting clever, and that getting ahead of bad news was a smart tactic. But this act of guile would not pay off.

11

BBC NEWSNIGHT CAR CRASH

The Newsnight interview was aired on the BBC on 16 November 2019. It was filmed in Buckingham Palace, so it clearly had at least the tacit consent of the Queen. In it Prince Andrew was, at the very least, disingenuous. First of all, he tried to explain his prevarication when it came to answering questions about his friendship with Epstein.

'There is no good time to talk about Mr Epstein and all things associated, and we've been talking to Newsnight for about six months about doing something around the work that I was doing, and unfortunately we've just not been able to fit it into either your schedule or my schedule until now,' he told interviewer Emily Maitlis. No long UK trade envoy, it is hard to see how his diary could be that full.

Asked how his friendship with Epstein started, Andrew said: 'I met through his girlfriend [Ghislaine Maxwell] back in 1999 who… and I'd known her since she was at university in the UK and it would be, to some extent, a stretch to say that, as it were, we were close friends.'

We've already seen that the date is dubious. He went on to say: 'It would be a considerable stretch to say that he was a very, very close friend.' However, he admitted that they met up two or three times a year and he would stay in Epstein's houses, even when the financier wasn't there.

It was also 'a bit of a stretch' to say that they shared an interest in partying—'you were perceived by the public as being the party prince,' Maitlis said.

'I don't know why I've collected that title because I don't… I never have really partied,' he said. 'I was single for quite a long time in the early 80s, but then after

I got married I was very happy and I've never really felt the need to go and party, and certainly going to Jeffrey's was not about partying, absolutely not.'

The newspaper headlines from the days before he was married provide good evidence for his love of partying—more recent revelations show that it is a taste that he has not given up.

Andrew interviewed in the Queen's south drawing room

The reason Andrew gave for getting to know Epstein was that he was about to become UK special representative for international trade and investment. His time in the navy had left him cut off and he needed to know more about the world of international business and Wall Street.

Maitlis then put it to him: 'He was your guest as well. In 2000 Epstein was a guest at Windsor Castle and at Sandringham, he was brought right into the heart of the royal family at your invitation.'

Andrew confirmed that this was true.

'Am I right in thinking you threw a birthday party for Epstein's girlfriend, Ghislaine Maxwell, at Sandringham?' asked Maitlis.

Andrew denied this, saying it was a simple shooting weekend.

'We now know that he was and had been procuring young girls for sex trafficking,' said Maitlis.

'We now know that, at the time, there was no indication to me or anybody else that that was what he was doing and certainly when I saw him either in the United States,' said Andrew. 'When I saw him in the United States or when I was staying in his houses in the United States, there was no indication, absolutely no indication.'

Andrew volunteered that, at the time, he was patron of the National Society for the Prevention of Cruelty to Children's Full Stop campaign… 'so I was close up with what was going on in those time about getting rid of abuse to children, so I knew what the things were to look for, but I never saw them.'

'You were a visitor, a guest on many occasions at his homes, and nothing struck you as suspicious?'

'Nothing.'

He confirmed that he had been on Epstein's private plane and stayed on his private island and at his homes in Palm Beach and New York, as well as Ghislaine Maxwell's home in London's Belgravia.

In May 2006 an arrest warrant was issued for Epstein for sexual assault of a minor. That July he was invited to Windsor Castle for Andrew's daughter Princess Beatrice's eighteenth birthday. Why would you do that? he was asked. Andrew said it was because he was inviting Ghislaine. Coincidentally Harvey Weinstein was at that party too.

At the time the invitation was sent Andrew said he knew nothing about Epstein's arrest.

'I wasn't aware until the media picked up on it because he never said anything about it,' he said. 'You see this is the problem—that an awful lot of this was going on in the United States and I wasn't a party to it and I knew nothing about it.'

Andrew said he ceased contact with Epstein when he discovered he was under investigation in 2006. Epstein was convicted of soliciting and procuring a minor for prostitution in 2008 and jailed.

'He was released in July, within months, by December of 2010, you went to stay with him at his New York mansion—why?', Maitlis asked. 'Why were you staying with a convicted sex offender?'

'Right, I have always… ever since this has happened and since this has become, as it were, public knowledge that I was there,' said Andrew, stumbling, 'I've questioned myself as to why did I go and what was I doing and was it the right thing to do? Now, I went there with the sole purpose of saying to him that because he had been convicted, it was inappropriate for us to be seen together.'

He said a number of people were advising him to go and see Epstein, while others advised him not to.

'I took the judgement call that because this was serious and I felt that doing it over the telephone was the chicken's way of doing it. I had to go and see him and talk to him.'

He said he was doing a number of other things in New York at the time, one of which was getting Epstein to pay off some of Fergie's debts.

'We had an opportunity to go for a walk in the park and that was the conversation coincidentally that was photographed, which was when I said to him, I said, 'Look, because of what has happened, I don't think it is appropriate that we should remain in contact,' and by mutual agreement during that walk in the park we decided that we would part company and I left, I think it was the next day, and to this day I never had any contact with him from that day forward.'

Epstein understood, but said he had accepted a plea bargain, served his time and was carrying on his life.

'I said, 'Yes but I'm afraid to say that that's as maybe but with all the attendant scrutiny on me then I don't think it is a wise thing to do".'

The decision to see Epstein and break off their relationship in person was Andrew's alone to make: 'Some people from my staff, some people from friends and family I was talking to and I took the decision that it was I who had to show leadership and I had to go and see him and I had to tell him, "That's it".'

Epstein had thrown a party to celebrate his release and Andrew was invited as guest of honour, but Andrew said he didn't go, then added: 'Oh, in 2010, there certainly wasn't a party to celebrate his release in December because it was a small dinner party. There were only eight or ten of us I think at the dinner.'

Andrew stayed several days at the New York townhouse of the convicted sex offender.

'It was a convenient place to stay,' said Andrew. 'I mean I've gone through this in my mind so many times. At the end of the day, with a benefit of all the hindsight that one can have, it was definitely the wrong thing to do. But at the time I felt it was the honourable and right thing to do, and I admit fully that my judgement was probably coloured by my tendency to be too honourable but that's just the way it is.' Clearly Prince Andrew had a highly refined sense of honour.

Maitlis then pointed out that, during the time he was staying at Epstein's house, witnesses said they saw many young girls coming and going, and there was video footage of Epstein accompanied by young girls while Andrew was there.

'I never…,' said Andrew stumbling again, '…I mean if there were then I wasn't a party to any of that. I never saw them. I mean, you have to understand that his house—I described it more as almost as a railway station, if you know what I mean—in the sense that there were people coming in and out of that house all the time. What they were doing and why they were there I had nothing to do with. So I'm afraid I can't make any comment on that because I really don't know.'

Another guest in Epstein's house was literary agent John Brockman, who had said he had seen Andrew getting a foot massage by a young Russian woman. Andrew said he could not remember and he did not know Mr Brockman. Then he said it was definitely not him getting a foot massage by a Russian girl.

Again casting doubt on Andrew's story, Maitlis said that he had chosen a funny way to end their relationship—'a four-day house party of sorts with a dinner. It's an odd way to break up a friendship.'

Andrew agreed, though said it was a 'difficult… stark way of putting it'.

'But actually the truth of it is that I actually only saw him for about, what, the dinner party, the walk in the park and probably passing in the passage.'

Was Epstein's slyly photographed walk in Central Park with Andrew part of his rehabilitation? Maitlis suggested. Andrew didn't think so, though he did not use the subsequent publication of the picture as an opportunity to announce the end of their friendship. He did not think that the well-composed photograph was staged by Epstein to compromise him. He did regret the trip, he said, but he did not regret his friendship with Epstein.

'Now, still not and the reason being is that the people that I met and the opportunities that I was given to learn either by him or because of him were actually very useful,' Andrew said. 'He himself not, as it were, as close as you might think, we weren't that close. So therefore I mean, yes, I would go and stay in his house but that was because of his girlfriend, not because of him.'

He claimed that his visit in December 2010 was the only time he had seen Epstein after his conviction, nor had he spoken to him since.

'Funny enough, 2010 was it, that was it because I went… well, first of all, I wanted to make sure that if I was going to go and see him, I had to make sure that there was enough time between his release because it wasn't something that I was going into in a hurry, but I had to go and see him, I had to go and see him, I had to talk.'

'And stay with him, and stay in the house of a convicted sex offender?' asked Maitlis.

'I could easily have gone and stayed somewhere else but sheer convenience of being able to get a hold of the man was… I mean he was in and out all over the place. So getting him in one place for a period of time to actually have a long enough conversation to say "look, these are the reasons why I'm not going to…" and that happened on the walk.'

In July 2019, Epstein was arrested again for abusing dozens of underage girls and sex trafficking, said Maitlis. One of Epstein's accusers, Virginia Giuffre, said she had met Andrew three times for sex in London and New York between 2001 and 2002.

Andrew said he had no recollection of ever meeting Giuffre. None whatsoever. Pushed, he repeated: 'I've no recollection of ever meeting her. I'm almost, in fact I'm convinced that I was never in Tramp with her. There are a number of things that are wrong with that story, one of which is that I don't know where the bar is in Tramp. I don't drink, I don't think I've ever bought a drink in Tramp whenever I was there.'

Andrew had long been a regular at Tramp, having met starlet Koo Stark there in 1981 and he had invited the club's co-founder Johnny Gold to his wedding to Sarah Ferguson. Customers on the dance floor pass within ten metres of the bar, which is next to the DJ's booth. The gents' is at the other end of the bar. So it would have been very difficult for him not know where the bar was. However, Andrew insisted he could not have been dancing at Tramp that night with Virginia Giuffre because he was at home with his children.

'On that particular day that we now understand is the date which is the 10th of March, I was at home, I was with the children and I'd taken Beatrice to a PizzaExpress in Woking for a party at, I suppose, sort of four or five in the afternoon. And then because the duchess was away, we have a simple rule in the family that when one is away the other one is there. I was on terminal leave at the time from the Royal Navy so therefore I was at home.'

Others recalled other occasions when he did leave the children in the care of the staff when Fergie was away. But why did he remember so clearly what he was doing that day?

'Because going to PizzaExpress in Woking is an unusual thing for me to do, a very unusual thing for me to do. I've never been… I've only been to Woking a couple of times and I remember it weirdly distinctly.'

Mischievous souls pointed out that Woking is only twenty miles from London, so it would have easily been possible to have a pizza there in the afternoon and have dinner and go dancing in London in the evening—even if you drove. Prince Andrew has a penchant for helicopters.

Then came the question of sweating—Giuffre remembered him sweating profusely on the dance floor, but not the prince.

'There's a slight problem with the sweating because I have a peculiar medical condition which is that I don't sweat or I didn't sweat at the time,' he said. 'I didn't sweat at the time because I had suffered what I would describe as an overdose of adrenalin in the Falklands War when I was shot at and I simply… it was almost impossible for me to sweat.'

The inability to sweat is called anhidrosis or hyperhidrosis. This can be a congenital condition, or it occurs during heatstroke when the body has no fluid to sweat. Otherwise it can be caused by skin damage such as burns, nerve damage or certain medications such as strong painkillers like morphine.

Andrew ruled out the possibility that he had met Giuffre on another occasion. Nor could he explain the photograph of him with his arm around her waist with Ghislaine Maxwell in her Belgravia home. Friends of his had suggested it was fake, though experts can find no evidence of that. Epstein was said to have taken the picture.

'I've never seen Epstein with a camera in my life,' Andrew told Maitlis on air.

Giuffre said that she had a small Kodak camera which she gave to Epstein to take the picture.

'Listen, I don't remember, I don't remember that photograph ever being taken. I don't remember going upstairs in the house because that photograph was taken upstairs,' said Andrew, beginning to get flustered. He did admit that it was a picture of him, but did not believe that it was a picture of him in London.

'When I go out in London, I wear a suit and a tie,' he said. 'Those are my travelling clothes if I'm going to go… if I'm going overseas. There's a… I've got plenty of photographs of me dressed in those sorts of… that sort of kit but not there.'

Pressed that it could have been taken at Maxwell's house on a different occasion, he pulled rank.

'I'm terribly sorry but if I, as a member of the royal family, and I have a photograph taken and I take very, very few photographs, I am not one to, as it were, hug, and public displays of affection are not something that I do'

These assertions were easily refuted.

'… So that's the best explanation I can give you and I'm afraid to say that I don't believe that photograph was taken in the way that has been suggested.'

Maitlis pressed him further: 'There's a photo inside Ghislaine Maxwell's house, Ghislaine herself in the background. Why would people not believe that you were there with her that night?'

'They might well wish to believe it,' said Andrew, 'but the photograph is taken upstairs and I don't think I ever went upstairs in Ghislaine's house.'

If he never went upstairs at Ghislaine's house, how did he know that it was taken upstairs? He was at a loss to explain it—because it never happened, he said. In April 2021, Ghislaine Maxwell's brother, Ian, was to confirm that Andrew's suspicion that it was taken upstairs in her mew's house was correct. Asked by the BBC Today Programme, 'do you recognise the setting of [the photograph]? Was it taken in Ghislaine's house in London?' Ian confirmed, 'I do recognize that setting'.

To Maitlis, the prince did not recall meeting Giuffre, dining with her, dancing with her at Tramp or going on to have sex with her in a bedroom in a house in Belgravia. He insisted that he never had any sexual contact with her, though in a court document in 2015 she said that they had sex three times—the first time when she was trafficked to London, the second time in Epstein's house in New York.

'Yeah, well I think that the date we have for that shows that I was in Boston or I was in New York the previous day and I was at a dinner for the Outward Bound Trust in New York and then I flew up to Boston the following day and then on the day that she says that this occurred, they'd already left to go to the island before I got back from Boston. So I don't think that could have happened at all.'

The aide who controlled Andrew's diary pointed out that there were plenty of gaps in his schedule. Johanna Sjoberg said that he visited the house at that time, though Andrew claimed that, on that trip, he had stayed with the British consul general nearby.

'I may have visited but no, definitely didn't, definitely, definitely no, no, no activity.'

The British consul Sir Thomas Harris said: 'I have no recollection of him staying at the address in April 2001. 'I don't have a note of the dates of all the visits.... It doesn't ring any bells whatsoever.'

The third occasion was, Giuffre said, on Epstein's private island with seven or eight other girls. Andrew denied everything and said he did not know why she was saying these things—though he stopped short of saying she was lying.

'If Virginia Roberts is watching this interview, what is your message to her?' Maitlis asked.

'I don't have a message for her because I have to have a thick skin,' he said. 'If somebody is going to make those sorts of allegations then I've got to have a thick skin and get on with it but they never happened.'

'For the record, is there any way you could have had sex with that young woman or any young woman trafficked by Jeffrey Epstein in any of his residences?'

'No, and without putting too fine a point on it, if you're a man it is a positive act to have sex with somebody. You have to have to take some sort of positive action and so therefore if you try to forget—it's very difficult to try and forget a positive action and I do not remember anything. I can't, I've wracked my brain and thinking oh... when the first allegations, when the allegations came out originally I went "well that's a bit strange, I don't remember this" and then I've been through it and through it and through it over and over and over again and no, nothing. It just never happened.'

Maitlis then turned to a legal deposition made by Epstein's housekeeper saying that Andrew visited the Palm Beach residence around four times a year and got a daily massage. Andrew insisted that he had only visited the Palm Beach mansion four times in the entire time that he had known Epstein.

'Is there a chance that those massages might have been the services of someone who is being sexually exploited or trafficked by Epstein?'

'No, I don't think... I mean I... no, definitely not, definitely not...'

Maitlis pointed out that Virginia Giuffre's legal team had said that one could not spend time around Epstein and not know what was going on.

Andrew's response was suitably royal: 'If you are somebody like me then people behave in a subtly different way. You wouldn't... first of all, I'm not looking for it, that's the thing, you see, if you're looking for it, then you might have suspected now with the benefit of a huge amount of hindsight and a huge amount of analysis—you look back and you go, well was that really the way that it was or was I looking at it the very wrong way? But you don't go into these places, you don't go to stay with people looking for that.'

Maitlis pressed the point. Again quoting Giuffre's legal team, she said: 'You could not spend time around him and not know.'

But Andrew was above such things: 'I live in an institution at Buckingham Palace which has members of staff walking around all the time and I don't wish to appear grand but there were a lot of people who were walking around Jeffrey Epstein's house. As far as I was aware, they were staff, they were people that were working for him, doing things. I… as it were, I interacted with them if you will to say good morning, good afternoon, but I didn't, if you see what I mean, interact with them in a way that was, you know, what are you doing here, why are you here, what's going on?'

Maitlis would not be thrown off track, saying: 'But you'd notice if there were hundreds of underage girls in Buckingham Palace, wouldn't you?'

Andrew conceded that he would notice if there were hundreds of underage girls around Epstein's house, but insisted there weren't, not when he was there.

'Now he may have changed his behaviour patterns in order for that not to be obvious to me so I don't…,' he said. 'You're asking me to speculate on things that I just don't know about.'

Maitlis found this hard to swallow.

'You seem utterly convinced you're telling the truth,' said Maitlis, who plainly had her doubts. 'Would you be willing to testify or give a statement under oath if you were asked?'

Andrew's reply was guarded.

'Well, I'm like everybody else and I will have to take all the legal advice that there was before I was to do that sort of thing,' he said. 'But if push came to shove and the legal advice was to do so, then I would be duty- bound to do so.'

Maitlis's thoughts were with the victims. There were many unanswered questions and they wanted closure. But this was not Andrew's concern. He was more concerned about himself.

'In the right circumstances, yes I would because I think there's just as much closure for me as there is for everybody else and undoubtedly some very strange and unpleasant activities have been going on. I'm afraid to say that I'm not the person who can shed light on it for a number of reasons, one of which is that I wasn't there long enough,' he said. 'If you go in for a day, two days at a time, it's quite easy, I'm led to believe, for those sorts of people to hide their activities for that period of time and then carry on when they're not there.'

Maitlis pointed out that Virginia Giuffre's lawyers had asked for a legal statement from him and the FBI were investigating. Again Andrew hid behind his lawyers, saying that he would provide a statement if that was what they advised.

Andrew said that he was shocked when he heard that Epstein was dead, but refused to speculate on the theory that he had not taken his own life. Nor would he address the question of whether Ghislaine Maxwell was complicit in Epstein's offences. Andrew insisted that his behaviour toward Epstein had been honourable when he had told him that he could not see him anymore after he had been convicted, but when it came to his old friend: 'If there are questions that Ghislaine has to answer, that's her problem, I'm afraid. I'm not in a position to be able to comment one way or the other.'

He had met her earlier that year on 5 June, when she had been in London to take part in the Monaco rally, but they had not discussed Epstein, even though US investigators had announced that they had reopened their investigation into the disgraced financier two weeks earlier.

'There wasn't anything to discuss about him because he wasn't in the news,' he said. 'We had moved on.'

Actually, Epstein was in the news, as there were calls in Congress for an investigation into US Secretary of Labor Alexander Acosta over the sweetheart deal he had arranged for Epstein in 2008, getting him just thirteen months in jail, when Acosta was US attorney general for Southern Florida. He was forced to resign from his cabinet post in July 2019.

Asked how he was moving on, Andrew said: 'I'm carrying on with what I do. I have a number of things that I have been doing since 2011. They're pretty well organised, pretty successful and so I'm carrying on and trying to improve those things that I'm already doing.'

He did not think that the Queen had been damaged by the scandal, but he had been. 'It's been a constant drip, if you see what I mean in the background that people want to know. If I was in a position to be able to answer all these questions in a way that gave sensible answers other than the ones that I have given that gave closure then I'd love it but I'm afraid I can't. I'm just not in a position to do so because I'm just as much in the dark as many people.'

His aim now was to reconnect with people by continuing to work with his entrepreneurial scheme Pitch@Palace and the Inspiring Digital Enterprise Award (iDEA). His judgment call when it came to visiting Epstein after he had been convicted still troubled him.

'It's almost a mental health issue to some extent for me in the sense that it's been nagging at my mind for a great many years. I know that I made the wrong judgement and I made the wrong decision, but I made the wrong decision and the wrong judgement I believe fundamentally for the right reasons which is to say to somebody "I'm not going to see you again" and in fact from that day forth, I was never in contact with him.'

The problem was social media. That was what was causing him difficulties. The allegations against him were 'surprising, shocking and a distraction. But… there are all sorts of things that are on the internet.'

Did he have a sense of guilt, regret or shame about his behaviour or his friendship with Epstein?

'As far as Mr Epstein was concerned, it was the wrong decision to go and see him in 2010,' he said. 'As far as my association with him was concerned, it had some seriously beneficial outcomes in areas that had nothing and have nothing to do with what I would describe as what we're talking about today.'

Meeting Epstein had been inevitable because of his friendship with Ghislaine Maxwell.

'Do I regret the fact that he has quite obviously conducted himself in a manner unbecoming? Yes.'

Maitlis was visibly shocked.

'Unbecoming? He was a sex offender.'

Andrew backpedalled.

'I'm sorry, I'm being polite,' he said. 'I mean in the sense that he was a sex offender. But no, was I right in having him as a friend? At the time, bearing in mind this was some years before he was accused of being a sex offender. I don't think there was anything wrong then.'

But after Epstein had been convicted, Andrew had stayed with him.

'I kick myself for [it] on a daily basis,' he said. 'It was not something that was becoming of a member of the royal family and we try and uphold the highest standards and practices and I let the side down, simple as that.'

Drawing the interview to a close, Maitlis asked if there was anything he felt had been left unsaid that he would like to say now.

'No, I don't think so,' he said. 'I think you've probably dragged out most of what is required and I'm truly grateful for the opportunity that you've given me to be able to discuss this with you.'

He did not take this opportunity to express his sympathy for Epstein's victims.

The establishing shot of Andrew walking through the palace with Maitlis was filmed after the interview. Maitlis said that Andrew was pleased with himself, confident that by facing the cameras he had drawn a line under the affair. He could not have been more wrong.

In July 2020, Maitlis gave *Radio Times* an insight into her own thougths at the time. She was 'incredibly nervous' as it could be the only chance ever 'to set the record straight'. But she knew 'within minutes of sitting down that it was going to be explosive'. Three things gave it away, 'First he was tackling the subject matter head on. Secondly the lack of apology or any real expression of regret', and the third was 'the level of detail'.

The BBC team had held out for an in-depth interview in the months of negotiations with the palace instead of a short, ten minute one. Until the last moment, Newsnight Editor Esme Wren expected a call that the interview was cancelled or curtailed. Not without reason. On behalf of the programme, Sam McAlister had made clear to the palace that Andrew would be asked about 'every piece of information in the public domain'. It couldn't have been further from a cloak-and-dagger interview. Even so, in order to avoid any gossip among BBC colleagues, Maitlis and Wren had kept the script very close to their chest and role-played together as preparation for the interview.

If anything could be said about the courtiers is that they didn't seem unduly worried. There was plenty of engagement after the programme aired and, Maitlis revealed, 'the palace was happy with the interview.'

12

FALLOUT

The day after Prince Andrew's Newsnight interview, it was condemned in the press as disastrous. He was lambasted from all quarters for his arrogance and poor judgement, while his eyebrow-raising defence that he was at a high street pizza chain, never sweated and only stayed at the disgraced financier's home because he was 'honourable' drew derision. But he drew most criticism for defending his friendship for Epstein while failing to show any empathy for his victims.

'Astonished Nation Watches Prince Squirm,' was the *Mail on Sunday*'s front-page headline. 'Many viewers shocked by 'total lack of empathy.' The newspaper also criticised the prince for uttering 'not one word of remorse'. The *Sunday Mirror* said: 'No Sweat… and No Regret.'

Catherine Mayer, co-founder of the Women's Equality Party, tweeted that Andrew had appeared 'too stupid to even pretend concern for #Epstein's victims'.

'I have never seen anything so disastrous. For any students of PR, that is how not to do it,' said image consultant Mark Borkowski. 'It was like watching a man in quicksand and, unfortunately, I don't think anyone would have thrown him a line to get him out.'

He also remarked on the prince's 'astonishing hubris. I've never watched a slow-motion car crash until now.' It was an example of 'doing all the wrong things really well'.

'I expected a train wreck," said Charlie Proctor, editor of the Royal Central, a website that covers the travails of the British monarchy. 'That was a plane crashing into an oil tanker, causing a tsunami, triggering a nuclear explosion-level bad.'

One Twitter user captured the reaction of many by posting a video of a man pouring gasoline on a fire under the headline, '#PrinceAndrew'. The ridicule was worldwide. The Agence France Press carried the headline: 'Britain's Prince Andrew Lambasted after "Catastrophic' Interview on Epstein links.' *The New York Times* said 'Prince Andrew Gets Candid, and Britain Is Appalled' and his answers were 'defensive, unpersuasive or just plain strange'. Pointing out that 'Prince Andrew claims liaison never happened because he couldn't sweat,' the *New York Post* carried the front-page headline: 'His Royal Dryness.'

Former Buckingham Palace press officer Dickie Arbiter described the interview as 'excruciating' and said the prince had 'done himself no favours'.

'If Prince Andrew thinks he's drawn a line in the sand over the Epstein saga he's in cuckoo land,' he said. 'Whomever advised he did this interview ought to collect his/her P45.'

The *Sunday Times* reported that Andrew's communications secretary Jason Stein had quit the role two weeks earlier, having advised against accepting Newsnight's request. It was feared that the interview would leave the prince 'terribly exposed' and risked coming across as 'an entitled idiot'. But his private secretary Amanda Thirsk managed to talk Andrew into doing it. She said: 'The duke has done nothing wrong… All he did was go and see his friend.'

Fergie also stuck by her ex-husband, saying that it 'is so rare to meet people that are able to speak from their hearts with honesty and pure real truth. Andrew is a true and real gentleman and is stoically steadfast to not only his duty but also his kindness and goodness.'

Kate Williams, a specialist in royal history at Reading University said: 'The royal household today will be in damage-control mode, trying to work out how to minimise the damage that has come from this. He has to go. Simply, last night was really a burning of the bridges, I think, for Prince Andrew.'

Dickie Arbiter told the BBC: 'They will be wondering: was this the right decision? Was the right decision made? Who made the decision to put him on? Did he make it himself or did he seek advice within the palace?'

There was controversy over whether the Queen had known and approved of the interview.

'My guess is that he bulldozed his way in and decided he was going to do it himself without any advice,' said Arbiter.

Afterwards Andrew reportedly told the Queen that the interview had been a 'great success'. A palace source told the *Sun*: 'He thinks he's done the right thing and has put the criticism to rest.' Even after the interview aired, he was seemingly unaware of the outrage it provoked and was seen with the Queen that Sunday.

'The duke went to church with the Queen and was heard telling her it's all been a great success,' a friend told the *Sun*. 'He thinks he's done the right thing and has put the criticism to rest. He was all smiles and was looking very buoyant and happy.'

The *Sun*'s political editor Tom Newton Dunn commented: 'I'm convinced Andy is as stupid as feared.'

Maitlis said the palace later informed the Newsnight team it thought they had done a 'fair job'. Of the Prince, she said: 'The impression I got was definitely that he had been happy with it.'

The interviewer told the *Radio Times* magazine: 'I didn't see it coming. It wasn't an attempt to bring down the royals, just a chance to understand the story.'

However, she admitted she 'never expected to hear' some of his answers and suspected there are words 'he wishes he'd chosen differently or better'. But she said she has a respect for him facing her questions head on.

'I think you have a curious duty of care towards your interviewees,' she said. 'I admire him for his candour and his engagement with the questions in an age of so much deviation and circumnavigation, and quite often a failure to put yourself up for scrutiny.'

She may have been playing down the incident because she was concerned that the resulting furore could put people off coming on the show.

'I didn't like people saying, "oh, it's a car-crash interview", because I thought, "that's not enticing, that's not encouraging",' she said. 'I don't want people thinking that's what happens at Newsnight.'

It is hard to imagine that she had damaged the reputation of the show and would not be drawn on whether she believed his side of the story.

'I don't feel that is for me, actually. It's not my job,' she said. 'I'm not a judge, I'm not a barrister, this isn't a court of law.'

However, the press were quick to pick apart the story Andrew told in his interview. Casting doubt on the photograph of him with his arm around Giuffre's waist, he had said: 'I don't believe it's a picture of me in London because… when I go out in London, I wear a suit and a tie. That's what I would describe as my travelling clothes if I'm going overseas.' However, there are pictures of him leaving London nightclub Chinawhite in July 2000, wearing almost the exact same outfit. Then Lisa Bloom, a lawyer for Epstein's victims said that she had two witnesses who saw Andrew at Tramp in with a girl they now believed to be the young Giuffre.

He also said he 'never really partied' and avoided 'public displays of affection'. The *Daily Mail* found footage of Andrew at a wild party thrown by wine tycoon Claude Ott on the French Riviera in July 2008, just weeks after Epstein had been prosecuted. It showed him embracing a number of women including socialite Christy Von Aspen, who he held by the waist before she later licked his face, at the party in Saint-Tropez. He was also seen dancing at close quarters with a Libyan model named Nadia Boejna. And there seemed to be a glimmer of sweat.

Andrew and Christy von Aspen

At a different party on the same trip Andrew was shown gripping Canadian socialite Pascale Bourbeau with one hand close to her bottom. At Heidi Klum's 'Pimps and Hookers' Halloween party held in New York in October

2000, Ghislaine Maxwell had her arm round him for much of the night.

Andrew and Pascale Bourbeau

Virginia Giuffre's lawyer David Boies spoke to the *Mirror* about Andrew's reaction to the 2001 photograph: 'He's had that picture for years and years and never once questioned it. If he had not been there, I think he would have said that years ago.'

In its leader, the *Mirror* dismissed Prince Andrew as 'toxic' and called for him to retire from public life.

Not only had Andrew tarnished his reputation by doing the interview, he had also made himself vulnerable legally.

Anna Rothwell, from criminal law firm Corker Binning, said: 'Prince Andrew is not entitled to any form of immunity by virtue of his position as a member of the royal family. His friendship with the convicted sex offender Jeffrey Epstein is under investigation by the FBI and he is vulnerable to extradition. It is therefore very unwise for the prince to give any account to the media, especially one which so starkly exposes the closeness of his relationship with Epstein, and again betrays yet another appalling lack of judgement.'

Celebrity lawyer Mark Stephens told the *Guardian*: 'If he'd kept his silence he'd have been able to remain outside of the case, as he's a witness and is entitled to diplomatic immunity. He was a private individual and now he's waived that privacy.' Andrew's strategy 'only works if you've got a complete and full answer to every possible question, and here there are too many loose ends.'

Former head of the royal protection squad Dai Davies called for a police investigation, saying he was 'utterly unconvinced' by the prince's denials and that he displayed the 'classic signs' of someone not telling the truth.

'It beggars belief the stupidity of his answers,' he added. 'I couldn't believe what I was hearing and seeing. This interview highlights why there should now be a full police investigation into these allegations. There are significant differences between the account of events given by Andrew and others. He is a primary witness and these allegations of sexual trafficking are extremely serious. Anyone who has material evidence should be interviewed. If that points towards a criminal offence having been committed then that questioning should be done under caution.'

Virginia Giuffre's allegations were investigated by the Metropolitan Police, which reviewed the evidence and decided not to conduct a full investigation. The matter was then closed. But the police investigation had not included the allegation of sex trafficking by the prince, a criminal offence in the UK.

Davies dismissed the prince's claim that he could not have slept with her as he was at a PizzaExpress party in Woking, Surrey, with his daughter at around 'four or five in the afternoon'.

'That alibi came as a surprise, to put it mildly,' Davies said. 'That party was in the afternoon. The allegation arises in the early hours of the morning. It's got no relevance. I was utterly unconvinced by his story. I have interviewed hundreds of people. To me he shows the classic signs of someone not telling the truth.'

The question of whether he was in the PizzaExpress in Woking or in Tramp nightclub could be cleared up if Scotland Yard released the logs kept by royal protection officers. One of the former officers, Paul Page, said that these would contain the times and dates of any such visits. Page, who was convicted in 2009 over a £3-million investment fraud, insisted he did not have a grudge against the prince but added that he was 'abusive and rude towards us as police officers'. He said about the TV interview: '[Andrew] made a compelling suspect. If that was a police interview he'd have been in the back of the van.'

Virginia Giuffre insisted that they dined in a Chinese restaurant that Sunday night, March 11. If so, that too would have been recorded.

Then, another protection officer made himself available to the lawyers of Epstein's victims and to the *Mail on Sunday.* The metropolitan policeman, who had an unblemished career of twenty three years and served on Scotland Yard's elite SO14 Royalty Protection Command at the palace, recalled the prince leaving in a green Jaguar earlier in the evening and returning to Buckingham Palace in the early hours that night with his bodyguard. He arrived at the North Centre Gate, which was closed. Flashing his lights, and honking his horn, the prince shouted through the police radio at a raised pitch, 'Open these gates, you buffoons!'

On taking the posting at the palace, the officer had been warned that the prince had a reputation for being rude. He would set off alarms at night and he was told only an inspector could go up to Andrew as he wouldn't speak to anyone below that rank. At the inspector he would then shout, 'I'll go where I want. It's my house.' Unlike other senior royals, Andrew resented the fact the police would keep records about guests. 'It's possible for people to come in at a moment's notice but it still gets put in the book on arrival', the duty officer told the paper.

The anonymous officer had received no payment for the interview, and gave the victims' lawyers a signed affidavit. The officer had also informed the duty inspector about the prince's behaviour on the night itself, but was then told, 'These stories about dealings with Prince Andrew go nowhere, so just swallow it.' The inspector confirmed he had said this to the officer, but could not remember the date on which the complaint was made.

The officer said he intended to use the Freedom of Information Act to access his own shift roster and other documents to confirm his recollection. He also pointed out that Andrew's bodyguards could confirm events that day, as 'with the police everything is written down.' He said that 'much of the evidence of what [Giuffre] and I are saying is held by the Metropolitan Police in its human resources department and the royal protection department'.

The duke's former bodyguards declined to comment, but the Metropolitan Police said they would consider the ex-officer's request. Although, these records could exonerate the prince, neither the Metropolitan Police nor the palace have made them available.

Psychologist Darren Stanton agreed that during intense periods of questioning Prince Andrew's behaviour was not consistent with somebody telling the whole truth. It was also noted that when Maitlis said that Epstein was dead, Andrew let out a small laugh. He kept his legs crossed throughout the interview and had trouble looking Maitlis in the face.

'The behaviour I observed during the documentary is consistent with someone being evasive and potentially deceptive,' Stanton told the *Mirror*. 'I am not convinced the account was consistent or congruent with the true emotion of the prince.'

He added: 'I noted Prince Andrew at times appeared to feign or overcompensate some expression of surprise. Either he was already aware of the information and tried to again distance himself from already knowing it, or he was trying to convey total surprise. Either way, it didn't appear to be genuine.'

Viewing the documentary with a forensic eye, Stanton, a former policeman, noted that the prince refused to categorically deny meeting the then teenager, instead using 'evasive, non-committal language'. A body language expert, he contended that the way Andrew was sitting was unnatural and appeared to have been considered prior to the interview.

'He has very stoic body language,' said Stanton. 'I believe he has been heavily coached.'

Another sign was that, at a number of points in the interview, he 'overcompensated' with the intensity and duration of his eye contact. 'That, along with periods of rapid blinking, is an indicator of dishonesty,' Stanton said.

He had other concerns about Andrew's behaviour.

'As the interview commences, the prince is sat still in the same position pretty much for the duration of the interview,' Stanton said. 'As he was questioned he begins to display some interesting gestures which are the body's unconscious gestures—in psychological terms, we call this "leakage".'

In an interview with the *Daily Mirror*, Stanton, aka TV's 'human lie detector', compared Andrew's demeanour to that of President Clinton when questioned about Monica Lewinsky.

'When he is asked about his time at Epstein's house and the photographs, he replied: "I have no recollection' or 'I've been trying to remember." This is not a straight-out denial. If someone was confident they had not been present in a location or behaviour, the response would be indigent and categorical. The use of this kind of language is reminiscent of President Clinton saying "I did not have relations with that woman".'

'There are lots of uses of what we call "distancing language",' Stanton went on, 'to create a distance between themselves and a person or situation. When asked if he would give a legal deposition he begins to move back to the fall-back position of "it's up to my legal team". Someone who was keen to help and had no knowledge of anything would simply answer "yes, I'll do anything I can". Not begin to waffle and talk about legal advisors.'

Lawyers for Epstein's victims urged him to speak to the FBI as he now faced the prospect of legal action in the US. One asked why he had maintained his friendship with Ghislaine Maxwell after allegations emerged against her in 2015.

Gloria Allred, who represented five of the women Epstein allegedly assaulted, said: 'If he has nothing to hide and has committed no crime, why did he not share what he knows about Jeffrey Epstein, and his suspicions, with the FBI? Anyone, whether a prince or a pauper, should provide what evidence they have to law enforcement in a criminal investigation. The only way we will know what happened is if Prince Andrew and anyone who has any knowledge passes it on to the FBI and prosecutors without delay and without excuse.'

Lisa Bloom, Allred's daughter, who is representing another five victims, said: 'Prince Andrew's interview was deeply disappointing. He is entitled to deny allegations and defend himself. But where is his apology for being so closely associated with one of history's most prolific paedophiles?'

The criticism had little effect on Andrew. A friend told the *Sun*: 'He's told his friends and advisers he is delighted because he thought he acquitted himself well. He's cock-a-hoop. He seriously believes he's pulled off a master triumph. It's astonishing. No one has the heart to tell him that he's delusional—and this is the overall problem. He's surrounded by people who tell him what he wants to hear. Yesterday he was looking happier than he has been for months, totally unaware his interview had caused a firestorm of criticism.'

However, when *The Times* asked him why he had done the interview, he said that he must 'seek approval from higher up'.

If things weren't bad enough for Prince Andrew, Rohan Silva, David

Cameron's senior aide on technology said that he had used the N-word in Buckingham Palace. At a meeting in 2012, Silva, who is of Sri Lankan heritage, asked Andrew whether the government department responsible for trade could be doing a better job, the prince said: 'Well, if you'll pardon the expression, that really is the n***** in the woodpile.' Former home secretary, Jacqui Smith, said Andrew has also made racist remarks about Arabs during a state banquet for the king of Saudi Arabia.

Medical experts said that excess levels of adrenalin caused more sweating rather than less. Professor John Hawk, a dermatologist at St Thomas' hospital in London, dismissed Andrew's claim of not sweating under pressure, telling the *Daily Mirror*: 'It is certainly possible to have problems with sweating, but an overdose of adrenaline would be likely to make a person sweat more, not less. Most cases are inherited, which does not seem to be the case here.'

He went on to imply that Prince Andrew had rewritten medical history: 'Other causes include heat stroke—which seems unlikely in the Falklands—severe dehydration, and certain medications including morphine could also cause it, but these are not likely. Maybe there was a supplementary event that happened which he cannot remember. Trauma is not a known cause of this condition.'

One doctor wrote in *The Atlantic* that the most charitable description was as a coping mechanism in high-pressure situations, such as battle zones. Habituated over time to controlling adrenaline surges, the 'tendency to not worry or panic becomes an outright inability to do so'. Its closest label, in its most extreme form, was 'sociopath'.

The newspaper also asked Ministry of Defence if it knew of any other service personnel who lost the ability to sweat after being fired at, but the MoD refused to comment.

In fact, Andrew had become a joke within the service. The suggestion that he was unable to sweat after experiencing an overdose of adrenaline during the Falklands had gone down particularly badly. Military sources told *The Times* that it 'came as a surprise to many of us who have also been in combat. It's just not viable. It's embarrassing to be represented by someone like that. A soldier would be expected to stand up for what he's done.'

Top brass also urged that he be stripped of his honorary military appointments, which include commodore-in-chief of the Fleet Air Arm, Colonel of the Grenadier Guards and four other regiments, and the Small Arms School Corps. The *New York Post* said that the military brass were 'giving prince a one finger salute'.

There were even calls for Prince Andrew to be stripped of his HRH title and the thirty-room Royal Lodge whose seventy-five-year lease cost him the equivalent of £250 a week.

Business and charities began to back away from him. Following the interview, KPMG, one of the world's biggest accountancy firms, confirmed it had pulled the plug on its sponsorship of Pitch@Palace, the prince's flagship initiative, with sources citing 'adverse media publicity'. Insurance company Aon requested that its logo be stripped from the Pitch@Palace website. Banking giant Standard Chartered pulled out. Adweek cut its backing. Bond University in Australia cut its ties and the pharmaceutical giant AstraZeneca reviewed its position, though its agreement was expiring at the end of the year anyway.

The organisation aimed to connect start-ups with investors. However, it turned out that, if successful, start-ups would have to pay Pitch@Palace Global Ltd, a company in which the duke had a significant controlling interest, 2 per cent of the business. The company would have to make no payment itself. It was legal but the UK operations, Pitch@Palace CIC, would be liquidated it was reported.

Andrew's patronage of the British Exploring Society, the Outward Bound Trust and the Jubilee Sailing Trust was called into question. Students at the University of Huddersfield, where Andrew was chancellor, called on him to resign. Former lecturer Stephen Dorril said: 'Students are very concerned about things like sexual harassment and the Me Too movement, and to be associated with someone who at the very least was a friend of a convicted sex trafficker and paedophile is not a good thing for the university.'

The NSPCC had already distanced itself from Andrew, and, while others were mulling over the situation, Prince Andrew stepped down from public duties. Barclays, the Royal Philharmonic and the National Ballet also stepped away, along with Yorkshire Air Ambulance and Action on Hearing Loss. The Women's Interlink Foundation, which helps sex-trafficked women in India, had second thoughts about his patronage.

In a statement issued by Buckingham Palace, Andrew said: 'It has become clear to me over the last few days that the circumstances relating to my former association with Jeffrey Epstein have become a major disruption to my family's work and the valuable work going on in the many organisations and charities that I am proud to support….

'Therefore, I have asked Her Majesty if I may step back from public duties for the foreseeable future, and she has given her permission. Of course, I am willing to help any appropriate law enforcement agency with their investigations, if required.' Months later, it turned out that the truth was a little different.

It was thought that Prince Charles supported Andrew's sacking from royal duties after his paranoia about the duke's attempted palace coup in the 1990s. 'If so, it's a fitting revenge,' said one ex-courtier. Charles refused to answer questions about his role in Andrew's downfall.

'Charles will be furious that his trip to New Zealand has been completely overshadowed,' royal biographer Tom Bower told the *Daily Mail*. 'The one thing Charles is determined to do is inherit the crown, and he won't let anyone get in the way.'

Prince William, the palace's number three, joined his father and insisted that Andrew was stripped of his royal duties. Palace sources said that he was not a huge fan of his uncle. Andrew's fall from grace cheered Australian republicans and Nicola Sturgeon, leader of the Scottish Nationalists, said there was a debate to be had over the future of the monarchy.

Andrew's rout was by now almost complete. A lavish party for Andrew's sixtieth birthday was cancelled. There would be a small family dinner instead.

New testimony surfaced on the cameras in Epstein's houses and it renewed the question whether Andrew might have been caught on one of them.

Maria Farmer, a young painter of nudes and adolescents engaged by Epstein as a receptionist in the 1990s, told CBS that he showed her the 'media room' in his New York townhouse. She said it contained closed-circuit televisions set up with feeds from secret surveillance cameras in bedrooms and bathrooms at the property.

She said: 'There was a door that looked like an invisible door with all this limestone and everything. You push it, and you go in. And I saw all the cameras… I looked on the cameras, and I saw toilet, toilet, bed, bed, toilet, bed. I'm like, I am never going to use the restroom here, and I'm never going to sleep here. You know, it was obvious that they were like monitoring private moments.... It was all videoed all the time. I asked him, "What do you do with all this?" And he said, "I keep it all in my safe".'

In 1996, while painting art work for Jack Nicholson hit As Good as It Gets at an artist-in-residence location arranged by Epstein, she was, she alleged, sexually assaulted by him and Maxwell—which included twisting her nipples—and broke off all contact. She had called her mentor Eric Fischl, who said, 'I just kept telling Maria, 'You've got to get out of there. You've got to get out of there'.

A former lap-dancer, who gave evidence under the name Tiffany Doe, then came forward to describe a party at Epstein's New York townhouse where Andrew put his head between her breasts and blew a raspberry and told her she should be in a magazine for big-breasted women.

'I guess being a prince gives you those privileges.'

She said normally she would have punched anyone who did that in the face, but it was a big night for Jeffrey.

'The girls had been specially selected to please Andrew,' she said. 'I believed the duke liked curvy girls like his ex-wife, Fergie. Epstein made it clear he wanted to keep Andrew happy. I was told to make sure he was looked after, that he had a drink, that he was OK. I saw the prince at parties a couple of times a year, if not more. I would flirt with him and he'd hit on me and was handsy. He would stand in close proximity, looking at my breasts. He would hold my hands, put his arm around my waist, stroke my cheek. He used royalty, his celebrity, to his advantage.' The woman also told the *People* about rooms 'where sex happened'. She hired teenagers to attend and said: 'The girls were younger sisters of other strippers, homeless kids, runaways. They were mostly older teens and were paid $200, $300. But the youngest girls would stay in the bedrooms because they couldn't look eighteen or nineteen.'

She also knew that the bedrooms had hidden cameras, adding: 'A huge staircase led to the bedrooms. There were strange artefacts, sex stuff, sex pics, nudes, and they would be moved from party areas so as not to freak people out when they arrived. The social party rooms were divided up and kept separate from where the sex happened.'

Chauntae Davies, who became Epstein's personal masseuse, gave the *Sun* an interview with pictures of 'Orgy Island' Little Saint James. A slew of powerful men including Prince Andrew came there, she said.

'I was very aware of Jeffrey Epstein's friendship with Prince Andrew and Fergie right away,' Davies said. 'It was one of several bragging tactics he used to further induce his power and privilege. He bragged a lot. He had framed photos of them in his residences. He bragged about how he'd lent money to the duchess.'

As for Andrew's denials about knowing his rich pal was a paedophile, Davies insisted, 'There is no way you could have been a friend of Jeffrey's and not know what was going on. I don't see how you could see somebody with another young girl all the time and there never being a conversation about it. It doesn't add up.'

The *Sun* newspaper then revealed more damning recollections by Steve Scully, Epstein's phone and internet contractor on the island. Though Andrew strenuously denied having ever met Giuffre, Scully said he was convinced he had seen them together. Called to fix Epstein's phone on the front porch he saw the prince with a bikini-clad blonde he grabbed and kissed by the pool between 2001 and 2004, 'He was grabbing her ass and stuff like that… grinding against her and groping her.' The girl seemed to enjoy the encounter and Scully swore it was the young Giuffre.

The three crossed each other on a pathway. 'Your Highness', Scully said, 'I'm Steve the phone guy'. But Andrew countered 'No, it's Andrew.' Scully responded 'I'm sorry, I really didn't know how to address you.'

'It was so obvious she was so young and she never said a word. I thought she looked particularly young. It bothered me,' Scully said and he told his wife and a friend at the time.

The royal family's official public diary, the Court Circular, showed Andrew flew from London to New York to stay with Epstein on the morning of 9 April 2001 and had the afternoon free. On the same day Giuffre flew into an airport near New York on Epstein's private jet.

A Buckingham Palace source told the *Daily Mirror*: 'Disturbing allegations of Epstein's lifestyle of underage sex and hidden video cameras has led to a fear in the palace there could be more devastating revelations to come. The enormity of the situation has hit the palace like a sledgehammer.'

The palace bowed out of representing Andrew in his Giuffre travails and issued a public statement, 'This issue is being dealt with by The Duke of

York's legal team. Buckingham Palace will not be commenting further on this particular matter.' The Queen, furthermore, took away from the duke the £249,000 she allocated from the Sovereign Grant to perform royal duties. She would nonetheless continue to pay her son an undisclosed allowance from her private Duchy of Lancaster income. She also told the prince he could no longer attend public events.

What this meant in practise became clear at his first public appearance in March, a memorial service at Windsor attended by eight hundred people—friends and relatives of a courtier who once had the cobblestones in front of Westminster Abbey hoovered. The prince wasn't permitted to represent his mother and the Court Circular expunged his presence as if he was never there—Stalin-style. In order not to embarrass his mother, Andrew also had to go to the Ministry of Defence to ask that his automatic promotion to admiral on reaching his sixtieth birthday be stopped. But was it too little too late?

Ostensibly the prince was left with only £20,000 a year from his navy pension. But it had long been questioned how the ex-couple lived a millionaire lifestyle, surrounded by valets, on just £270,000 a year. Then there was the ex-couple's £13-million ski chalet in the Swiss mountain-village of Verbier (the duke owned the top half and the duchess the bottom half as a legal tweak to strict canton ownership rules) with a staff of six, to give daughters Beatrice and Eugenie a permanent base in the glitzy playground for billionaires. With its living quarters full of priceless antiques, seven bedrooms, massive indoor pool, sauna, sun terrace and bar, Chalet Helora cost nearly £25,000 a week to rent. The sale went through in January 2015, a week after Giuffre made her allegations in court. A decade earlier, the duke splashed out £7.5 million to refurbish Royal Lodge, his thirty-room home in Windsor Great Park.

In 2020, the prince wore the latest £12,000, 18-carat Apple watch and he drove a £200,000 Bentley with the personal number plate DOY. Otherwise he is seen at golf courses and the resorts of St Tropez.

No one knew where the money came from. But it was speculated that Andrew earned money in countries such as Azerbaijan and Kazakhstan with dodgy regimes. A series of emails—which Buckingham Palace first claimed were false and then conceded were genuine—signed by 'The Duke' detailed a 1 per cent commission proposal on a £385 million deal to build sewage works in Kazakhstan sent to a local business man on behalf of a Greek company.

The duke's secretary Amanda Thirsk was to make the introductions.

The exchange was part of a secret cache of emails made public by Kazakh activists to reveal dubious practices in their country's business world. One email included in the cache was by a Kazakh boasting to Russian businessmen of house parties with Russian prostitutes while on holiday near the Black Sea. Attached to his message was video footage of each of the girls, stick-thin and incredibly young, dancing in tiny bikinis next to a pool.

By this time, the prince was an embarrassment. He was forced to pull out of a trip to Bahrain for Pitch@Palace and did not attend a memorial for one of his oldest friends. Being edged out of Pitch@Palace was a particular blow in view of the 2 per cent cut from every deal made—effectively the company charged British fledgling entrepreneurs twice the 1 per cent commission the duke intended to charge the Greeks and Kazakhs, or the 1 per cent Fergie proposed to charge an Indian businessman during the *News of the World* sting. The previous year the Global company had made a profit £600,000. There were calls for his finances to the scrutinised by parliament. Meanwhile more of Epstein's victims were coming forward and their lawyers renewed their calls for Andrew to speak to the FBI. Andrew said that his company never claimed the 2 per cent it was entitled to on deals it had brokered.

The duke's Pitch@Palace Global Ltd limped on with only Amanda Thirsk and one other director remaining on its board of directors, while the organisation mooted rebranding its initiatives. Thirsk left the Queen's employment with a settlement in January—after having lost her job as the prince's private secretary, a role she had had since 2004. In the same month she resigned from Pitch@Palace CIC and in April also as Pitch@Palace Global director upon finding a job elsewhere—though she remained a director of Pitch@Palace Innovations, incorporated under the prince's control eight days before the unsealing of Giuffre's court papers in August 2019. The duke's £1.4 million charity connected with Pitch@Palace CIC and the iDEA awards was liquidated following 'a serious incident report' to the Charity Commission. One of the trustees had been paid in contravention of charity rules. The prince refunded the payment to the charity from his own pocket. But it was too late by then to undo reputational dent.

The *Sunday Times* reported: 'There's been active discussions between the FBI and Department of Justice about interviewing Prince Andrew in relation to the Jeffrey Epstein case. If he agrees to an interview, he could potentially provide some very unique and helpful insights and make a considerable difference to the investigation.'

Without some diplomatic deal it was going to be hard to get Andrew to tell what he knows.

'It's not going to be easy to subpoena someone like Prince Andrew,' Lisa Bloom told the BBC. 'He's obviously not walking down the street, where a process server can just hand him a piece of paper.' Giuffre's lawyers had twice tried to serve legal papers on the prince, once via the Embassy in Washington DC and another time by recorded delivery to Buckingham Palace. On both occasions, receipt of papers was refused.

Shelby Patrick, sister of Skye who died of a heroin overdose after being abused by Epstein from the age of sixteen, said that, now the Queen had stripped him of his duties, 'the only duty you have left—that you must tell the truth in the name of my sister and each and every victim. No one believes you could not have seen something. Please tell the FBI everything you know.'

If he would not come back voluntarily, he should be extradited. Another Jane Doe said: 'They should haul him back. If he has nothing to hide, then he'll have no problem coming back.'

13

THE MYSTERIOUS MS MAXWELL

By 28 November 2019, a video deposition made by Ghislaine Maxwell as part of the 2015 Giuffre defamation action surfaced. In it she said: 'My job included hiring many people. There were six homes. I hired assistants, architects, decorators, cooks, cleaners, gardeners, pool people, pilots. I hired all sorts of people. A very small part of my job was to find adult professional massage therapists for Jeffrey. As far as I'm concerned, everyone who came to his house was an adult professional person.'

She strenuously denied Virginia Giuffre's allegations she was loaned out by Epstein for sex to rich and powerful men, including Prince Andrew. At one point during her questioning, Maxwell became so angry she smashed her hand down on to a table.

'I can only go on what I know,' she said. 'What I know is a falsehood based on what Virginia said. Everything Virginia has said is an absolute lie, which is why we are here in this room. At seventeen, you are allowed to be a professional masseuse. There is nothing inappropriate about her coming at that time to give a massage.'

Maxwell explained she recruited masseuses—'I would receive a massage and if it was good I would ask them if they did home visits.'

Asked how often Giuffre massaged Epstein, she said: 'When I was at the house he received a massage on average once a day.'

Her memory was cloudy though. In her video testimony, Maxwell said: 'What I can say is that I barely would remember her, if not for all of this rubbish.... I probably wouldn't remember her at all, except that she came from time to time.

But I don't recollect her coming as often as she portrayed herself.'

She was clear she was not involved in any abuse.

'I have never participated at any time with Virginia in a massage with Jeffrey. I have been absolutely appalled by her story,' she said.

Maxwell also said she knew nothing of abusive activity and denied procuring underage girls for Epstein.

'It's important to understand that I wasn't with Jeffrey all the time,' she said. 'In fact, I was only in the house less than half the time, so I cannot testify to when I wasn't there how often she came.'

Maxwell disappeared from the public eye following Giuffre's sex allegations. But after Epstein's death, it was reported that she had been living in the quiet Massachusetts town of Manchester-by-the-Sea in the mansion of former boyfriend Scott Borgerson.

Borgerson flatly denied any involvement with Maxwell, surprisingly in view of later developments.

'I am not dating Ghislaine. I'm home alone with my cat,' he told the *New York Post.*

Asked about the status of their friendship, he said: 'I don't want to comment on that. Would you want to talk about your friends?'

When reporters arrived in Manchester-on-Sea in the summer of 2019, Ghislaine was nowhere to be seen. Other reporters scoured the US and Europe. Some said she was in Russia out of reach of the FBI. Others pointed to Israel or Brazil. The *Sun* even offered a £10,000 reward to anyone who could find her.

Tatler published a profile on the elusive Maxwell, asking where on earth she was and asked everyone listed in her 2005 address book, a *Who's Who* of A-listers that could be found in its Florida-court facsimile online. Most declined to talk, but once Maxwell was at every glittering party in New York.

When she arrived in Manhattan after the collapse of her father's fraudulent business empire in Britain made her name toxic, she had to start from scratch. Someone who knew her at the time said, 'She didn't have money—so she moved in with Epstein, having a fabulous time, private planes, being a helicopter pilot, all that. He was working class, a fraud, while she had an entrée: she knew all the upper-class English coming through New York and reeled them in. She was very much on the scene; she knew how to give a dinner party.'

Disturbingly, press-baron Lord Hartwell's daughter Eleanor Berry recalled that, as a teenager, she was once told by nine-year-old Ghislaine that she was about to be given a hiding by her father Robert Maxwell. 'Daddy has a series of things lined up in a row. There's a riding crop with a swish to it, another straight riding crop and a few shoehorns. He always asks me to choose which one I want', she told the writer.

An anonymous friend remembered seeing Maxwell in New York around 2010 and asking what are you up to? Maxwell replied, 'I'm selling this product—stainless-steel mini dumb-bells—that you put up your fanny. For exercising your vaginal muscles, exercise your pelvic floor, learn the Singapore Grip. I'm giving seminars in LA and they all turn up and I tell them, this is how you keep your man.'

New York Banker Euan Rellie, one of the few speaking on the record, said, 'She was at the epicentre of the social scene in New York. She knew everybody. It wasn't just teenage girls who Epstein was interested in cultivating. Every single interesting, pretty, new girl to arrive in New York, would end up going for tea with Ghislaine then being introduced to Jeffrey. She was the acceptable face of a rather mysterious billionaire. I found him creepy.'

A source close to Maxwell claimed in *Vanity Fair* spoke about Maxwell's relationship with Epstein.

'Ghislaine was in love with Jeffrey the way she was in love with her father. She always thought if she just did one more thing for him, to please him, he would marry her,' the source said. 'When I asked what she thought of the underage girls, she looked at me and said, "They're nothing, these girls. They are trash".'

Laura Goldman, a friend of Ghislaine's sister Isabel, added that Maxwell had a 'super power' when it came to attracting men.

'One of her talents is finding a man to take care of her,' Goldman told the *Sun*. 'She's good at that. It's like a superpower. Her superpower is she finds men to take care of her.... But I get her appeal to guys. All she ever talked about was "sex, sex, sex".' Maxwell also frequently discussed the techniques of oral sex in public, it was said.

Artist and former employee Maria Farmer told the *New York Times* that Maxwell would habitually leave the New York mansion in the early nineties saying, 'I've got to go get girls for Jeffrey', casting for models. 'It was really weird to me. I'm like [the] "models are so young", and she said: "Yeah, but they need these models for Victoria's Secret. They go as young as thirteen now in modelling".' Farmer also alleged that Maxwell recruited teenagers from schools on the Upper

East Side and in Central Park.

Farmer was also a witness in the criminal case against Maxwell. 'Ghislaine was key in making me feel safe,' Farmer told CBS. 'I trusted her because she is a woman.' It was why Farmer's sister, Annie, aged sixteen, came for a visit from Arizona and was allowed to go unaccompanied to Zorro Ranch with Maxwell by her mother. Expecting other students, Annie was there alone. While the girl massaged Epstein's foot, Maxwell gave tips. She also told the high school girl to lie topless on her back as she massaged her.

Maxwell was magnetic, Farmer recalled, 'My sister even said that she would feel so special if Ghislaine paid attention to her because she had that way about her, you know, the popular girl in school, she was one of those. She knew everybody… . She was so dangerous.' Farmer said Maxwell would do anything to get what she wants, 'and all of it for her is about power and money'.

When Maxwell found out around 2002 that Farmer had spoken out about her and her young sibling's experiences, she made threatening calls, Farmer alleged.

Farmer went into hiding, 'Ghislaine kept threatening my life. She found out where I was living, and she would send messages to me or I would get a call and I would have to move again. Most of her threats were veiled, like: "You better look over your shoulder because there's someone coming for you." She told me she was going to burn all my paintings, my career was burned.'

She went to the police, as well as more than one FBI agent, none of whom took action. She also spoke to journalist Vicky Ward, who included the story in a profile of Epstein for *Vanity Fair* in 2003. Ward wrote later that the then-editor Graydon Carter cut out the entire part about Farmer and her sister after being pressured by Epstein. A spokeswoman for the magazine responded, 'Epstein denied the charges at the time and since the claims were unsubstantiated and no criminal investigation had been initiated, we decided not to include them in what was a financial story.'

Ward's 2003 'financial' profile said that a Victoria Secret model was once summoned by Maxwell to a concert at Epstein's New York mansion. Mar-a-Lago style, women far out-numbered the men. 'These were not women you'd see at Upper East Side dinners' the model said, 'Many seemed foreign and dressed a little bizarrely.' The same woman attended a party by Maxwell with Prince Andrew filled with Russian models. 'Some of the guests were horrified.'

Maxwell's deposition was contradicted in court by former bodyguard Tony

Figueroa who said, 'Maxwell personally requested that he find and bring girls to Epstein for sex.' Virginia told him that she had threesomes with Epstein and Maxwell involving strap-ons.

Alfredo Rodriguez, Epstein's butler, testified: 'Maxwell kept a list of the local girls who were giving massages at her desk, and that Maxwell kept nude photos of girls on her computer.' Maxwell's purported address book, impounded in 2005, detailed under 'massage' many names per Epstein property in alphabetical first-name order. There were close to a hundred and included in the list was Virginia Roberts.

Another witness said in a deposition they had seen 'a fifteen-year-old Swedish girl crying and shaking because defendant [Maxwell] was attempting to force her to have sex with Epstein and she refused'.

Epstein victim Jennifer Araoz chose this moment to file a new lawsuit against Maxwell, even though she'd never met her, alleging, 'Maxwell participated with and assisted Epstein in maintaining and protecting his sex trafficking ring, ensuring that approximately three girls a day were made available to him.'

Lawyer Dan Kaiser, representing Jennifer Araoz said: 'From what we know, Ghislaine Maxwell was a principal enabler to Jeffrey Epstein when he was alive. She was integral in maintaining the sex trafficking ring. She provided important administrative services in terms of the hiring of recruiters, and management of those employees, the making of appointments and dates for interactions between Mr Epstein and the underage girls that were providing sexual services to him. She also maintained the ring by intimidating girls, by ensuring their silence. Jeffrey Epstein couldn't have done what he did for as long as he did it without the services of somebody like Ghislaine Maxwell. She is as culpable, in my judgment, as Jeffrey Epstein himself.'

Like the prince, Maxwell has consistently denied all allegations against her. When she was arrested and charged in New York in July 2020 she made clear from her detention centre in Brooklyn that she would vigorously fight the sriminal charges in court.

While Maxwell had gone to ground, the *Sun* said that Andrew had not cut his ties with her.

'They have remained constantly in touch by phone and email,' a source told the newspaper about the time before she was charged. 'The duke has an unswerving loyalty to Ghislaine and she is very loyal to him. They both share the view they have done nothing wrong. They talk regularly. If he wasn't in the spotlight at the moment he would have found a way to meet up with her.'

A former adult friend of Maxwell's told the Daily Beast: 'Ghislaine procured women like me for Andrew. It was a network. She was on the party circuit and she was bringing Andrew around, meeting young women.'

Maxwell invited her friend to Andrew's private apartment in Buckingham Palace.

'Ghislaine was there,' she said, 'and it was clear immediately that I have been brought to the dinner as a sex object. Andrew sat next to me on the sofa and kept reaching over to hold my hand.'

To distract Andrew, she asked him to take her on a tour of the palace.

'The next thing I knew, I was walking hand in hand with Prince Andrew through Buckingham Palace,' she said. 'As a joke, he took me out on the balcony and I waved to the non-existent crowd.' Several other women had reported on the duke's trusted dating technique, including the model Caprice Bourret.

Andrew suggested that they went to a club, but the woman begged off saying she had to go to work the next day.

Maxwell arranged massages for Andrew as she did for Epstein. Professional masseuse Monique Giannelloni said she was sent to the palace, recommended by Maxwell. Andrew greeted her at the door of his apartment in a robe.

'He said, "Excuse me" and went into the bathroom. He came out and he was naked. He got onto the table. I didn't know where to look,' she said. She also revealed that she had given Maxwell massages upstairs in her Belgravia house, where the picture of Andrew and Giuffre was taken. An old girlfriend of Andrew's then came forward to say that the prince was particularly fond of being given a massage by two women at a time.

Though none of these reports concerned illegal activity, London's Met was now firmly on the back foot and was forced to explain why it had dropped its investigation into Giuffre's complaint of 2015. Alex Murray, commander for specialist crime, admitted the Met had received an 'allegation of non-recent trafficking for sexual exploitation' against Epstein and a British woman at the time.

'Officers assessed the available evidence, interviewed the complainant and obtained early investigative advice from the Crown Prosecution Service,' he said, 'Following the legal advice, it was clear that any investigation into human trafficking would be largely focused on activities and relationships outside the UK' and so the Met 'was not the appropriate authority'. In November 2016 a full criminal investigation was dropped. Ironically, parliament had just passed the Modern Slavery Act 2015, which clearly fell at its first wicket.

Harry Fletcher, of the Victims' Rights Campaign, challenged the Met's claim that it was not the appropriate authority to investigate because any inquiry would be largely overseas, pointing out that the law at the time, the Sexual Offences Act 1956, forbade procuring a girl under twenty one to have sexual intercourse with a third party anywhere in the world.

Giuffre tweeted: 'At first the Scotland Yard told me they were going to forensically examine GM's [Ghislaine Maxwell's] house in London—next thing I hear, just like the FBI, they were not allowed to pursue the investigation. Corruption in the highelevels [sic] of gov.'

Scotland Yard also claimed it had liaised with 'other law enforcement organisations but has not received a formal request asking for assistance in connection with this allegation'. The Met later said it was assisting the FBI in its investigation after all.

Prince Andrew—despite his strenuous denials of what was being alleged—had by now become a lightning rod for bad headlines and was not present at a reception for NATO leaders, including President Trump, at Buckingham Palace. He was so toxic that Trump denied knowing him—even though they had played golf and been photographed together on numerous occasions since 2000, after first meeting in 1999 at Jeffrey Epstein's Manhattan mansion.

14

'ONLY ONE OF US TELLING THE TRUTH'

With the airing of Virginia Giuffre's Panorama interview just days away, Prince Charles called for a 'tell-all' summit at Sandringham. He had consulted his father and his friend Sir Nicholas Soames, the veteran MP and grandson of Sir Winston Churchill, on how best to handle the crisis. The palace had played the duke first and it had blown up spectacularly in their faces.

Virginia Giuffre's interview finally aired on 2 December. Usually a half-hour show, Panorama was extended to an hour. In it Virginia appealed for the support of the British people.

'I implore the people in the UK to stand up beside me, to help me fight this fight, to not accept this as being ok,' she said. 'This is not some sordid sex story. This is a story of being trafficked. This is a story of abuse and this is a story of your guys' royalty.'

Giuffre rehearsed how the alleged encounters with Epstein and other wealthy men often began with the code word 'massage' before turning overtly sexual. She said during the interview that she 'went from being abused by Epstein to then being passed around like a platter—a platter of fruit'.

She said that she was instructed only to talk when she was spoken to and be polite and friendly with Epstein's friends, and laugh when they tried to be humorous. She recalled flying on private jets and going to places she never imagined she would visit.

Giuffre pushed back against the idea that the widely circulated photograph that showed Andrew standing with his hand around her waist was doctored. She insisted that the photograph was real and that she had handed the original to the FBI in 2011.

'I think the world is getting sick of these ridiculous excuses,' she said, adding that there was a date on the back of the photo showing when it was printed—just two days after they met.

'The people on the inside are going to keep coming up with these ridiculous excuses like his arm was elongated or the photo was doctored,' she said, 'I mean I'm calling BS on this, because that's what it is. He knows what happened. I know what happened. And there's only one of us telling the truth.'

Michael Thomas, a freelance photographer who copied the original picture before it was handed over, said it was in a pile of photographs Virginia had given him.

'It wasn't like she pulled the photo of Prince Andrew out—it was just in amongst the rest of them,' he said. 'These were five-by-seven photos that looked like they had come from Boots, nothing more complicated than that. They were just typical teenage snaps. There's no way that photo is fake.'

An affidavit from a man Virginia was dating in 2001 reportedly confirmed he saw the original picture and that she told him she was forced to have sex with the prince.

Her account of the evening of the 11th of March began with tea at Maxwell's house, where he spoke about his former wife, Fergie, who Maxwell was 'bad-mouthing'.

She continued with her tale at Tramp, 'We went to the VIP section. There was no waiting in the lines obviously—you were with a prince. Andrew asked what I wanted to drink then asked me to dance,' she said. 'He is the most hideous dancer I've ever seen in my life. It was horrible and this guy was sweating all over me, his sweat was like it was raining basically everywhere. I was just like grossed out from it, but I knew I had to keep him happy because that's what Jeffrey and Ghislaine would have expected from me.'

When they left the club instructions were issued. 'In the car Ghislaine tells me that I have to do for Andrew what I do for Jeffrey and that just made me sick,' she said. 'I just didn't expect it from royalty. I didn't expect it from someone who people look up to and admire, you know, in the royal family.'

She grew emotional when she said that later that evening she had sex with Andrew upstairs at Maxwell's mews house in Belgravia.

'There was a bath, and it started there, and then it led into the bedroom,' she said. 'It didn't last very long, the whole entire procedure. It was disgusting. He wasn't mean or anything but he got up and said 'thanks' and walked out, and I sat there in bed just horrified and ashamed and felt dirty. I had to get up and have a shower. I had just been abused by a member of the royal family.' The following morning, according to Virginia: 'Ghislaine said, "You did a really good job," and pats me on the back and says, "You made him really happy".'

Virginia said, 'It was a wicked time in my life. It was a really scary time in my life. I had just been abused by a member of the royal family… I wasn't chained to a sink, but these powerful people were my chains,' Giuffre said, beginning to cry. 'I couldn't comprehend how in the highest levels in the government powerful people were allowing this to happen. Not only allowing it to happen, but participating in it.'

The interviewer asked if she would like to stop the interview.

'If you don't mind, just for a moment,' she said.

In the interview, she acknowledged that a 'foggy memory' might mean she was sometimes wrong on dates or places, but she stood by the substance of her allegation.

'One thing that I can tell you is you never forget the face of someone who has heaved over you,' she said.

Panorama said that it has discovered more damning evidence. In a 2015 email from Andrew to Maxwell he asked for help dealing with the allegations being made by Giuffre. He wrote: 'Let me know when we can talk. Got some specific questions to ask you about Virginia Roberts,' to which Maxwell replied: 'Have some info. Call me when you have a moment.' The emails were sent just hours before Virginia appeared on a US website claiming she was forced to have sex with Prince Andrew.

Another victim, Sarah Ransome, was also interviewed for the programme. She said that Maxwell 'controlled the girls. She was like the madam. She was like the nuts and bolts of the sex trafficking operation and she would always visit Jeffrey on the island to make sure that the girls were doing what they were supposed to be doing… She would be the one getting all the girls in check. She knew what Jeffrey liked. This was very much a joint effort.' Maxwell denied all the allegations.

Ransome, who said she was kept for six months on Little Saint James and claimed she was raped several times a day, also said Epstein had 'full erotic sex' in front of everyone on his private jet and that his private island, was 'very much set up for orgies'. Having observed Epstein and Maxwell at close quarters, she told the *Guardian*: 'They were never like a couple. Jeffrey and Ghislaine were best friends, or like brother and sister. Never holding hands or kissing. And she wasn't his employee.'

Court documents cited in the documentary said Andrew had spent weeks in Epstein's Florida home and got daily massages.

The FBI confirmed that Ghislaine Maxwell was the main focus of their investigation.

15

FEDERAL WITNESS

The day after Panorama aired, Giuffre's father Sky Roberts appeared on ITV's Good Morning Britain. He stuck up for his daughter and her version of events.

'I have no doubt at all that she is telling the truth. I've seen the interviews with Prince Andrew and it shows to me, and I think most of Britain, that he is not telling the truth,' he said. 'She has no reason not to tell the truth about this and he has every reason to deny it because of him being a royal and what he has done. These are young girls, these are kids.'

He said he feared for her life. 'There are still a lot of powerful people alive now,' he said. 'But she's just telling the truth and letting the world know who these people are and what they are doing. And these people have families too and that's why they're denying it, because they do have families and they have children, but they should not be preying on young girls, some of these girls are fifteen years old.... I am sure that why Jeffrey Epstein is not alive right now, is because somebody didn't want to see his books or whatever he's got on everybody.'

After reading a tweet that said 'FBI will kill her to protect the ultra-rich and well connected', Giuffre replied: 'I am making it publicly known that in no way, shape or form am I suicidal. I have made this known to my therapist and GP. If something happens to me—for the sake of my family do not let this go away and help me to protect them. Too many evil people want to see me quieted.'

She also retweeted a message saying, 'if you die in an 'accident', it wasn't no accident.' She said that she had been informed by the FBI there'd been a credible death threat against her.

In her private journal she had recorded her fears of Epstein and his pals.

'Epstein also trafficked me for sexual purposes to many other powerful men, including politicians and powerful business executives,' she said. 'Epstein required me to describe the sexual events I had with these men, presumably so he could potentially blackmail them. I am still very fearful of these men today.' She added: 'I also hope that this information is treated in a way that will keep me safe from Epstein and others criminals identified here so as to encourage more victims of similar crimes to come forward.'

In the media's post mortems of their TV accounts, it was not Andrew who was favoured. The *New York Post* did not mince its words, saying straightforwardly: 'The BBC has come to bury Prince Andrew', having framed the documentary as an exploration of 'the prince's friendship with a prolific sex offender'.

'Some of Epstein's victims are believed to have been as young as eleven or twelve years old,' the *Post* continued. 'Sure, Prince Andrew may have had his office at the palace shut down (hardly a consequence; he doesn't really work) and lost corporate sponsors after his disastrous sit-down with the BBC just two weeks ago, but the queen has continued to message support for her favourite child. And Andrew, the BBC pointed out Monday night, continues a friendship with Maxwell, long accused of sexually abusing the underage girls she procured for Epstein.'

Generally, the media thought that Virginia Giuffre's recollection of events was in strong contrast to the duke's. She was emotional and straightforward; he was cold and evasive. Panorama painted Giuffre as a victim fully aware of the weight of her accusations; Newsnight left many feeling that he was devoid of a conscience, full of entitlement and self-importance.

Known only as Jane Doe 15, another Epstein victim stepped forward after US attorney Berman's appeal for witnesses. She piled on the moral pressure for Andrew to make good on his public promise on BBC Newsnight to help the victims with what he knew. She said that one of Epstein's assistants had taken her to Epstein's Manhattan townhouse where she had been photographed. Then she was invited out to his Zorro Ranch in New Mexico where she says she was sexually assaulted.

'Epstein took my sexual innocence in front of a wall of framed photographs of him shaking hands and smiling with celebrities and world leaders,' she claimed in her statement. 'After, he wanted to talk with me about what had just been my first sexual experience and directed me to take time to myself that night to cry. He said that would be beneficial for my growth.'

Epstein then asked her how much money she wanted from him towards her university bills, she alleged. She took just $5,000.

'I left Zorro Ranch with a deep sense of shame, not just a shame of his having sexually abused me, but the shame of knowing that I had somehow been duped,' she said. 'It was the weight of Epstein's wealth, the isolation to which he subjected me and his discussion of his social connections that crushed me into submission, far more than his physical strength.'

After that, she said, she was enticed to come to Little Saint James to meet Prince Andrew. She turned down the offer 'out of fear'. Her lawyer, Gloria Allred, wrote to Prince Andrew saying:

> We write now to seek your cooperation to bring out the truth about his predatory behavior. You are no doubt aware by now that Mr Epstein was a skilled manipulator and abuser of minor girls. A central element of that predatory behavior was to present himself as having connections to the world's most powerful people.
>
> After Mr Epstein sexually assaulted Jane Doe 15 in New Mexico, his representative contacted her again to attempt to lure her to Mr Epstein's private island. In trying to persuade her, Mr Epstein's representative conveyed to Jane Doe 15 that Mr Epstein was close to you, that you would be among the guests and that she would have an opportunity to meet you. Your prestige and reputation were directly touted in his attempts to engage in further harm.
>
> We urge you now to actively participate in providing sworn testimony to the FBI, and voluntarily to submit to a sworn deposition in Jane Doe 15's lawsuit.

If he did not, pre-trial witness subpoenas had been prepared in the civil cases in the US, which could be served on Andrew if he returned to the US.

These would compel him to give evidence on what he saw while staying at Epstein's home. It was thought that he might have vital information about Epstein's sex trafficking operation.

Prince Andrew was deaf to all appeals. Representing another five victims, Lisa Bloom, who had a witness who said she saw Andrew with Virginia in Tramp, also appealed to Andrew, stating, 'You've said you're going to cooperate, let's do it. Don't make us subpoena you. Don't make law enforcement chase you. Come to the US, sit down with the FBI and attorneys and answer questions. Give us the documents, calendars, journals, all of the information that is customarily turned over in investigations like this and have your staff who travel with you, security who have eyes and ears, have them answer questions as well.'

As to her witness Bloom stated, 'She says that in 2001 she was at the Tramp nightclub and recalls seeing Prince Andrew. It was pointed out to her by a member of her group. The woman remembers it vividly. She had never seen a royal before or since. It was a very big moment for her—she stared at him. She says he was with Virginia—who looked very young and not happy—but Andrew was smiling and seemed to be very much enjoying himself on the dance floor.'

A second witness to seeing the couple dancing at Tramp also now came forward, along with another woman who had been abused by Epstein and said she had sex with Andrew.

Being subpoenaed as a witness might, however, be the least of the duke's worries, despite his consistent and insistent denial of the allegations.

Josh Schiller, a lawyer representing Giuffre, warned that Andrew could be the target of an FBI investigation and not just as a witness but 'because he is accused of participating in a sex trafficking ring'. If the federal prosecutors could show reasonable suspicion, Prince Andrew could face extradition to the US to face federal charges.

Buckingham Palace shuddered. If this ever came to pass, it would rip open the abyss for the monarchy.

On 9 June 2020, there must have been a small sigh of relief. Further to news reports that US Attorney Berman had issued an official request to the UK government for Prince Andrew's testimony as a witness in the Epstein case, Berman's boss, US Attorney General William Barr, himself clarified on

Fox News that this had little to do with extradition. 'I don't think it's a question of handing him over' confirmed Barr. All it meant, Barr said, was that the US government wanted the prince to 'provide some evidence'.

Bypassing the prince, the US government had issued the request under the Mutual Legal Assistance Treaty (MLAT) 1994. It obliged the British police and National Crime Agency to assist the FBI investigation. In addition to a witness statement before a high-court judge, for example, extradition specialists Bindman's said that investigators could ask that Andrew 'provides documents and /or property relating to the investigation.' The prince could refuse to cooperate, but that might prompt more invasive inquiries.

16

BUCKINGHAM PALACE RETREAT

Dissolute living on a palatial scale, failed marriages, mistresses, financial ruin. These words summarised the state of Britain's Hanoverian royals in 1837. Where does the Epstein Affair fit in today in the history of the Saxe-Coburg/Windsor branch of the royal family that replaced them?

1837 was the year Queen Victoria came to the throne. She had grown up isolated from her royal relatives, in quarantine almost from her relatives' lewd behaviour and outlook. As Queen, she and her prim, German-provincial husband Albert sought to expunge the excesses of the hard-living royal family and refashion the British royal family. Instead of projecting power, they would stand for small-time domesticity, hard work and wholesomeness. The monarchy would have to be seen as a paragon of rectitude and provide an example to the population of the British Isles, as opposed to exemplifying the male lust and dominance as it had under Victoria's Hanover uncles.

The effect of their two-person social crusade was modest to say the least, not only on vice in Britain but even on their own children. Their eldest son Bertie, the Prince of Wales, resumed the freestyle sexual appetites of his royal relatives and great uncles as if his parents' rebranding exercise had never happened. His life as a playboy was a continuing act of rebellion against his exacting father (whose name he dropped as king, preferring Edward VII instead) and, later, his memory. Public knowledge of Bertie's hectic amorous life was only narrowly avoided when, instead of being named as the correspondent, he was called as a witness in divorce proceedings of a disgusted MP in 1869. The scandal created headlines but did not otherwise tarnish the Saxe-Coburg brand of monogamy and industriousness covering the royal family.

Albert and Victoria's curveball had, however, created a deep appetite for stories on both sides of the coin among the population at large. In 1885, almost half a century into Queen Victoria's reign and some years after her acceptance of the florid title 'Empress of India', the *Pall Mall Gazette* ran a series of articles called 'The Maiden Tribute of Modern Babylon'. The *Gazette*'s sex investigation was aided by religious leaders, the Salvation Army and early suffragettes. With borderline pornographic headlines such as 'The Violation of Virgins' and 'Strapping Girls Down', the paper described London as a cesspit of moral turpitude, awash with brothels, child prostitution and vile slum mothers selling daughters as slaves. The spectacular sales led to a mass demonstration of some 250,000 people in Hyde Park. It was an awkward moment in an election year with a ballot extended to an additional million working voters. In order to put out the fire rapidly, Britain's MPs hurriedly passed the Criminal Law Amendment Act of 1885. It criminalised the industry catering to the urges of the upper classes, homosexual acts between men, and raised the age of consent for girls from thirteen to sixteen.

No royal family members were swept up in the Babylon Maiden scandal, but it was open season after this clarion call. Fortunately for him, Bertie seemed to confine his activities to actresses and other men's wives—as a sensible measure he only otherwise frequented the elegant brothels of Paris. Bertie's oldest son and heir, however, 'Eddy'—Prince Albert Victor—was linked to the Cleveland Street Scandal of 1889 where teenage telegraph messenger boys as young as fourteen were employed as male prostitutes in the eponymous brothel.

As Edward VII, Bertie himself sought to clean up the royal family's act yet again. He balanced the books financially, and the courtiers buttressing the royal family's image became adept at massaging the news and papering over cracks. 145 Piccadilly, Queen Elizabeth's childhood home (nowadays the location of the enormous 400-room Park Lane Intercontinental) was successfully branded as 'not a palace'. Even the Abdication Crisis of 1936, when Edward VIII stepped down to marry American double-divorcee Wallis Simpson, was presented as a great love story despite the many tawdry sexual elements kept hidden from the public.

Under the new king, George VI—Edward VIII's younger brother 'Bertie', who was named after his grandfather Prince Albert—the royal family once again fully lived up to the 'Victoria & Albert' ideal of male domesticity and application.

Although Bertie had had the induction to sex that was customary for a male member of the royal family, he was otherwise shy and insecure about himself, having rarely excelled at anything before he became king. It also helped that the royal household now consisted of no more than four members, three of them women, two of which were still young girls.

When Elizabeth II ascended the throne, she continued the royal brand her father and the Queen Mother had assiduously burnished. Her exemplary reign easily trumped her rival in longevity, Queen Victoria. The flame of industry that Albert had lit with Victoria seemed to waver after his death, and as queen she enjoyed semi-retirement for forty years, palming off most of her work to her son.

Nonetheless, the one male member of Elizabeth's royal household of four was an entirely different type of man from her father. Even in the early stages of their marriage, there were rumours about Prince Philip's close involvement with actresses and various other women, especially when he undertook official trips alone. They appeared to be just rumours, but the Queen's sister Princess Margaret, an adult in the swinging sixties, had a colourful private life that could easily rival that of a traditional male royal. The palace managed to steer the royal brand away from most of the damage as the press was generally still respectful and stayed out of the private lives of members of the establishment, royals included. Nonetheless, Princess Margaret's marriage didn't survive the headlines created by pictures of her on a beach in Mustique with the strapping gardener Roddy Llewellyn frolicking in speedos.

Over the length of Queen Elizabeth's reign, the royal household swelled to a dazzling size as more children continued to be borne to the monarch's family. The Firm became a sprawling enterprise. It was thought that over a hundred royals relied on the public purse for money, protection or accommodation in one of the grace-and-favour palaces. Yet while doff-the-cap respect for authority had gone, the royal brand aspired to be the same one of wholesomeness, rectitude and industry. This branding of The Firm came to be seen as the sole reason for continuing the institution in Britain; it was no longer a matter of choice for the royal family. And since the public were footing the bill for The Firm, Britain, as stakeholder, came to expect to be informed in some detail when the brand frayed.

Thus crises came in thick and fast. Prince Charles barely survived the collapse of his marriage to Diana, the Princess of Wales, but managed to claw his way back into public acceptance, or toleration at least, by reuniting with the woman he wanted to marry. In a subtle blaming of 'them', the suggestion lingered that courtiers had stood in the way of true love at the time. Princess Anne's love travails went almost unnoticed; so dedicated was she to public duties that she received a pass for effort. Prince Harry gained something of a reputation, prior to his marriage, but was forgiven because of the tragic circumstances of his mother's untimely death.

The wild card, however, was always the Queen's second son, Prince Andrew. Handsome as a young man, he displayed from an early age all the characteristics of royal privilege. Like the young Donald Trump, he liked to have beautiful women as arm candy to show off. And there was the litany of lovers before and after his marriage, including starlet Koo Stark and a number of nude models. As time went on, that exceptional privilege atrophied into rigidness in the case of Andrew, whereas his father had tried to leaven it during his life with a sense humour and his brother Charles had turned to promoting new-age ideas.

Prince Andrew's reputation soured considerably since his 'Randy Andy' days of having a model on each arm. After stepping back from royal duties in November 2019, Andrew was soon dragged back into the public eye when a large, American-style yellow school bus was parked outside Buckingham Palace. The bus was covered with two headshots of the prince alongside the words, 'If you see this man please ask him to contact the FBI to answer their questions.'

The stunt came from lawyer Gloria Allred. Allred claimed that Andrew had failed to cooperate with the FBI's probe into Epstein's purported sex trafficking scheme, despite Andrew saying he would cooperate on more than one occasion. Surprisingly, US Attorney for the Southern District of the State of New York, Geoffrey Berman agreed and issued a similar complaint against the prince.

'Contrary to Prince Andrew's very public offer to cooperate with our investigation into Epstein's co-conspirators, an offer that was conveyed through press release, Prince Andrew has now completely shut the door on voluntary cooperation,' said Berman at a press conference on 9 March 2020.

At least at this stage of the proceedings, Andrew could still have offered to work with the FBI behind the scenes. His lawyers, among them extradition law expert Clare Montgomery QC, whose past clients include dictator and mass murderer Augusto Pinochet and fugitive businessman Nirav Modi, might have been able to negotiate for the prince merely to answer written questions.

If Andrew refused to cooperate, the risk was that the US might go directly to the UK government with a mutual legal assistance request. If approved by the Home Office, the request could in theory end up requiring Andrew to appear in a UK court to give evidence. It would be up to the judge to decide if the hearing was in open court. Ominously Berman's office had said it was 'considering its options,' suggesting anything could happen—including such a request.

Colleagues of Berman's thought that he was escalating his campaign against the prince. Ex-prosecutor Elie Honig opined, 'I think it's really unusual'. But, he added, 'I think it's the right tactic'. He continued, 'I applaud Geoffrey Berman for not allowing Prince Andrew to put on a public face of cooperation when really he's stonewalling.' Former New York prosecutor and law professor Jennifer Rodgers added that the prince could be arrested in the US. 'In theory, if he comes to the US, he could be arrested pursuant to a material-witness warrant'.

Megxit, which gave Andrew a brief break from the spotlight, took away a lot of the pressure that was building up around the prince. When Harry and Meghan first announced their departure from their roles as senior royals, their decision was met with anger from parts of the British public and press, and criticism over their cost to the British taxpayer. The Queen was angry too, at least according to former royal spokesman Dickie Arbiter on TV show Good Morning Britain.

'The Queen will be very angry,' said Arbiter. 'Probably more angry than she felt after Andrew's car crash interview last year,' he said, referring to Andrew's disastrous appearance on Newsnight and his attempts to justify his relationship with Epstein. Indeed, the public response to Megxit was voluble, and dominated the media.

Prince Charles, the heir to the throne, was not a fan of his sibling. He once memorably described Andrew as, 'like a fizzy drink that has been shaken up and the top taken off'. The tension between the two brothers only increased over the years in a quasi war of the roses. A royal source said, 'Charles has disapproved of quite a lot of Andrew's friends and acquaintances over the years, and Epstein is no exception. I was told he was very concerned about the friendship for a long time and saw it as a disaster waiting to happen. This story isn't going away, and no one knows what will come out next.'

It was not quite clear, whether the Queen's anger would ever be directed at her favourite son. Part of his funding always came through her private Duchy of Lancaster income. And whenever she heard Andrew was by himself in

Buckingham Palace, she sent him a hand-written note and he'd change into a suit to go up and see her. He'd greet her with a bow, kissing her hand and both her cheeks. 'It's a little ritual that she adores', palace aides confided. At Windsor, the Queen would also see him on Sundays after church for drinks before lunch at Royal Lodge. She particularly enjoyed it when Beatrice and Eugenie were also there. If Fergie was up, too, she'd go for a walk with her. Whenever they had dinner together, Andrew's favourite dessert, *crème brulée* with Sandringham oranges, would be on the menu.

It was Andrew's spontaneous quality that popped for the Queen. Andrew and Philip were the two people who made the monarch the happiest person in the world. Andrew delighted her—in the same way that the older Princess Beatrice had entertained and protected her mother Queen Victoria a century ago. He was the son who put his life at risk defending her crown at war without hesitation and she still felt immensely proud of him. He was the only relative with that chivalric distinction. For the Queen the horrors of World War II were part of her formative memory, and Andrew had an unassailable place in the middle years of her reign. Prominently on her desk in Buckingham Palace was a photograph of him in naval dress. It was inconceivable that she would not shield him when he most needed her. The prince assured her and Philip in March 2011, when the photograph with Virginia Giuffre was first published, that he had not been part of anything untoward and she trusted her son's promise. And ever since the prince had strenuously and consistently denied all allegations of wrongdoing that were reported, and had even gone on TV to counter them in person and in detail during the BBC interview conducted in her private rooms in Buckingham Palace.

During her reign, which exceeded Victoria's long rule, Elizabeth's close family made many mistakes and gave plently of ill-advised interviews, creating a tsunami of headlines that travelled world-wide. If she recognised many of Philip's awkward traits in Andrew, they were also the ones of the man she had always loved. She also saw clearly that as a father Andrew could not be faulted. He would do anything for his two daughters—much in the way her father worshipped her and Margaret. And while the relationship between Andrew and Fergie was unconventional, it was full of companionship, good will and affection, even if filled by jejune bread-roll jousts rather than matters of state. The Yorks' marriage was a media disaster, but as a family they weathered their storms remarkably well and not just for the children. Their Hanoverian ancestors—whom Queen Victoria so loathed and never met—would have recognised the duke and duchess's amicable arrangements as business as usual. After all what was the point of being a royal if it did not mean freedom from more common conventions that determined the lives of the monarch's subjects?

Princess Beatrice, Andrew's oldest daughter, and Edoardo Mapelli Mozzi revealed their wedding plans on 6 February 2020. It wouldn't have escaped the Queen or members of the royal family that the announcement was made on the day her father died and Elizabeth ascended to the throne. Prince Charles had proposed to Diana two days before in 1981. The princess's February announcement made headlines around the world, but invariably the connection was made between Beatrice's wedding details and Prince Andrew's being forced to retire from public life due to the controversy over his friendship with Jeffrey Epstein.

Engaged in September 2019, the pair's wedding details added more royal noise to the Meghan and Harry cacophony and helped draw attention away from Andrew. He himself announced that he would walk Beatrice down the aisle, but that announcement had little chance of diverting the media spotlight. As the US Epstein cases continued, he risked being thrust back into the limelight even if he chose not to assist voluntarily with the FBI's investigation into crimes committed by Epstein's associates.

A few months later the *Mail on Sunday* interviewed three models who had visited Epstein's mansion in December 2010 while Andrew was staying there for a total of six days. In his BBC interview, the prince had said that the stay was meant to terminate their friendship because of Epstein's 2008 conviction. The models revealed, however, that Epstein himself had bragged about an exclusive event at the house. He had organised a private, pre-release showing of The King's Speech which he had arranged for the prince. Once again, the royal's own words seemed open to interpretation.

And the legal battle lines inched forward. While Andrew continued to strenuously deny all allegations or knowledge of illegal or criminal behaviour of hist host, the palace would no longer speak for the prince on the issue. It had already stated, 'Buckingham Palace will not be commenting further'. The duke appointed his phalanx of heavy-weight lawyers and media experts to help manage the matter from hereon.

Claire Montgomery QC, the duke's legal knight in shining armour, was from Cherrie Blair QC's Matrix chambers. Slightly stuffily (as one might expect from the prince) Montgomery QC was instructed by Gary Bloxsome, a top-defence solicitor, rather than directly by the duke himself. Bloxsome was also able to deal with any assistance sought by Scotland Yard with regards to Epstein's dealings in London.

The problem for the prince's legal team was always going to be that the prince liked to take the initiative, undoubtedly as a result of his active duty as a navy officer. The rarefied atmosphere in the navy and the palace however had not equipped him well for when he was out of his depth. The realisation of a false rally would come to him in the end, but often when it was too late; such as when he told the Queen that the BBC interview was a great success. The law was another area of which the prince knew little, apart perhaps from the snippets he received as an adolescent when he was still understudy to the heir to the throne. Would he allow his lawyers to do their work, or would he take charge himself and create more headlines?

For good measure, public relations whisperer Mark Gallagher was also appointed by Andrew. Gallagher previously represented the British establishment figures accused of paedophilia by Carl Beech. That allegation proved to be a hoax from beginning to end and the prince and Buckingham Palace must have hoped that Gallagher could once again put the genie back into the bottle.

Giuffre's lawyer David Boies claimed in the press that other evidence 'will come out that undercuts his assertion that [Andrew] didn't know Virginia'. Moreover, the lawyer said this evidence would also undermine the prince's categorical statement that he 'had not been with her'. Boies flatly contradicted the prince's repeated statements that he had never met Giuffre.

Bradley Edwards—the Florida lawyer who had been involved since the first complainant and had spent more than a decade on the matter—had previously put this question to Epstein's lawyer, Alan Dershowitz. Deposing Dershowitz under oath, Edwards asked whether Giuffre had met Andrew. Though Dershowitz stated that Giuffre was lying 'from beginning to end', he evaded answering this simple question. When asked whether Giuffre was lying about being paid to have sex with the duke, the emeritus Harvard professor again tried not to answer the question. Instead he addressed a different one, 'if she was paid fifteen thousand dollars to have sex with Prince Andrew at the age of seventeen, she would be guilty of prostitution.' However, ultimately Epstein's lawyer was forced to concede, 'I have no idea'.

The affair had dragged on since the picture with Andrew first appeared in 2011. It seemed to find no conclusion. There was growing anger at Andrew among courtiers. In truth, it had been their job to guard the crown from the kind of turbulence it was in. They let the Queen down for almost four decades, if not longer. It was well-known that the prince floundered in public. A sabbatical from royal engagements in 2011 would have taken the prince out of the public eye. Instead, the court let headlines fester for the Queen and only acted after the prince's Newsnight debacle. If anyone's apology to the victims and the Queen was overdue it was theirs.

In the Spring of 2020, during the COVID-19 epidemic, Andrew appeared for a photo opportunity, packing care packages for Windsor's Thames Hospice with the duchess. Someone had put temporary tables up in Royal Lodge's expansive gardens so that they could catch the sunshine in the pictures. Beautifully designed, the purple bags—casually held up like a tray of turnips for the camera by Prince Andrew—looked more like another collection of up-market goodie bags than acts of contrition. Presumably it was Gallagher's first blow on behalf of the duke—he had previously helped the Queen with her Diamond Jubilee. 'Pathetic' was the response of Britain's largest newspaper on this occasion.

Then, on 2 July, days after William Barr tried to sack Geoffrey Berman, the FBI arrested Ghislaine Maxwell in her house in Maine. It was reported she had hidden after agents had identified themselves and the front door had to be broken down to retrieve her. The trial date was set for 12 July 2021 and included among the charges was perjury, highly likely in Virginia Giuffre's defamation case. Now casting a very long shadow, it was this lawsuit that had featured the prince himself in allegations made by Giuffre in court in January 2015.

As if Gallagher's job couldn't get any worse, a February 2015 video capture of Donald Trump was released late at night, days after Ghislaine Maxwell's bail application was denied. On the clip Trump talked to journalists about Epstein's Little St James property. The US President said, 'just ask Prince Andrew. He'll tell you about it. The island was an absolute cesspool.'

The next morning, the news broke that the palace had taken down all content from the Yorks' personal website, thedukeofyork.org. The site merely redirected to a single page on the Queen's website, royal.uk/the-duke-york. Links to the princesses only referred back to their father's page. According to public internet information the redirection dated to around the time when the US made its official

MLAT request to the UK government.

The House of York's rout continued when it was announced a few hours later that Princess Beatrice had that day married Edoardo Mapelli Mozzi. It wasn't a royal marriage spectacle as planned. The event was downgraded to a secret ceremony in Windsor, attended by no more than twenty guests, including the Queen, Prince Phillip, Andrew, Fergie, and the groom's parents. It made history nonetheless. The last royal wedding to have happened behind closed doors took place 235 years before in order to avoid tongues wagging.

The palace went to great lengths to avoid scandal in 2020. The wedding involved no public expense on police protection palace sources confirmed and, in order to project frugality, Beatrice had even borrowed her wedding dress from the Queen. Acknowledging that a crisis loomed in the background, the duke was not in his daughter's public wedding pictures in order not to 'overshadow' the event, palace sources said.

In 2021, the duke was once again seen in public after the private memorial service at Windsor following the death of Prince Philip. The duke broke his self-imposed eighteen-months' silence and stepped away from his relatives to address the assembled TV crews. Purporting to speak on behalf of the royal family, Andrew said, 'Thank you very much indeed for for coming to see us this morning at our private chapel where we've been able to as it were give our prayers and head on for the next few days before the funeral'. He also commented on himself, 'occasionally we in the family are asked to stand up and show compassion and leadership and unfortunately with my father's death it has brought at home to me not just our loss but actually the loss that everybody else has felt for so many people who've um as it were died and lost loved ones during the pandemic um and so we are all in the same boat slightly different circumstances because he didn't die from Covid'. He added, 'the messages that I'm getting are absolutely outstanding um and I just want to say how grateful I am we are um for these tributes'.

Some good news came for the duke in October when the Metropolitan Police completed its review of Giuffre's allegations for the third time following the lawsuit brought by her in Manhattan. Again, it decided that it would not open an Epstein investigation. In a public statement the police force said, 'As a matter of procedure, MPS officers reviewed a document released in August 2021 as part of a US civil action. This review has concluded and we are taking no further action.'

There was also good news for Ghislaine Maxwell. Evidence had been passed on to the police in June purporting to indicate that she was involved with sex-trafficking in the UK. Here, too, the Metropolitan Police stated that no further action would be taken following its inquiry into the Maxwell information it had received.

17

ANDREW'S COUNTER ATTACK

The dramatic break-through in Virginia Giuffre's court case against Prince Andrew came on 27 August. On that day, more than two weeks after the lawsuit was filed in Manhattan, the Head of Security at Royal Lodge accepted the papers served on the prince on a third attempt, stating he would send them on to the prince's lawyers. Andrew himself was at Balmoral in talks with the Queen and her advisors. He had arrived on 10 August, a day after the filing in New York.

It followed a confused period during which Giuffre's lawyers served papers on four of Prince Andrew's lawyers and advisors, two of whom responded directly that they were not authorised to accept service on behalf of the royal while the other two did not respond directly to their counterparts. After further legal skirmishes, the matter appeared resolved when the High Court in London accepted Giuffre's request to serve papers on the prince in Britain on 15 September, giving his lawyers seven days to challenge its decision. This happened two days after celebrity lawyer Andrew Brettler joined presiding Judge Kaplan and Giuffre's lawyers to represent Andrew during the first oral conference of the case.

During the conference Brettler still disputed that his client had been served properly of the proceedings. Confusingly, Brettler also told Kaplan that Giuffre wasn't permitted to bring her lawsuit as a result of an agreement with Epstein in 2009. As David Boies, Giuffre's lead lawyer, pointed out, that was a legal matter to be decided in Kaplan's courtroom after argument from both sides. It required, by definition, acceptance that his client had been served. Brettler appeared to be wanting his to have his cake and eat it.

To move things forward, Judge Kaplan mooted during the conference that papers could now also be served on Andrew at his lawyer's Los Angeles office in the US and warned, 'Cut out all the technicalities'. Even so, he gave Brettler until Friday 17 September to submit his arguments that the prince had not been served. On that day, the judge himself also issued letters rogatory to the UK government to service notice on the prince of the case before him through the same Mutual Legal Assistance Treaty under which the FBI sought to interview the prince.

Andrew was known to be a stickler for protocol and it seemed his lawyers were too. It proved a boon to his accuser. David Boies pressed his client's case in the media for a month without opposition. He said that Giuffre wanted to send a message that the behaviour described in her lawsuit 'is not acceptable and that you cannot hide behind wealth and power and palace walls'. She would donate any proceeds to charity, he stated. She had 'tried every way she can to resolve this short of litigation', but that 'litigation is the only way to establish once and for all what Prince Andrew's evidence actually is'.

In the end, Brettler filed a letter by the close of day on the 17th on behalf of the royal that stated, 'Oral argument on the Duke's previously anticipated motion challenging service … will not be necessary'.

Although 'service of proceedings' was now conceded by the prince, it remained uncertain what would happen next since it had taken such a long time for Andrew's lawyers to accept that this was the case. It was still considered possible that the prince would file no response, even if letting the proceedings in New York continue in absentia would carry the risk that Kaplan might enter a default judgment against him. In a timeline approved by the judge, Andrew was given until 31 October to file a rebuttal of Giuffre's allegations ahead of the second conference of lawyers before the judge on 3 November.

In the end, the 31st of October turned out to be just as dramatic as the 9th of August when Giuffre filed her lawsuit. Brettler launched a blistering counter attack. It seemed as if Andrew relished the opportunity of finally dealing with his opponent's accusations head-on.

No one would be better suited. Brettler was a prominent partner at the firm founded by Hollywood's 'Mad Dog' Marty Singer, known as the 'the man who can make any problem go away'. He was also defending Call Me By Your Name film star Armie Hammer who denied accusations of rape and other sexual impropriety, as well as comedian Chris D'Elia who denied allegations of soliciting pornography from a 17-year-old girl and exposing himself.

The submission's first paragraph couldn't be clearer: 'Prince Andrew never sexually abused or assaulted Giuffre. He unequivocally denies Giuffre's false allegations against him.'

The submission's second paragraph went for the jugular: 'For over a decade, Giuffre has profited from her allegations against Epstein and others by selling stories and photographs to the press and entering into secret agreements to resolve her claims.... This presents a compelling motive for Giuffre to continue filing frivolous lawsuits'. In other words, 'Giuffre has initiated this baseless lawsuit against Prince Andrew to achieve another payday at his expense and at the expense of those closest to him. Giuffre's pattern of filing a series of lawsuits against numerous highprofile individuals should no longer be tolerated'.

In addition to calling Giuffre's facts against the prince 'threadbare', 'inconsistent', 'lurid' and 'outrageous', Brettler went on to set out her prior role in Epstein's underage sex ring in a manner that cast doubt on whether she was a 'victim of sexual abuse'.

She was 'climbing the ladder', the submission stated, and became 'one of the few [who Epstein] trusted'. Brettler quoted a former boyfriend who said 'She was like the head b***h' and a female acquaintance who said that Giuffre would ask 'do you know any girls who are kind of slutty?' And when Epstein told her she would accompany him on a six-week trip to Europe and Nort Africa in 2001—the year of her allegations against Andrew—'she threw her arms around [Epstein]'. 'It is a striking feature of this case that while lurid allegations are made against Prince Andrew by Giuffre, the only party to this claim whose conduct has involved the willful recruitment and trafficking of young girls for sexual abuse is Giuffre herself, including while she was an adult', Brettler concluded.

Having attacked the truthfulness of Giuffre's facts, motives and character, the duke's lawyer also set out his key legal argument in a Motion of Dismissal of Giuffre's case. Three days after Giuffre had brought her case, Brettler observed, she had voluntarily withdrawn a claim of battery against Epstein's lawyer Alan Dershowitz brought under the same extension of the deadline of bringing sexual abuse cases in New York State.

The reason for this 'voluntary' dismissal was the 2009 settlement agreement she had signed with Epstein in exchange for dropping her nine causes of action for sexual abuse as 'Jane Doe 102' against the billionaire. The agreement had been drawn up by in 2009 by Dershowitz. On 12 August, 3 days after beginning proceedings against Andrew, Brettler stated, Giuffre agreed the settlement precluded her from suing the lawyer as a fellow-releasee besides Epstein. As the 2009 agreement was based on her claims to have been sexually abused by "'royalty" and other of Epstein's "adult male peers'", Brettler argued that Andrew was a releasee like Dershowitz under the settlement. For good measure, he added that the extension of the statute of limitations by New York State was in any case 'unconstitutional' and that the passage of time also barred her from sueing his client.

The prince's spirited defence of his position made headlines around the world and also appeared to strongly support the position of Ghislaine Maxwell, whose criminal trial was due to start a few months later and which included two charges that involved Giuffre's testimony.

Apart from the 2009 settlement, the Dershowitz case contained another filing that bore on the prince's arguments. It was a transcript of an 80-minute conversation in 2019 between journalist Sharon Churcher and Dershowitz's New York publisher Tony Lyons. Churcher published the first interview with Giuffre in 2011. It was 'checkbook journalism' Churcher conceded to Lyons (Brettler's submission showed Giuffre was paid $160,000). About Giuffre's 2009 settlement Churcher stated to the publisher that Giuffre was 'a big spender' and had 'taken half a million, I think it was' from Epstein.

Other circumstantial facts were filtering through. Investigating the prince's itinerary in 2001, the *Daily Mail* discovered that he flew to New York on 9 April for a visit as chairman of a trust relating to the school his father, Prince Charles and he had attended to Britain's consul general whose residence was at 4 East 66th Street, five blocks from Epstein's mansion on 9 East 71st Street. In Andrew's diary, 1:45pm to 6:45pm were set apparently aside for 'private time'. In the end this private time took place between 2:30 to 5:30pm. In addition, it was discovered that a puppeteer called Steve Wright was at a Buckingham Palace reception in 2003 where the prince told him, 'Oh my God, puppets! Spitting Image—do you know that my friend bought my Spitting Image puppet'.

During the BBC interview, Andrew himself recalled about the visit, 'I was staying with the consul general which is further down the street on Fifth so I wasn't... I wasn't staying there. I may have visited but definitely didn't, definitely, definitely no, no, no activity.' The *Daily Mail* found, however, that the prince did spend the night at Epstein's on 11 April, two days later, with his body guard in his 'usual' room. Andrew had flown in at night at his own expense from his engagement for the school's trust in Boston. By then Epstein's mansion was empty as Epstein, Maxwell and Giuffre had left for St Thomas on Epstein's private plane on that day. In 2001, all this was of course uncontroversial as Epstein would only be convicted in 2008. The prince himself was on his way from Boston to join Fergie and the children in the West Indies.

The real problem remained that, as Andrew made his case in court, it was his mother as Britain's Head of State who got drawn in further and further into the Affair. In 2011, when Churcher published Giuffre's first interview, royal lawyers had first got involved (though it may even have been as early as September 2007 when Sjoberg first published her Spitting Image story with Andrew months after Epstein pleaded guilty to soliciting underage sex in Florida). When the prince lost his role as the UK's Special trade envoy in July 2010 following the first rumblings of the Epstein Affair, the palace had brushed off the fall-out and maintained his role as a senior royal. Andrew received yearly payments from the Privy Purse and the Queen's income from the Duchy of Lancaster and could claim considerable expenses when on official palace duties.

It was hardly surprising the Queen was unwavering in her support for her second son. She knew Andrew held an impossible position, like her younger sister Margaret, and was thwarted in love because of it. When his relationship with his first love Koo Stark fizzled out, he was lost. Having taken up photography because of Stark, he had thrown himself into his new hobby and converted a bathroom on the third floor of Buckingham Palace. Asked whether there was a theme to his work the prince had replied, 'Dare I say it? The theme, in fact, is loneliness'. It explained much of the close relationship that was to follow with Fergie even after their marriage was dissolved.

In 2020, the makers of the Crown IV suggested in their portrayals that the Queen was losing patience with the situation the prince found himself in. But there was little real evidence of this. Wherever it was within her gift, she made no changes. Andrew retained his HRH title where Meghan and Harry lost theirs. Against questions from within the armed forces, Andrew also continued to keep his honorary military titles, including Commodore-in-Chief of the Royal Navy's air fleet and he remained as Colonel-in-Chief of multiple units.

If there was a removal of titles, it only occurred in a royal tweet on the occasion of his birthday in 2021. Instead of mentioning his titles as in previous years, the tweet merely read '#OnThisDay in 1960 the Queen was safely delivered of a son, the first child born to a reigning Monarch since 1857'. She had, of course, also offered the prince sanctuary at her private estate Balmoral in August 2021. It was true that, in 2020, the prince did not receive his promotion to Honorary Admiral. Under a policy adopted by the Navy in 2009, the royal could count on 'automatic' promotions every five years on crown years. But it was he himself who had begged two weeks before his sixtieth, 'if this promotion [to Admiral] might be deterred' until he returned to 'public duty'.

Worryingly, however, the Queen reportedly underwrote her son's mounting legal expenses. The prince's finances had taken a turn for the worse after the BBC interview. He no longer received £250,000 from the Queen through the Privy Purse, nor twice that in expenses on the job. In November 2021, Bloomberg furthermore revealed that the prince had borrowed £125,000 every quarter from 2015—the year Giuffre first made her allegations against him and when he bought a chalet in Verbier—with a final £250,000 for 'general working capital and living expenses' in November 2017. This made a total debt of £1.5 million. There was also his half of a reportedly £13 million mortgage on the Verbier chalet—though it appeared to have finally sold in September 2021, clearing the prince's debts in Switzerland.

Experts believed that Andrew's final legal bill would reach stratospheric levels. His Los Angeles lawyer Andrew Brettler was thought to be charging the prince $2,000 (£1,475) an hour. And he was just one of the prince's ten-thousand-dollar-a-day men. His UK lawyer Gary Bloxsome, for example, was not far off at over £1000 ($1,350) an hour.

The thorny problem underwriting the duke's legal expenses was that it reportedly came from the income from the Duchy of Lancaster. Although it paid around £20 million a year in income to the Queen, the Duchy is not inherited by her the way, for example, her Balmoral estate was inherited as private property. The Queen received the Duchy's income every year in her official capacity as Britain's Head of State. Should she ever decide to abdicate, it would no longer be hers. By contrast, abdication would make no difference to her continued private ownership of Balmoral.

Increasingly, the Epstein Affair was raising constitutional issues as Buckingham Palace got further and further drawn into its centre alongside the prince. As

Giuffre's claims against Andrew went beyond matters of state, the palace crossed the Rubicon and unleashed potentially far-reaching consequences for the monarchy in Britain. Legal experts in New York opined in August 2021 that cases such as the one against Prince Andrew rarely ended up in court. However, if the monarch's financial might had aided Andrew in a private matter this required justification to avoid public outcry. What justification there could be was, however, hard to imagine. Andrew was not the only one on trial in the public court of opinion. Buckingham Palace and the entire monarchy had been complicit in deploying its might to cover up ugly fact. It would have to the pay the price, too.

18

A THRONE IN PERIL?

When Andrew was stripped by Buckingham Palace of all of his royal status on 3 November 2025—a long delay of four years after Andrew settled the Giuffre lawsuit for £12 million—Andrew ceased to be a representative of the British head of state only by one last silken thread. Though shorn of all royal honorifics and now the plain Mr Mountbatten-Windsor, Andrew still remained 8th in the line of succession to the throne. The monarch alone could not change this with just the stroke of a pen. It required an act of Parliament as well as the agreement from fourteen other Commonwealth realms to remove Andrew. In fact, until such time he remained one of Britain's Counsellors of State as one of the four adults in the line of succession to whom the monarch could delegate royal functions. Everything remaining equal, Andrew's counsellorship wouldn't terminate for another decade until William's daughter Charlotte would turn twenty one and become the fourth adult in the line of succession. On that day, the message was clear to anyone, however: if it were up to Charles III he would also have severed this last legal connection of his brother's to the crown. The government duly let it be known that it was considering legislation to begin the long-winded process to remove this last vestige of Andrew's involvement with the head of state.

The events that followed made clear how powerful the invisible shield was that covered all royals, even one as controversial as Andrew, from the consequences of unacceptable behaviour. The British royal family called itself The Firm, but it became clear that unlike any ordinary firm Andrew would be given opportunity after opportunity to prove himself after leaving his job at the Ministry of Defence in 1999. Meanwhile he received all the historical deference and dispensations that government officials extend to honourable members of the head of state's family and which, in effect, lift them above and beyond the measures and actions that such officials would apply to British citizens as a matter of course.

From 3 November, Andrew was a subject of investigation by no fewer than eleven police forces in the UK according to news reports following ever increasing excruciating details that circulated in the press. This did not in any way imply that he was guilty of any wrongdoing, but it did show that officials were now free to do their job and establish the facts first, where they might have decided to step back from doing so for decades previous to that date.

On 23 February 2026, for example, the BBC's Sean Coughlan reported conversations with three civil servants involved with Andrew's claims as UK Trade Envoy from 2001 to 2011, and the unique treatment he received compared to other British functionaries. One of them recalled refusing to refund Andrew's cost of 'massage services' during a trip but found he was then overruled by senior civil servants. As a matter of course, checks on Andrew's expenses were given a 'rubber stamp' and the costs were spread over different budgets, disguising the aggregate costs. 'I couldn't believe it… it was like it wasn't real money', the second one said, adding 'they weren't spending any of their own money'. There were charges for flights, hotel rooms and Andrew's entourage, but little control on spending or the record keeping the civil servant was used to in his own department. The third civil servant said he had tried to prevent Andrew from visiting the Middle East, but had been reluctant to speak out because 'no one would complain'. Paradoxically, it would be counterproductive as 'it wouldn't help your reputation', suggesting there were career implications for civil servants who scrutinised Andrew's costs as they were trained to do.

By now, eleven police forces in the UK were involved in looking into the FBI's Epstein files and otherwise, with three forces acting as the core investigators into the facts surrounding Epstein including a connection to Andrew if any:

Metropolitan Police (core investigators)

Reviewing Andrew's protection officers further to the Epstein files which suggested Andrew had asked his protection officers to look into Virginia Giuffre; liaising with US authorities regarding UK airports. Former Prime Minister Gordon Brown, also sent them 'new and additional information' with the request to review the use of taxpayer funded flights to facilitate meetings between Andrew and Epstein including potential landings on RAF bases.

Thames Valley Police (core investigators)

Leading the investigation into Andrew for misconduct in public office and searching his former home, Royal Lodge. Received the same letter from Gordon Brown. In addition, it is probing a claim that a woman in her twenties was dispatched to the UK by Epstein in 2010 for an encounter with Andrew at Royal Lodge.

Surrey Police (core investigators)

Stating the core investigators are 'seeking access to unredacted versions of the material to enable a full and independent assessment... to understand any potential impact arising from the millions of documents that have been made publicly available.' Received the same letter from Gordon Brown.

Bedfordshire Police

Received the same letter from Gordon Brown.

Essex Police

'We are assessing the information that has emerged in relation to private flights into and out of Stansted Airport following the publication of the US DoJ Epstein files.'

Police Scotland

Investigating Scottish landings of Epstein's airplane with registration N908JE, nicknamed the Lolita Express.

Wiltshire Police

Announced it is assessing the Epstein files.

West Midlands Police

Announced it is assessing the Epstein files.

Sussex Police

Received the same letter from Gordon Brown.

Berkshire Police

Assisting with searches.

Norfolk Constabulary

Received the same letter from Gordon Brown.

The criticism in the press of Andrew was not new, but this was the first time the police were actively investigating claims. If anything, it would finally create clarity about the constant criticism of Andrew over the years with an opportunity for him to prove that the criticism of him was unfounded and that there was no wrongdoing.

The cause for the investigations was primarily Andrew's official role as UK Trade Envoy. He was not a civil servant as such, but the official terms stated that the envoy has 'a duty of confidentiality in relation to information received. This may include sensitive, commercial, or political information shared about relevant markets/visits'. In addition, the Official Secrets Acts applied to Andrew's role. Lawyers pointed out that the circumstances were crucial in assessing whether such duties were broken.

It was highly unusual for former Prime Minister Gordon Brown at the time to write to the police forces, but the main driver were the FBI files released on 28 January 2026. One email of 30 November 2010 from 'The Duke' to Epstein forwarded reports on trips to 'Vietnam, Singapore, Hong Kong and Shenzhen' that Andrew received from civil servant Amit Patel, who had cc-ed them to Andrew's then secretary Amanda Thirsk. A month later (having told the BBC he had cut off contact with Epstein in December), Andrew forwarded on 24 December a 'confidential brief' to Epstein on Helmand Province, Afghanistan, where the UK government was funding reconstruction projects, adding 'I am going to offer this elsewhere in my network (including Abu Dhabi) but would be very interested in your comments'. When asked for his reaction to the news, Sir Vince Cable, the then business secretary said, 'I was unaware of Andrew... sharing information about investment opportunities [in Afghanistan] before, this is the first I've heard of it.' In another email of 9 February, Andrew said he had visited a private equity firm and asked Epstein whether he might want to take a stake.

The other new allegations centred around Andrew's private life. One email in the 28 January batch that stood out was by Amanda Thirsk, responding to the *Mail on Sunday*'s publication of the photograph of Andrew with Virginia Giuffre a few days earlier. At that point, the paper had for legal reasons gone further than stating that Andrew had met Virginia and Johanna Sjoberg in Epstein's New York apartment and that Sjoberg alleged he had touched her breast. But behind the scenes the paper was asking further probing questions about any sexual relations and Thirsk advised 'The Duke' to respond. She advised, 'I would go with the following… The allegations that are made … are completely untrue and without foundation. The only time I recall them meeting was at my home in 2001 in London—you have published a photo. They did not have sex. They may have met again in New York but I categorically state that Prince Andrew did not grope Ms [Sjoberg] and [Giuffre] nor did they have sex. There was no orgy in Little St James.'

On 31 January, a US lawyer for some 200 Epstein victims, Brad Edwards, told BBC News, 'We're talking about at least one woman who was sent by Jeffrey Epstein over to Prince Andrew [at Royal Lodge in 2010] And she even had, after a night with Prince Andrew, a tour of Buckingham Palace.' However, Thames Valley Police said 'At this time, these allegations have not been reported to Thames Valley Police by either the lawyer or their client'. Andrew always strenuously denied any wrongdoing. It made the absence of a decision by the Metropolitan police to reopen the investigation into Virginia Giuffre's claims regarding her London visit to Ghislaine Maxwell's home where the famous photograph was taken even more incomprehensible. Since the photograph appeared to be genuine on all accounts published by the FBI, it would be the chance to prove Andrew's innocence for once and for all.

After Andrew had become a commoner, Buckingham Palace seemed caught in the headlights. It issued once again exceptional statements, 'I can confirm that the Prince and Princess of Wales have been deeply concerned by the continuing revelations. Their thoughts remain focused on the victims.' The other statement was by Charles III himself, who let it be known that 'The King has made clear, in words and through unprecedented actions, his profound concern at allegations which continue to come to light in respect of Mr Mountbatten-Windsor's conduct. While the specific claims in question are for Mr Mountbatten-Windsor to address, if we are approached by Thames Valley Police we stand ready to support them as you would expect. As was previously stated, Their Majesties' thoughts and sympathies have been, and remain with, the victims of any and all forms of abuse.'

To an increasing number of people, however, it seemed that these

INDEX

Acosta 34, 125, 126, 167
Air Miles Andy 108, 110
Albert 35, 43, 106, 203, 204, 205
Anderson 42, 46
Andy King 52
Andy Pandy 42
Andy's Harem 54, 55, 103, 107
Andymania 60, 81
Anne 27, 42, 43, 44, 46, 59, 89, 94, 206
Annie 190
Arbiter 27, 171, 172
Assange 35
Baby Grumpling 3, 42
Balliol 82
Balmoral 6, 7, 25, 45, 46, 57, 85, 213, 218, 219
Barbados 88
Beatrice 43, 97, 112, 125, 148, 158, 162, 184, 208, 209, 211, 212
Beauvoir 84
Berman 128, 129, 130, 150, 199, 201, 202, 206, 207, 211
Blair 36, 209
Boies 7, 34, 119, 174, 210, 213, 214
Borten 49
Brockman 35, 160
Brown 34, 102, 125
Bryan 95
Buckingham Palace 3, 5, 6, 22, 23, 25, 27, 29, 30, 31, 32, 35, 39, 41, 43, 46, 47, 64, 70, 71, 75, 76, 77, 80, 87, 89, 90, 93, 95, 98, 99, 102, 103, 106, 112, 114, 116, 155, 156, 165, 171, 176, 178, 180, 183, 184, 186, 192, 193, 201, 203, 206, 207, 208, 209, 210, 217, 219
Cairoli 49
Camilla 94, 96
Canada 32, 52, 53, 54, 57, 59, 71, 79, 121
Carey 31
Castro 30, 149
CCTV 130
Central Park 24, 35, 113, 127, 152, 160, 190
Chalet Helora 184
Charles 30, 31, 33, 37, 38, 44, 45, 46, 47, 48, 50, 51, 53, 56, 57, 58, 59, 60, 62, 63, 65, 66, 67, 71, 74, 75, 77, 78, 80, 81, 86, 88, 89, 92, 94, 96, 97, 98, 106, 148, 181, 194, 205, 206, 207, 209, 216
Chelsea FC 49
Clarence House 92, 93
Clinton 22, 125, 131, 136, 140, 152, 177, 178
Club Pigalle 63
Commonwealth Games 57
COVID 211, 212
Cowes 49, 77, 97
Crown Estate 99
Curry 78
Dance of the Decades 27, 121, 148
Dartmouth 60, 61, 62, 63, 77, 97
Davies 120, 151, 175, 182, 183
Davos 29
Deas 78, 80, 86, 96
DecepTech Voice Stress Analysis Machine 29
Dershowitz 34, 125, 210, 216
Diana 2, 45, 62, 75, 77, 78, 79, 80, 81, 82, 88, 89, 91, 92, 94, 97, 205, 209
Dispatches 27, 28, 29, 108
Duchess 28, 41, 91, 94, 95, 96, 103, 106, 155, 162, 182, 184, 208, 211
Duke of Edinburgh 64, 79, 96
Edward 39, 41, 42, 46, 47, 48, 49, 51, 59, 69, 89, 90, 93, 96, 98, 203, 204
El Brillo Way 118, 122
Elizabeth 5, 7, 204, 205, 208, 209
Extradition Act 2003 36
Falkland 65
Falklands 28, 40, 65, 66, 68, 69, 71, 72, 73, 75, 76, 77, 80, 81, 83, 89, 97, 162, 179
FBI 5, 23, 31, 33, 35, 117, 125, 128, 142, 144, 147, 151, 152, 166, 174, 178, 185, 186, 188, 190, 193, 195, 197, 198, 199, 200, 201, 202, 206, 209, 211, 214
Fergie 3, 28, 43, 88, 89, 90, 91, 92, 93, 94, 95, 96, 97, 98, 99, 100, 101, 102, 103, 105, 114, 118, 155, 159, 162, 171, 182, 185, 195, 208, 212, 217, 218
Firm 3, 22, 31, 40, 64, 79, 96, 115, 117, 118, 174, 205, 214
Gates 5, 59, 62, 93, 130, 176
Gazelle helicopter 63
George V 43, 44, 80
George VI 41, 66, 204

Giannelloni 35, 192
Giuffre 5, 6, 7, 22, 23, 24, 26, 27, 28, 29, 30, 31, 34, 35, 38, 103, 105, 113, 114, 126, 127, 130, 134, 135, 136, 137, 141, 142, 144, 145, 146, 147, 155, 161, 162, 163, 164, 165, 166, 173, 174, 175, 176, 183, 184, 185, 186, 187, 188, 192, 193, 194, 196, 198, 199, 201, 208, 210, 211, 212, 213, 214, 215, 216, 217, 218, 219
Golden Eagle 63
Gordonstoun 40, 50, 51, 54, 55, 57, 58, 60, 77, 107, 121
Gore 34, 119
Hamza 36
Harry 32, 33, 41, 45, 90, 94, 193, 206, 207, 209, 218
Hawking 127
Heatherdown 48, 49, 50
Hernandez 124
His Royal Heartthrob 77
HMS Brazen 89, 90
HMS Cottesmore 100
HMS Invincible 64, 65, 66, 67, 72, 74, 75, 76, 79, 81, 88, 97
HMS Norfolk 50
IRA 37, 50, 53, 54, 55, 56, 66
Johnson 38, 109, 152
Kaplan 213, 214
Kate 30, 48, 90, 106, 114, 171
Keating 25, 127
Kilroy 37, 38
Klosters 62
Klum 105, 121, 173
Kulibayev 99, 112, 114
Lakefield College School 52
Lightbody 45, 46
Linley 48
Little Saint James 26, 28, 101, 127, 128, 144, 151, 152, 182, 196, 200
Lolita Express 120, 128, 130, 142, 144, 151
Macmillan 44
Maitlis 30, 156, 157, 158, 160, 161, 163, 164, 165, 166, 168, 169, 172, 177
Mar-a-Lago 22, 38, 39, 118, 135, 136, 143, 190
Margaret 27, 40, 57, 62, 65, 78, 79, 85, 86, 93, 96, 107, 148, 205, 208, 217
Maria 181, 182, 189
Marra 128
Marylebone Boy Scouts 59
Maxwell 3, 6, 22, 23, 25, 27, 28, 34, 35, 38, 39, 82, 102, 105, 108, 114, 118, 119, 120, 121, 125, 126, 127, 128, 130, 133, 135, 136, 139, 140, 141, 142, 143, 144, 145, 146, 148, 149, 150, 156, 157, 158, 162, 163, 166, 168, 174, 178, 182, 187, 188, 189, 190, 191, 192, 193, 195, 196, 197, 199, 211, 212, 216, 217
Meghan 32, 33, 41, 90, 207, 209, 218
Melania 39, 119
Monaco 35, 42, 106, 167
monarchy 5, 23, 33, 39, 40, 41, 64, 65, 66, 77, 109, 171, 181, 201, 203, 219
Montreal Olympics 51
Mountbatten 44, 54, 55, 56, 66
Munich Olympics 51
Musk 22
Mustique 85, 86, 87, 205
nanny 42, 45, 46, 47
Nathaniels 54
Nazarbayev 112
Newsnight 3, 30, 32, 33, 36, 73, 96, 99, 155, 156, 169, 170, 171, 172, 199, 207, 211
Nightingale 53
OJ 34, 125
Palm Beach 22, 23, 26, 27, 118, 122, 125, 126, 129, 130, 131, 133, 134, 135, 137, 138, 145, 148, 149, 150, 158, 165
Philip 2, 32, 42, 43, 44, 47, 48, 49, 50, 54, 57, 59, 60, 66, 78, 79, 85, 90, 92, 93, 96, 97, 101, 103, 108, 205, 208, 212
Phuket 104, 105, 106, 107
Pimps and Hookers 105, 121, 173
PizzaExpress 162, 175
Playboy Prince 2, 28, 96
Port Stanley 69, 70, 71, 72, 75
Queen Mary 80
Queen Mother 27, 43, 47, 49, 67, 90, 92, 98, 103, 205
Queen's Silver Jubilee 56
RAF 50, 51, 63, 78, 109
Randy Andy 28, 52, 64, 74, 80, 81, 83, 86, 88, 206
Recarey 123, 125, 131, 132
Robach 30
Robert 22, 51, 82, 95, 118, 119, 128, 147, 189
Rodgers 23, 142, 207
Rose 24, 67, 72, 74, 117
Royal Ascot 88, 96
Royal Lodge 6, 7, 98, 99, 114, 180, 184, 208, 211, 213
Royal Navy 40, 60, 64, 78, 162, 218
Sandringham 45, 55, 87, 89, 121, 148, 157, 194, 208
Savile 30
Scully 26, 183
Sea King 63, 64, 66, 67, 68, 72
Seymour 48, 118
Shelby 186
Sjoberg 25, 34, 137, 138, 164, 217
Skye 139, 186
Spacey 7, 120
St Tropez 107, 184
Stark 83, 85, 89, 95, 135, 160, 161, 206, 217
Starr 34, 125
Sunninghill Park 98, 99, 111
Task Force 65, 73, 74, 75
The Boss 42, 47, 94, 142
Theresa 29
Thirsk 99, 171, 184, 185
Tokyo Joe 55
Tramp 49, 55, 83, 134, 145, 161, 162, 164, 173, 175, 195, 201
Trinity 57
Trump 22, 34, 38, 117, 118, 119, 131, 135, 136, 137, 140, 143, 144, 145, 193, 206, 211
Vatican 30
Verbier 108, 184, 218
Victoria 43, 105, 118, 141, 190, 203, 204, 205, 208
Weinstein 7, 106, 119, 125, 158
William 33, 34, 45, 75, 94, 97, 114, 148, 181, 202, 211
Windsor Castle 27, 47, 78, 88, 91, 96, 121, 125, 148, 157, 158
Witherow 72, 74, 97
Woking 162, 175
Woody 24, 77, 141
Zorro Ranch 120, 121, 128, 151, 190, 200

www.ingramcontent.com/pod-product-compliance
Lightning Source LLC
LaVergne TN
LVHW091536010926
846999LV00030B/288
* 9 7 8 1 7 8 3 3 4 2 9 5 2 *